Political Cultures in Asia and Europe

Political Cultures in Asia and Europe is a study of attitudes to political and social life among the citizens of eighteen countries in Western Europe and East and Southeast Asia. Drawing on data from the largest cross-national survey on political culture for the last half a century, this book assesses how political culture differs across the two regions and whether this can be drawn back to a profound difference in basic societal values, or 'Asian values'. Examining geographical, religious and socio-economic factors, the authors discuss whether there really is a common political value in the two regions or a profound difference as these countries move towards modernity and beyond.

This unique and comprehensive study of the values, norms and beliefs held by citizens of the East and West will appeal to students and scholars of political culture, comparative politics, Asian politics and European politics.

Jean Blondel is Professor Emeritus at the European University Institute and the University of Siena, Italy.

Takashi Inoguchi is Professor Emeritus at the University of Tokyo and Professor of Political Science at Chuo University, Tokyo.

Politics in Asia series
Formerly edited by Michael Leifer
London School of Economics

ASEAN and the Security of
South-East Asia
Michael Leifer

China's Policy towards Territorial
Disputes
The case of the South China
Sea islands
Chi-kin Lo

India and Southeast Asia
Indian perceptions and policies
Mohammed Ayoob

Gorbachev and Southeast Asia
Leszek Buszynski

Indonesian Politics under Suharto
Order, development and pressure
for change
Michael R.J. Vatikiotis

The State and Ethnic Politics in
Southeast Asia
David Brown

The Politics of Nation Building and
Citizenship in Singapore
Michael Hill and Lian Kwen Fee

Politics in Indonesia
Democracy, Islam and the ideology
of tolerance
Douglas E. Ramage

Communitarian Ideology and
Democracy in Singapore
Beng-Huat Chua

The Challenge of Democracy in
Nepal
Louise Brown

Japan's Asia Policy
Wolf Mendl

The International Politics
of the Asia-Pacific,
1945–1995
Michael Yahuda

Political Change in Southeast
Asia
Trimming the banyan tree
Michael R.J. Vatikiotis

Hong Kong
China's challenge
Michael Yahuda

Korea versus Korea
A case of contested legitimacy
B.K. Gills

Taiwan and Chinese
Nationalism
National identity and status in
international society
Christopher Hughes

Managing Political Change in
Singapore
The elected presidency
Kevin Y.L. Tan and Lam Peng Er

Islam in Malaysian Foreign Policy
Shanti Nair

Political Change in Thailand
Democracy and participation
Kevin Hewison

The Politics of NGOs in
Southeast Asia
Participation and protest in the
Philippines
Gerard Clarke

Malaysian Politics under Mahathir
R.S. Milne and Diane K. Mauzy

Indonesia and China
The politics of a troubled
relationship
Rizal Sukma

Arming the Two Koreas
State, capital and military power
Taik-young Hamm

Engaging China
The management of an emerging
power
Edited by Alastair Iain Johnston
and Robert S. Ross

Singapore's Foreign Policy
Coping with vulnerability
Michael Leifer

Philippine Politics and Society in
the Twentieth Century
Colonial legacies, post-colonial
trajectories
Eva-Lotta E. Hedman and
John T. Sidel

Constructing a Security
Community in Southeast Asia
ASEAN and the problem of
regional order
Amitav Acharya

Monarchy in South-East Asia
The faces of tradition in transition
Roger Kershaw

Korea after the Crash
The politics of economic recovery
Brian Bridges

The Future of North Korea
Edited by Tsuneo Akaha

The International Relations of
Japan and South East Asia
Forging a new regionalism
Sueo Sudo

Power and Change in
Central Asia
Edited by Sally N. Cummings

The Politics of Human Rights in
Southeast Asia
Philip Eldridge

Political Business in East Asia
Edited by Edmund
Terence Gomez

Singapore Politics under the
People's Action Party
Diane K. Mauzy and R.S. Milne

Media and Politics in Pacific
Asia
Duncan McCargo

Japanese Governance
Beyond Japan Inc.
Edited by Jennifer Amyx and
Peter Drysdale

China and the Internet
Politics of the digital leap forward
*Edited by Christopher R. Hughes
and Gudrun Wacker*

Challenging Authoritarianism in
Southeast Asia
Comparing Indonesia and Malaysia
*Edited by Ariel Heryanto and
Sumit K. Mandal*

Cooperative Security and the
Balance of Power in ASEAN and
the ARF
Ralf Emmers

Islam in Indonesian Foreign Policy
Rizal Sukma

Media, War and Terrorism
Responses from the Middle East
and Asia
*Edited by Peter Van der Veer and
Shoma Munshi*

China, Arms Control and
Nonproliferation
Wendy Frieman

Communitarian Politics in Asia
Edited by Chua Beng Huat

East Timor, Australia and
Regional Order
Intervention and its aftermath in
Southeast Asia
James Cotton

Domestic Politics, International
Bargaining and China's Territorial
Disputes
Chien-peng Chung

Democratic Development in
East Asia
Becky Shelley

International Politics of the
Asia-Pacific since 1945
Michael Yahuda

Asian States
Beyond the developmental
perspective
*Edited by Richard Boyd and
Tak-Wing Ngo*

Civil Life, Globalization, and
Political Change in Asia
Organizing between family and
state
Edited by Robert P. Weller

Realism and Interdependence
in Singapore's Foreign Policy
Narayanan Ganesan

Party Politics in Taiwan
Party change and the democratic
evolution of Taiwan,
1991–2004
Dafydd Fell

State Terrorism and Political
Identity in Indonesia
Fatally belonging
Ariel Heryanto

China's Rise, Taiwan's Dilemmas
and International Peace
Edited by Edward Friedman

Japan and China in the World
Political Economy
*Edited by Saadia M. Pekkanen and
Kellee S. Tsai*

Order and Security in Southeast
Asia
Essays in memory of
Michael Leifer
*Edited by Joseph Chinyong
Liow and Ralf Emmers*

State Making in Asia
Edited by Richard Boyd and
Tak-Wing Ngo

US–China Relations in the
21st Century
Power transition and peace
Zhiqun Zhu

Empire and Neoliberalism in Asia
Edited by Vedi R. Hadiz

South Korean Engagement
Policies and North Korea
Identities, norms and the
sunshine policy
Son Key-young

Chinese Nationalism in the
Global Era
Christopher R. Hughes

Indonesia's War over Aceh
Last stand on Mecca's porch
Matthew N. Davies

Advancing East Asian
Regionalism
Edited by Melissa G. Curley and
Nicholas Thomas

Political Cultures in Asia and
Europe
Citizens, states and societal values
Jean Blondel and Takashi Inoguchi

Political Cultures in Asia and Europe

Citizens, states and societal values

Jean Blondel and Takashi Inoguchi

Routledge
Taylor & Francis Group

LONDON AND NEW YORK

First published 2006
by Routledge
2 Park Square, Milton Park, Abingdon, Oxon OX14 4RN

Simultaneously published in the USA and Canada
by Routledge
270 Madison Ave, New York, NY 10016

*Routledge is an imprint of the Taylor & Francis Group,
an informa business*

Transferred to Digital Printing 2009

© 2006 Jean Blondel and Takashi Inoguchi

Typeset in Sabon by
Newgen Imaging Systems (P) Ltd, Chennai, India

British Library Cataloguing in Publication Data
A catalogue record for this book is available from the
British Library

Library of Congress Cataloging in Publication Data
Blondel, Jean, 1929–
    Political cultures in Asia and Europe: citizens, states and
societal values / by Jean Blondel and Takashi Inoguchi.
        p. cm. – (Politics in Asia series)
    Includes bibliographical references and index.
        1. Political culture–Asia. 2. Political culture–Europe.
    I. Inoguchi, Takashi. II. Title. III. Series.

    JQ36.B56 2006
    306.2095–dc22   2006003773

ISBN10: 0–415–40415–0 (hbk)
ISBN10: 0–415–54685–0 (pbk)
ISBN10: 0–203–96690–2 (ebk)

ISBN13: 978–0–415–40415–0 (hbk)
ISBN13: 978–0–415–54685–0 (pbk)
ISBN13: 978–0–203–96690–7 (ebk)

Contents

List of figures		xi
List of tables		xiii
Preface		xv

1 Introduction — 1

2 The nature and content of the notion of 'Asian values' — 20

3 How opposed are 'basic societal values' in the two regions? — 41

4 A common political culture in Western Europe? — 64

5 A common political culture in East and Southeast Asia? — 89

6 Political culture at the level of individual states — 113

7 Conclusion — 148

Appendix I: characteristics of the Asia–Europe Survey — 165
Appendix II: profiles of the eighteen countries of the Asia–Europe Survey — 168
Appendix III: recodes undertaken for Chapter 3 — 172
Notes — 174
Bibliography — 177
Index — 181

Figures

3.1 Spread of answers to human rights, communitarian and
     socio-economic questions, divided between the two
     regions by country   50
4.1 Spread of answers to human rights, communitarian and
     socio-economic questions, divided between northern and
     southern Western Europe by country   81
5.1 Spread of answers to human rights, communitarian and
     socio-economic questions, divided between East and
     Southeast Asia by country   106
6.1 The relationship between responses on the two
     liberalism questions   140
6.2 The relationship between responses on the two
     government restraint questions   140
6.3 The relationship between responses on the two
     decision-making questions (consensus and influence
     which old people should have)   141
6.4 The relationship between responses on the two *social
     relations* questions   141

Tables

2.1	Factor analyses	34
3.1	Distribution of 'agree', 'disagree' and 'not deciding' answers to the thirteen 'basic societal value' questions (percentages)	44
3.2	Intra-regional differences: spread (in percentage points from −100 to +100)	53
3.3	Intra-regional differences: overlap (number of countries)	55
3.4	First-level linkages between countries	56
3.5	First-level linkages between countries by answer	57
3.6	Type of relationship between background variables and societal values among Asian and European countries (number of cases)	61
6.1	Range of dispersion between regions, sub-regions and countries (percentages)	121
6.2	Cases of links between variables (number of countries)	131
6.3	Four models of dimensions linking human rights and communitarian questions	137
6.4	Number of times a country is at the Asian and European ends of country groupings	144
7.1	Distribution of 'pro-' and 'anti-Asian values' standpoints (percentages)	150

Preface

This book is the product of a close academic collaboration between the two of us over a decade, a collaboration which also includes Ian Marsh, now at the University of Sydney, and which started with the preparation and subsequent publication in 1999 of the edited book on *Democracy, Governance and Economic Performance* (Tokyo: United Nations University Press). That volume concentrates on East and Southeast Asia, but the many discussions we had at the time about politics in the region among the three of us and with the colleagues who had joined us in the preparation of that book turned frequently on the question of the attitudes of citizens to democracy and society in both East and Southeast Asia and the West. We became increasingly concerned with the fact that, amazingly, there was an almost total gap of comparative empirical evidence in this respect so that one could not find out whether these attitudes were or were not vastly different. The feeling that something had to be done to fill that gap was naturally strengthened by the fact that this was also the time when 'Asian values' and the 'clash of civilisations' were presented in some quarters as axiomatically correct interpretations of the present and future of East and West. To say the least, it seemed rather strange that we should not be able to know what attitudes ordinary citizens hold on democracy and society, not just between the two regions but within each of the two regions: it also seemed rather strange that, despite the absence of empirical evidence about what citizens feel, one should none the less be prepared to believe in a sharp divide between the attitudes of citizens in East and Southeast Asia, on the one hand, and in Western Europe, on the other. This book was therefore born out both of the impatience about these a priori standpoints and of the desire to begin to remedy this situation by attempting to find out how far what elites said about attitudes held in the society at large was indeed shared by the people.

We were most fortunate to be able to realise our desire to undertake such a study as a result of the generosity of the Japanese Ministry of Education and Science which provided us with a grant (#11102001 with principal investigator, Takashi Inoguchi) large enough to conduct identical surveys in eighteen countries, nine in each of the two regions. We thus had the opportunity to study simultaneously how far attitudes to democracy and society differed between the two regions and from one nation to another. We wish to express our profound gratitude to the key officials of the Ministry for having made this study possible in an atmosphere of complete freedom in terms of the questions which would be asked in the inquiry.

A study of this kind naturally includes a large number of participants and entails building a substantial technical infrastructure. The codebook was prepared during a series of meetings which took place in 1999 and 2000 and involved, alongside the two of us, Ian Marsh, Richard Sinnott of the University College Dublin and Ikuo Kabashima of the University of Tokyo. Our team was helped during these preparatory meetings by Ms Emiko Tomiie and Ms Kaori Kojima from the Nippon Research Centre, the polling organisation in charge of the organisation of the overall survey, of its administration in Japan and of the selection and overall supervision of the relevant survey organisations in the various countries in which the study was to be conducted. We wish to thank most warmly our three colleagues, these having been involved, as a matter of fact, in other aspects of the study. We wish to express our greatest thanks to the staff of the Nippon Research Centre and in particular to those of its members who attended our meetings and displayed extreme patience during the slow progress of the development of the codebook.

Our thanks go also to a large number of researchers from the countries concerned by the study, many of whom attended a conference which took place in Tokyo on 26–28 November 2002, at which they presented papers concerned with a variety of aspects of the study. We wish also to thank most warmly for the help they provided Professor Paola Palmitesta and Dr Filippo Tronconi, both of the University of Siena, as well as the collaborators of the Institute of Oriental Culture at the University of Tokyo, Mr Ken Firmalino and Mr Hideaki Uenohara with Ms Sakiko Doi and Ms Kimiko Goko who handled the administrative part of the project. We wish to thank the members of our families, and in particular Tess and Kuniko, for having been so patient during the whole of the process of preparation and maturation of the project, given the many meetings and the long periods of writing and rewriting the various drafts of this work. We would be dishonest not to say, however, that we did enjoy the adventure, an adventure which made us come closer to and therefore reflect on the attitudes held by the people of the countries concerned, even if the medium of the survey remains typically more abstract than one might ideally wish it to be.

Florence, London and Tokyo
Jean Blondel and Takashi Inoguchi

1   Introduction

This is a study of the political culture of citizens in eighteen countries of Western Europe and East and Southeast Asia; it is based on the answers to surveys undertaken at the end of 2000 in both areas with an identical questionnaire. Another volume is inquiring about the extent to which the citizens of the two regions react to the state (forthcoming), while a third examined how far these citizens were aware of and, if so, felt affected positively or negatively by the processes which have come under the general label of globalisation (forthcoming). The present volume aims at delving more deeply into the political culture itself. It is designed to elicit how far the political culture, at the level of the citizens, differs across two regions of the globe and within these regions in terms of basic attitudes to politics and society. The key question with respect to this objective can be summarised in the following way: is there convergence of citizens' values across the world and in particular in the regions which have moved towards what used to be called 'modernity' and may be labelled, according to some, 'post-modernity'?[1]

This work follows the example of the pioneering study of Gabriel Almond and Sydney Verba, *The Civic Culture*. That study, which was published in 1963, opened a line of systematic empirical inquiry into the social and political universe of the 'common man'. It did so by using the survey method, not just in the context of the electoral process, as had primarily been the case up to then, but in order to discover broader sets of attitudes and of judgements of populations about politics and society. It did so also by undertaking the analysis with the help of techniques which made it possible to go beyond impressionistic statements backed by little evidence.

The socio-political values of citizens: *The Civic Culture* and beyond

Naturally enough, as Verba stated in *The Civic Culture Revisited*, edited by Almond and Verba and published in 1990, 'the concerns expressed in *The Civic Culture* were products of their times. This, as I have pointed out, was reflected in the use of survey techniques and the focus on democratic stability' (1990, 408). However, *The Civic Culture* provides lessons which go beyond 'the concerns of the times' as these can guide efforts made, half a century later, to understand political culture in a truly general manner. The profound intellectual contribution of *The Civic Culture* results from the fact that the work develops an approach which places the political attitudes of citizens within a framework which is neither time- nor space-bound. First, the model is not time-bound because it propounds a tripartite distinction into parochial, subject and participant culture (as well as mixed types), these types being regarded as covering variations among all states. Admittedly, the distinction emerged in the context of 'modernisation theory': it is based on the notion that the 'participation state' 'should' characterise all nations. However, it does not consider such a move as 'inevitable'. In the very first paragraph of the volume, the authors note that there are 'serious doubts about the inevitability of democracy in the West' (1963, 3), let alone elsewhere. Indeed, as far as the 'new nations' are concerned, there are two major worries. One is that the 'participation explosion' can take two forms, totalitarian and democratic; the other is that there are special 'difficulties among the new nations [with respect to] the objective problems confronting these nations' (1963, 6). While the authors clearly hope that democracy in the Western sense will prevail, they propose a model which, precisely because of the doubts they have about the future, has to be independent from the question of the success or otherwise of democracy. Thus the model *does not postulate* that there will necessarily be a move from one of the types to the other. Moreover, and this is the second fundamental contribution of *The Civic Culture*, the work does not postulate either that the four Western countries to which it is devoted together with Mexico, albeit located in a common geographical universe, have to be part of a common culture. *The Civic Culture* does not *imply* that there will be 'convergence'; nor is it based on the notion of the search for 'geographical clusters': in this it differs sharply from studies which followed it, in particular on 'modernisation' and 'post-modernisation', but not only on these.

The model which is proposed in this study differs markedly from the model put forward in *The Civic Culture*, however. It does so in three ways. It differs, first, in that it aims at examining the extent to which what are widely regarded as two distinct cultures are indeed truly distinct. It differs, second, in that, contrary to what the authors of *The Civic Culture* state about their work, this study is concerned with 'orientation to the substance of political demands and outputs' (1963, 29): it seems impossible to do justice to the presence or absence of a fundamental distinction between two cultures without entering the field of the substance of political culture, even if in a broad manner. This study differs, third, in that the focus is not, as in *The Civic Culture*, on 'democratic stability', and thus not on the *nature* of support for the political system, but on the *extent* of this support. This has to be the case, since this study covers two regions, one of which is composed of states, the great majority of which have been highly authoritarian up to the last decades of the twentieth century and some of which were indeed still at least semi-authoritarian at the beginning of the twenty-first.

Yet, *The Civic Culture* did provide the key lesson that the main effort had to be the search for fundamental distinctions, without constraining these distinctions in terms of time – that is to say without postulating that there was to be 'convergence' – or in terms of space – that is to say without postulating that there was to be a search for 'geographical contiguity'. *The Civic Culture* provided another basis, and in this it has been followed by subsequent studies of political culture. That basis is that the state was to be the unit of analysis of the political culture of citizens. The case for such a unit of analysis was not argued in *The Civic Culture*: it was presumably assumed that it went without saying. After much questioning has taken place about the role of the state and in a different century, this assumption needs to be examined; one must reflect as to whether the state should continue to be the basis of the study.

This chapter examines therefore the components of the model which is adopted here and have just been outlined. These are, first, that 'convergence' over time cannot be assumed and therefore that it is more prudent to adopt a framework which is not based on time as a factor of 'development'. Second, geographical contiguity cannot be assumed either, that is to say that the culture of citizens who live in neigbouring states cannot be regarded as being axiomatically broadly similar. Third, the state remains the unit of analysis because it continues to be, by and large, even in the twenty-first century, the channel through which political culture is passed on to citizens. Fourth, political culture includes two distinct types of attitudes, both of which have to be explored. They are the attitudes which concern the values held by citizens about the 'good society' and those which relate to the support of citizens for the state. While this volume deals with the first aspect, another volume is concerned with the character of the support of citizens for the state.

Why it is not prudent to assume either that the political culture of citizens will become uniform across political systems or that differences in political culture across regions are fundamental

The key difficulty with the analysis of the political culture of citizens stems from the fact that we have barely any means, so far at least, of monitoring the dynamics of the process. We do have evidence of the dynamics of the process of economic change and of those aspects of social change which are 'objective', for instance in relation to health, welfare or education – though, even in the latter case, conclusions about literacy achievements are subject to substantial debates. We do not know, on the other hand, except to a very limited and indeed controversial extent, about changes in citizens' values. Indeed, we do not even know well what these values are, at least for most parts of the world, let alone what they were and are becoming. All that is said about dynamics in this field is therefore in the realm of speculation.

Modernisation, post-modernisation and 'convergence'

There has naturally been much speculation, however, and this speculation falls under three categories. One of these – and such a view is typically labelled 'modernisation theory' – consists in assuming a close relationship between economic, social and political change: when there is economic change, social and political change follows. There is therefore a further assumption, namely that, somehow, economic change precedes and 'explains' social and political change. That 'theory' leads to the notion of 'convergence': since industrialisation began, a process started to take place which led all countries to move in the same direction. Not all countries are at the same point on the road towards that goal, naturally, but all are going along it. The idea of convergence is therefore the cornerstone of the edifice of 'modernisation theory'.

This question is particularly relevant to the present study for, if the theory of convergence is to be valid, it has to apply to East and Southeast Asia, given the extremely rapid development of that region in the last decades of the twentieth century. Western Europe and East and Southeast Asia are the two regions which have come to be the most economically and indeed socially 'developed' areas of the globe together with North America: many of the problems which East and Southeast Asia faces are therefore likely to be of the same character as the problems which are faced by Western countries: the matter had to be explored. While a genuinely worldwide study of political cultures poses very difficult problems of analysis and even of inter-pretation,[2] it seemed possible and it was truly imperative to undertake an in-depth and geographically representative comparative examination of the political culture of the two regions which are most similar in their economic achievements, in order to discover whether they were different in other ways. If there was to be a way of exploring the validity of the convergence idea, a matter which, as we shall see, is in serious doubt, this had to be by examining in parallel the cultural characteristics of Western countries and of East and Southeast Asian countries.

Although 'modernisation theory' was attacked on a variety of grounds and it did suffer a decline from the late 1960s, it was never abandoned alto-gether. It was even somewhat revived in the last decades of the twentieth century, partly as a result of the fall of communism and partly as a result of the other 'waves' of democratisation which characterised the period, as these events seemed to manifest the existence of a close link between eco-nomic and political change. This link had indeed been suggested by Lipset and others from the early 1960s, the most sophisticated of these analyses having been those conducted by Vanhanen since the 1980s (Lipset, 1960, new edn 1983; Vanhanen, 1997, 2003).

Meanwhile, 'modernisation theory' itself underwent a change as a result of the studies of Inglehart, who suggested, first in his 1977 volume which was devoted to Western Europe and subsequently, on a wider front, in his 1997 volume, that societies were moving towards 'post-modernisation' (Inglehart, 1977, 1990, 1997; Inglehart and Baker, 2000). Inglehart stated categorically that 'post-modernisation' was part of 'modernisation theory'. He also suggested that there was some evidence that the political culture of citizens did change from a 'modernisation' to a 'post-modernisation' set of attitudes, but on the basis of data which related to Western countries only (Inglehart, 1977, 53).[3]

He thus claims at the opening of the 1997 volume:

> Economic, cultural, and political change go together in coherent patterns that are changing the world in predictable ways.
>
> This has been the central claim of Modernisation theory, from Karl Marx to Max Weber and Daniel Bell. The claim has given rise to heated debate during the last two centuries. This book presents evidence that this claim is largely correct.
>
> (ibid., 7)

Inglehart's 1977 study was based on Western European countries only; that of 1997 was based on 40 countries from around the world, but the sample was fundamentally biassed: Western states constituted about half the total of the forty countries, while a further quarter was made up of Eastern European countries, with the result that the number of Latin American cases is small (four) and that of East and Southeast Asian cases tiny (Korea and Japan, with China being included, somewhat surprisingly). Yet, despite the fact that this evidence is biassed geographically and does not provide any dynamics, except to a limited extent for Western Europe, Inglehart proceeds to express in the strongest manner the view that there is 'convergence' while correspondingly asserting that political culture is in some sense the consequence of economic change.

> Although frequently stereotyped as having authoritarian cultures, China, Japan, and South Korea all emerge near the pole that emphasises thrift rather than obedience. The three East Asian societies in this survey rank highest on Achievement Motivation.... The scale reflects the balance between two types of values: one type of values – emphasising thrift and determination – supports economic achievement, while the other – emphasising obedience and religious faith – tends to discourage it, stressing conformity to traditional authority and norms. These two types of values are not necessarily incompatible: some societies rank high on both, while others rank relatively low on both. But the relatively (*sic*) *priority* accorded to these two types of values is strongly related to a society's growth rate.
>
> (ibid., 221–2)

He adds:

> Brilliant and instructive books have been written about the ways in which given societies differ from others. This book focuses on the general themes underlying the cross-national pattern, not because we are uninterested in the unique aspects of given societies – few things are more fascinating – but because the common themes are *also* interesting, and because any book that undertakes to deal with more than 40 societies almost inevitably *must* focus on what is common, rather than on what is unique. The evidence examined here indicates that common underlying themes *do* exist: it suggests that roughly half of the cross-national variance in these values and attitudes can be accounted for by the processes of Modernisation and Postmodernisation, while the remaining half of the variation reflects factors that are more or less nation-specific.
>
> (Inglehart, 1997, 84, italics in the text)

One should note in this respect that if 'roughly half of the cross-national variance in these values and attitudes can be accounted for by the processes of Modernisation and Postmodernisation', 'roughly half of the cross-national variance in these values and attitudes' *cannot* be accounted for by these processes. It therefore is not prudent to assume such dependency of political culture on economic change and to assume convergence among citizens' values before being even clear as to what these values are across the world.

Political culture as accounting for economic and social change

The view that there might be 'convergence' about political culture across the world is thus speculative: it is perhaps not surprising that it should be rejected by many, in particular by those who feel that it has a pro-Western bias, the West being expected to lead the path towards modernisation and post-modernisation. This is the second form, equally speculative, which has thus been put forward. It consists in claiming that political culture is the engine of development including economic and social development. Whether such a view also means that there will or not be convergence is not clear; the main purpose is not to consider what the future might hold but to claim that the political culture of regions other than the West, in this case East and Southeast Asia, is 'better' for economic and social change, and for society in general than the political culture of the West. This view was adopted in its most extreme form by some academics and politicians of East and Southeast Asia who suggested that 'Asian values' were indeed what made the region so dynamic economically. It was claimed in particular that the socio-political relationships prevailing among East and Southeast Asian populations were based on a more 'collective' or 'communitarian' view of society, in contrast with the equally widely believed notion that Western citizens display greater 'individualism'[4]: this was the reason, according to those who held this view, why East and Southeast Asia had been so successful. The same kind of approach was also adopted, albeit in a somewhat 'softer' manner and in the context of business only, by a variety of scholars and commentators from both East and West who pointed to the superiority of the Japanese model of industrial management over the Western one.

While, at any rate for some decades, it was clear that economic change was more rapid in East and Southeast Asia than in the West, the link between this performance and the values of citizens was not proven. Broad studies of the values of citizens at large were not undertaken in that part of the world; there were a number of empirical studies of the values of managers and of key employees of firms from the late 1970s onwards, admittedly, and these began to cover areas outside the West: but they did not – and could not – demonstrate that the economic performance of firms and of the economy in general in East and Southeast Asia was due to the political culture of these managers and key employees.

Political culture as distinct from economic and social change

If both the claims that economic and social change leads to 'convergence' and that the values of citizens account for economic and social change are purely speculative, it is understandable that a third, somewhat intermediate line should have been taken, namely that political culture is scarcely affected by economic and social change. This view has been expressed most emphatically by Pye, who both agrees with the 'convergence' aspects of economic development and rejects the notion that political culture will ever be uniform.

> The degree to which cultures converge during the process of modernisation is significant since they are all participating in the spread of a world culture based on advanced technology. Yet political cultures will always have a strongly parochial dimension because every political system is anchored in its distinctive history, and the central political values of loyalty and patriotism and the phenomenon of national identity mean that differences are certain to persist, and possibly even to increase with modernization.
>
> (Pye, 1985, 342)

The author then goes on to find evidence in the fact that Western European countries, while including ' "modern" societies composed of "modern" people' have 'profoundly different' political cultures (ibid.).

Such a view is seemingly more realistic in that no great claims are being made, indeed quite the contrary; yet it is as speculative as the other two. It seems even difficult to hold it literally as it is too 'modest'. It is hard to believe that there is no relationship whatsoever between the political culture of citizens and 'objective' social and economic change. It seems more probable the case that some relationship exists, but that it is reciprocal and that it is subjected to lags of an indeterminate character. In the last resort, the demonstration that there are such relationships has to be made on the basis of evidence collected over time, an evidence which scarcely exists, as we noted, outside the very limited amount which Inglehart presented about Western Europe.

Before such a dynamic analysis can be undertaken, moreover, there is a need to acquire straightforward knowledge about what the political culture of citizens consists of. This is surely the first step to take, whether or not the dynamics of the process can also be documented. What needs to be discovered is whether, *currently*, differences in value patterns among citizens are vast or small from one region of the globe to another. By limiting the analysis to two regions which have reached a high level of economic development and therefore by controlling to an extent for economic development, one can more easily concentrate on the characteristics of these values. In this way one does at least find out whether 'Asian values' prevail in East and Southeast Asia (as well as, presumably, whether Western values prevail in the West). While not being able to help to determine whether there is 'convergence' or not with respect to these values or whether they depend or not on, or influence or not economic and social change, an examination of the current values of citizens will at least make it possible to discover whether, indeed, these values are fundamentally different in the two regions.

Why it is not prudent to assume that the political culture of citizens is uniform within each region

No one has suggested so far that a common world political culture already exists: the debate on the matter is about whether there is a convergence process and, if such a process is taking place, it is at best expected to take a long time to reach its ultimate goal. In the case of 'regional political cultures', on the other hand, it is often suggested that there *are* already common cultures and that these cultures are part, perhaps a large part, of what distinguishes one region of the globe from another. The question is therefore not whether countries within regions are converging in terms of their political culture: it is whether such a common political culture does exist or not.

The controversy about the existence of regional political cultures

As a matter of fact, there are major controversies in this respect, but these have not led to a systematic analysis of the problem of 'regional' political cultures: the judgements which are passed seem to be on two parallel planes. On the one hand, the West is regarded by most, if not by all, as having a common political culture which is distinct from the political culture of other parts of the world; on the other hand, at least the political culture of Northern Europe and that of Southern Europe are so often presented as being different that they seem to be regarded as two wholly distinct cultures. A similar contrast arises in relation to East and Southeast Asia: on the one hand, it is sometimes viewed as a region with a common culture, though this is said less frequently than about Western Europe – not surprisingly perhaps, since, apart from Japan and China, the countries of the region became independent recently only and the area had difficulty in becoming truly one cultural region afterwards, in large part because of the impact of communism; meanwhile, the difference between a 'Chinese' and a 'Malay' culture is often emphasised as being so deep that the idea of a common East and Southeast Asian culture may be unrealistic.

It is possible to reconcile to an extent these contrasting viewpoints. One can, for instance, play up the 'higher' level and play down the 'lower' level and state that the more fundamental element is the common political culture of the region; differences within the region should then be regarded as being merely 'sub-cultures'. This kind of interpretation is probably widespread in the Western European case.

On the contrary, one can play up the 'lower' level and play down the 'higher' level: this is likely to be often done with respect to East and Southeast Asia, the common regional element being regarded as somewhat symbolic rather than real. Pye thus refers to 'the East Asian Confucian cultures of China, Japan, Korea and Vietnam' and to 'the Southeast Asian patron-client systems of Burma, Thailand, Indonesia and the Philippines' (to which he adds a third element constituted by South Asia) (1985, 30). The idea of a common regional culture can be regarded as wishful thinking, more in the nature of a political gesture designed to assert East and Southeast Asia's position with respect to America and perhaps Europe. However, the fact that Japan is the economic leader and that Southeast Asia depends markedly on Japanese capital and knowhow tends to bring the two segments of the region closer to each other and unquestionably much closer to each other than they ever were, given the fact that most of Southeast Asia was composed of colonies of Western Europe before 1939 and thus had to look more to the West than to the North at the time.

As a matter of fact, there is also an element of wishful thinking in the context of Europe. Admittedly, the idea of (mainly Western) Europe as a common cultural area is rather old, but, until the nineteenth century at least, the Europeanness of Europeans was exclusively at the level of the elites. Subsequently, wars and changes of political regimes meant that there was relatively little ground for Western Europeans to see themselves as Europeans: not surprisingly, therefore, as is well known, most European citizens feel primarily nationals of their country and not Europeans. Thus, even if Europe is viewed as gradually becoming a political unit, to claim that its component parts are merely sub-sets of the bigger whole is an obvious exaggeration.

Yet the fact that the citizens of the various European countries see themselves as different from each other – and that the citizens of the countries of East and Southeast Asia perhaps feel that way even more – does not signify that a common regional culture does not exist in either case. Citizens of a region may feel different from each other and yet may have broadly the same political culture. The question of the existence of a common regional culture cannot be resolved on the basis of the feelings of 'belongingness' of citizens: what has to be determined is whether the attitudes which these citizens hold differ and differ sufficiently from one part of the region to another to warrant the conclusion that their political culture is truly distinct and not merely a variant of a common political culture.

Regional or sub-regional political cultures?

Since the question is not whether there will be convergence at some point in the future but whether the citizens of the region have a common political culture, an answer to the puzzle can be found by asking representative samples about their values. Such surveys have began to be administered, on a limited scale, since the 1970s, although the aim has been more to discover the values held by managers and by key employees of firms, sometimes multinationals, than to discover in a general manner the broad pattern of the political culture of all citizens, especially outside the West.

These studies were designed to discover, at a time when Europe was uniting economically, whether those who were in charge of important firms in the region could be said to hold attitudes which were sufficiently similar to each other to be part of a common culture. As a result, especially in the earlier work and partly because this type of data was easier to obtain, emphasis was placed more on the work culture than on political culture in general and in Europe than on the rest of the world. The samples were therefore geographically biassed, indeed often as much as and in some cases more than had been the case with Inglehart's sample of the 1990s (Ronen and Kraut, 1977; Hofstede, 1980; Woliver and Cattell, 1981; Smith *et al.*, 1996; Brodbeck *et al.*, 2000).[5]

Among the authors of these studies, however, Hofstede stands apart as, in his *Culture's Consequences*, published in 1980, he endeavoured to go beyond work culture, to base his conclusions on a sample of countries which was more representative and to look for general dimensions. His work has therefore been a leader in the field for a generation, as the references made to *Culture's Consequences* by those who wrote after him do show. His aim is descriptive: having found, by means of factor analyses, that there were four dimensions of culture, he attempts to see whether certain combinations of dimensions tend to occur and whether they occur in some regions rather than in others.

One of the key purposes of these 'management' studies, typically undertaken by social psychologists, is indeed to find out whether there are common regional or 'sub-regional' cultures. Factor analyses make it possible to do so and, in order to provide a more immediate grasp by the readers of the conclusions of these statistical findings, visual presentations in the form of maps show the way in which countries can be grouped. Ronen and Kraut were among the first to do so by using data from two earlier surveys of, respectively, 15 and 14 countries (1977, 92–4). Hofstede did the same (1980, 316, 324) as well as some of his successors. Inglehart also provided maps in his 1997 volume (1997, 93, 335, 349), but these are not based, as those of Hofstede and other social psychologists, on dimensions of the personality. There are based, in line with the general goals of the work, on aspects of societal development: two variables are identified as critical, 'rational-legal authority' and 'post-modern values'.

The most general conclusion which can be drawn from these analyses is that sub-regional cultures, but not uniform regional cultures, are found to exist. Western Europe, for instance, cannot be reduced to a single 'cultural region'. In Inglehart's study it is divided into 'Northern Europe' and 'Catholic Europe', though, in one case, Britain and Ireland are said to be part of the 'English-speaking' group (1997, 93, 335, 349); Hofstede's analysis leads to suggest, as is also suggested by other authors, that there is a more specifically Scandinavian cultural area, which includes also Finland and the Netherlands. Indeed, all of those who have studied the culture of managers have distinguished between at least a Northern or Germanic Europe and a Latin Europe. The sample of East and Southeast Asian countries is so small in Inglehart's study that these cannot be subdivided, but Hofstede is able to distinguish between a Southeast Asian and an East Asian cluster. Empirical analyses thus lead to rejecting the view that either Western Europe or East and Southeast Asia should be regarded as single cultural areas.

These findings do not make it possible to answer with certainty, however, whether sub-regional distinctions constitute 'sub-cultural' differences which might well be integrated in more general regional cultures. The maps provide somewhat ambiguous results in this respect, apart from the fact that, even in Hofstede's analysis, East and Southeast Asia is not fully represented. The reason these results are ambiguous may have to do with the fact that the search for uniform 'sub-regional' cultures may be as illusory as the search for uniform regional cultures.

The limits of sub-regional political cultures and the need
not to make assumptions about the 'geographical contiguity'
of political culture

As was noted earlier, the socio-psychological studies, of which Hofstede's is the most prominent, were triggered by the desire to find out whether there were 'supra-national' managerial cultures, so to speak; Inglehart, on the other hand, was anxious to demonstrate that the move from 'materialism' to 'post-materialism' was sweeping across Western Europe and even extending beyond that region. Thus, all the authors have been eager to look for possible combinations of states rather than for a set of 'independent' country results. They do not, in the end, truly consider each state as a unit of analysis in its own right: they aim at showing that, if there is no regional culture, 'sub-regional' cultures do exist. In reality, the examination of all the maps which are published in these studies indicates that even the smaller geographical groupings which are elaborated are difficult to sustain and that what emerges from the data is markedly less clear-cut. The 'forced' character of the groupings is particularly noticeable in the contours which Inglehart gives to these groupings. In the map which appears at page 349 of the 1997 volume, the Northern European group is made to include countries which are very distant from each other on the map and which are often closer to countries which are described as belonging to other groups: thus Switzerland (which is noted as belonging to the Northern European group) is closer to Britain and Canada (which are presented as belonging to the English-speaking group) than to any other country of its own group; Germany is closer to Japan than to any other country of its own group. 'Geographically-contiguous' groups seem therefore to have been created arbitrarily and not to emerge from the data itself.

Hofstede's presentation does not suffer from this drawback to the same extent: some of the circles which are drawn include countries which do not all belong to one geographical area. Thus, France and Italy are placed in the same group as several Latin American countries in the map appearing at page 316, and Italy and Belgium are placed in the same group as several Latin American countries in the map appearing at page 324. Yet, even Hofstede does not appear prepared to abandon entirely the idea of geographical contiguity. Some of the circles which he draws include countries which are geographically close to each other, although, according to the clusters, these countries may well be appreciably closer to countries belonging to other groups. For instance, in the map at page 316, Germany is appreciably closer to the Netherlands than it is to Austria, although Germany and Austria, but not the Netherlands, are circled as belonging to the same group; in the map at page 324 Finland is appreciably closer to Thailand than it is to Denmark, although Finland and Denmark, but not Thailand, are circled as belonging to the same group.

Empirical analyses have been conducted in order to discover whether one can refer to uniform regional cultures: such a conclusion does not appear valid; but it is equally uncertain as to whether even the sub-regional groupings which emerge from the statistical analyses are composed of countries which are sufficiently close to each other to constitute blocks of common cultural areas. It seems therefore not prudent to expect 'geographical contiguity' to constitute the basis for common political cultures.

On the contrary, empirical analyses show sharp cultural differences among countries which are geographically contiguous; these differences, rather than the similarities, need to be taken into account. The only sensible approach thus consists in examining similarities and differences in the values of citizens *of each country* and to determine, each state genuinely being the unit of analysis, whether the values of citizens of different states are sufficiently close to each other to constitute the basis of a common political culture.

It still is right to adopt the state as the basic unit of analysis in the context of political culture studies: the announcement of the state's demise is unquestionably premature

Yet if the examination of the attitudes of citizens shows that the political culture of these citizens varies even within what is widely regarded as a common geographical cultural area, would it not be also prudent to cease adopting the state as the unit of analysis? The existence of 'sub-cultures' below the level of the state is well known. In some cases, cultural differences are vast and seem overwhelming, for instance in Belgium, Switzerland, Malaysia or India, where these cultural differences are embedded in the language of different groups; but, even if they are typically less funda-mental, substantial 'sub-cultural' differences exist in every country, not only between ethnic and religious groups in particular, but also between classes. Why then stop at the state and why not look at the political culture of the citizens belonging to the key groupings which are within each state?

This problem is simply not mentioned at all in *The Civic Culture*: states are the units of analysis. For the authors of that study, the supremacy of the state was not regarded as problematic. One must even go further: it must be inferred from the lack of discussion of this problem that the state was regarded as the framework within which political culture emerged and that it was regarded in this way because it was the socialising agent for (the broad mass of) citizens. Yet what was simply obvious or incontrovertible in the early 1960s may not be so in the twenty-first century. The events which have occurred in the last decades of the twentieth century seem to have appreciably eroded the status of the state, in 'objective' terms at least. First, many new states have been created and these often appear to have a limited 'capacity'. Second, secessions have taken place, in particular in Eastern Europe and North Asia, and these have also led to the creation of new states whose capacity may not always be large. Moreover, and generally, states appear to be increasingly in question at the international level as a result of the growth of international organisations, intergovernmental or supra-national, public or private, economic or social. Finally and somewhat more unexpectedly perhaps, states seem also to be undermined by a num-ber of 'sub-national' bodies which appear to have acquired prominence in the second half of the twentieth century. Is it therefore still the case that there are strong enough grounds for continuing to maintain that the state is the level at which the analysis of political culture can be legitimately undertaken?

What is at stake here, however, is not whether the state is, objectively, less powerful than it was, but whether the citizens feel that way. Ideally, one would have wanted to know whether, as a result of the setting up of new states, of the break-up of some of the older ones, of the growth of international organisations and of the emergence of powerful 'sub-national' bodies, citizens believe that the 'weight' of the state has markedly declined. The answer to this question cannot be given, as we have no means of knowing with any degree of precision what citizens thought in the past about the state to which they belonged, whether because there were no surveys on the subject at the time or because, in the more recent past, such surveys on the subject were not permitted. What can be discovered is only how far the state, at present, is regarded by citizens as being the key institution to which they refer.

Support for the state must be substantial if the state is to remain the unit of analysis of political culture. For, if the support for the state is strong, if, in a nutshell, citizens see themselves as 'owing their allegiance' above all to the state, they are more than likely to continue to be socialised by the various instruments which the state has at its disposal, by education in particular, and more generally by the many ways in which state authorities have an impact on citizens in the course of their life. Where the state does not only have the opportunity to affect citizens, above all because it does not play a major part in the education of children, but also because it does not reach citizens in many localities (as is often the case in the Third World and as is indeed the case in several Latin American states), it becomes questionable as to whether the state should be the basic unit of analysis of studies of political culture. Where, on the other hand, the state does play a major part in educating future citizens and in administering all those who live on its territory, as is manifestly the case in Western countries but also in East and Southeast Asia, the state can be regarded as the framework by excellence within which attitudes are formed, including those formed against the state and its policies. One of the reasons why a worldwide inquiry about the political culture of citizens is at best premature is indeed that the validity of such an inquiry depends on the extent to which the state can be regarded as the 'true' 'provider of political culture' in various parts of the world. Meanwhile, one of the reasons why attention has been paid in another volume to the part played by the state in the minds of the citizens is in order to be able to assess whether it was indeed justified to regard the state as the unit of analysis of the study.

As a matter of fact, while the part played by the state in the West and in East and Southeast Asia may be declining and may even have already declined, the grounds for believing that the state continues to be the main frame of reference of citizens in these two regions continue to be strong.

This is true even in Western Europe, where, as is well known, despite the substantial development of the European Union, the large majority of citizens continue to refer primarily to the state to which they belong (Blondel *et al.*, 1998). Perhaps even more to the point, despite the apparent rise in prestige and even power of a number of sub-national bodies in a number of states, the state does continue to be regarded by citizens as the major frame of reference. There are a number of exceptions to that general 'rule', admittedly; but, in Western Europe and in East and Southeast Asia, these are indeed exceptions. They affect a minority of states, Belgium being probably the prime example, and, almost everywhere, a minority of citizens within these states. Local and, where they have been set up, 'regional' authorities are important in many aspects of decision-making, to be sure, and many, probably most, citizens are aware of this fact: but citizens appear none the less able to distinguish between the power which these authorities exercise and the fact that they operate within the framework of the state.

It seems therefore entirely legitimate, at any rate within the context of the two regions which are studied here, to continue to regard the state as the proper unit of analysis for the inquiry into the political culture of citizens. A proviso must be made, however: reference must be made to the way the citizens themselves consider the state. This is one of the key reasons why, alongside the examination of substantive attitudes of citizens to the 'good society' undertaken in this volume, another volume is devoted to the way in which these citizens regard the state. Ultimately, it is to the extent that the state constitutes a reference point that the examination of the attitudes of citizens in a given state can legitimately be undertaken. There was therefore an overwhelming case for looking in parallel at the attitudes of the citizens to the 'good society' and towards the state, as has been undertaken in two of the volumes which are based on the surveys in the two regions.

The analysis of the political culture of citizens must be based both on the examination of views about the 'good society', which is the object of the present volume, and on attitudes relating to the support for the state, undertaken in another volume

'We would mislead the reader if we were to suggest that our study treats proportionately each aspect of political culture. Our study stresses orientation to political structure and process, not orientation to the substance of political demands and outputs' (Almond and Verba, 1963, 29). The authors of *The Civic Culture* were no doubt influenced by the systems approach which was fashionable at the time and which was in the process of being systematised in the political context by Easton. This meant stressing the part played by *support* rather than by the content of the policies which the state was putting forward (Easton, 1965, *passim*).

Attitudes to the 'good society' or to 'basic societal values'

This volume concentrates on attitudes to the good society in the eighteen countries covered by this study. As was pointed out at the outset, an approach based exclusively on support and not on content would simply be wholly unrealistic when one aims at understanding the political culture of Western European and East and Southeast Asian countries. So much of the literature on the subject is devoted to the demonstration that attitudes to the 'good society' are substantively different in East and Southeast Asia from what they are in Western Europe that, perhaps above all and unquestionably in a major way, the study of the political culture of the two regions must examine whether or to what extent the propositions which are put forward about the differences are correct.

Indeed, most, if not all of the literature which is concerned with the difference between East and Southeast Asia and Western Europe focuses on attitudes to the 'good society' which can also and perhaps more accurately be referred to as attitudes to 'basic societal values'. One reason was, as noted earlier, that a substantial part, probably the largest part, of that literature was aimed at discovering the attitudes of managers: as a result, views about work and about the firm are more emphasised than views about the society at large. Yet attitudes about society are also examined, would it only be because attitudes about work have to be placed in context; moreover, Hofstede's approach in particular is broad, although the author stops short of undertaking a study of political culture as such, given that he, too, was examining attitudes of employees, in this case of a single large multinational firm.

What Hofstede aims at doing in *Culture's Consequences* is to present the basic 'dimensions' of culture which may exist among nations. As the author states at the beginning of his work:

> This book explores the differences in thinking and social action that exist between members of 40 different modern nations. It argues that people carry 'mental programs' which are developed in the family in early childhood and reinforced in schools and organisations, and that these mental programs contain a component of national culture. They are most clearly expressed in the different values that predominate among people from different countries.
>
> (ibid., 1980, 11)

The proof that Hofstede is concerned, not merely with attitudes of employees to work and firm, but in the widest possible manner about what he refers to as 'basic problems of humanity' (1980, 312) can be found in the broad framework within which he brings together the replies to the questions which were administered in the surveys which he analyses. He discovers that there are four dimensions within which he can order the value systems of respondents from the forty countries which these surveys covered. These four dimensions are 'power distance', 'uncertainty avoidance', 'individualism' and 'masculinity'. He then locates each country in relation to these dimensions and it is in this context that he draws two maps, one which relates 'power distance' to 'uncertainty avoidance' while the other relates 'uncertainty avoidance' to 'masculinity' (1980, 316, 324). This makes it possible for him to state that Scandinavian countries are 'feminine', have a 'small power distance' and are weak on 'uncertainty avoidance', while most Latin American countries are 'masculine', have a 'large power distance' and are strong on 'uncertainty avoidance'.

Hofstede's data seems to justify the view that there are four separate dimensions, although he himself notes that there is a high correlation between the power distance and individualism dimensions; but intercorrelations among the other indices are weak (1980, 314). Yet studies which have been undertaken since Hofstede published his work have strongly suggested that these dimensions should be reduced, at least to three and perhaps even to two, as strong correlations were indeed found to exist between the individualism and the power distance dimensions (Smith *et al.*, 1996, 234). Smith and his colleagues proceed to examine studies which have been undertaken since Hofstede published his *Culture's Consequences* before giving the results of their own analysis. They note that some studies claimed that only two dimensions were truly relevant, these two dimensions being labelled, in one case, 'openness to change versus conservatism' and 'self-enhancement versus self-transcendance' (ibid., 235). Having analysed data from slightly more nations (43) than Hofstede, the authors of the study conclude that one can discover three dimensions but that the third 'only accounts for a further 7 per cent variation in the proximities data' (ibid., 246). Basically, the two dimensions which seem to account for substantial variations in the attitudes of citizens are 'achievement versus ascription' or 'universalism versus particularism' or 'conservatism versus change-supporting', on the one hand, and 'utilitarianism versus loyalty' or 'individualism versus collectivism' (ibid., 247–53). The conclusion is that Hofstede's 'uncertainty avoidance' and 'masculinism–feminism' dimensions 'are not readily apparent (ibid., 259), while his other two dimensions, 'power distance' and 'individualism–collectivism' are important.

The current study thus examines the attitudes of the citizens of the two regions with respect to 'basic societal values'. It follows the approach which Hofstede and other social psychologists have adopted in being descriptive and in not assuming that attitudes of citizens can be located within a single overall dimension. This study is more specifically political than that of Hofstede and other social psychologists, however: it does not originate from the examination of responses of employees in relation to firms; nor does it inquire into the fundamentals of the personality which these studies tend to explore. The emphasis is on the basic values which correspond to the general position which the individual perceives to have in society.

This makes it possible, for the first time, to assess how strong is the evidence for the claim that citizens of East and Southeast Asia hold a cluster of 'basic societal values' which correspond to what has been often described as 'Asian values' and how strong is the evidence for the claim that Western European citizens hold different values in this regard. It is also possible to determine the extent to which there are variations among the citizens of each region with respect to these values and thus to conclude whether the two regions are indeed separated by a massive 'fault line' or whether one is confronted with a markedly more complex panorama.

Yet, one must not exaggerate the extent to which conclusions can reasonably be drawn on the basis of responses, typically given rapidly, to a conventional survey. This study has therefore to be viewed as the first foray into the comparative study of attitudes to democracy and society in East and Southeast Asian and Western Europe. Its ambition is to delineate some of the main contours of the similarities and differences in these attitudes in the eighteen nations concerned; but it also expects to start a trend and naturally to be followed by many comparative studies designed to examine these and other attitudes in the years to come.

The structure of this book

One can obtain in the way which has just been described an overall picture of the 'basic societal values' which for citizens are likely to result in the 'good society'. This is done in this book by looking successively at three levels at which citizens react to 'basic societal values'. To begin with, Chapter 2 looks at the way in which the debate between Asian and Western values has been presented in the literature. Chapter 3 then examines the evidence, on the basis of the surveys conducted for this study, for the view that there is a fundamental conflict of attitudes between East and West. The subsequent two chapters examine the extent to which there are differences in attitudes towards 'basic societal values' within each of the two regions of this study: Chapter 4 deals with Western Europe and looks especially at the possible contrast between North and South; Chapter 5 deals with East and Southeast Asia and is concerned with the possible consequences of various cleavages, religious as well as geographical, among the countries of East and Southeast Asia. Chapter 6 considers the variations which may exist at the level of individual countries; an attempt is made to see to what extent countries can be grouped on the basis of there being similarities in the attitudes of respondents to 'basic societal values'. Finally, in conclusion, Chapter 7 attempts to give a balanced judgement about the extent to which the political culture of citizens does differ between East and West, within regions and at the level of individual states.

* * * * *

This volume aims at providing a comprehensive picture of the political culture of citizens in East and Southeast Asia and Western Europe. Such a task cannot be achieved without abandoning some of the assumptions ('taboos' to an extent) which prevail about 'civilisations' and about the differences among these civilisations. It means being 'inductive' rather than 'deductive' in the approach to political culture: daily experience, for instance about election results in Western democracies, have repeatedly shown that the views that elite groups may have about certain relationships are distinct, indeed often divorced, from the views of the citizenry at large. This does not entail passing a judgement about who is right or who is wrong: it is unquestionably the function of political elites in the broadest sense of the word to attempt to form or transform opinion. What is manifestly wrong is to believe that what the members of these elites state about the views of the citizenry at large is necessarily correct. The purpose of this book is to find out how 'correct' is received opinion (received, that is, from the elite) about the views which the citizens hold on attitudes to 'basic societal values'. It is hoped that debates about values and about the relationship between the citizen and the state might be better informed by being based on a more realistic assessment of what citizens feel on these matters.

2 The nature and content of the notion of 'Asian values'

If there is to be a regional political culture in East and Southeast Asia and, correspondingly, in Western Europe, two conditions have to be met: on the one hand, the attitudes of respondents in each of the two regions have to be profoundly different; on the other, the attitudes of respondents within each region have to be similar. This is presumably what was meant by the strongly worded statements which were made in East and Southeast Asia, especially in the 1980s and early 1990s, a period which can be considered as the hey-day of what might be described, without more than a tinge of exaggeration, as the 'Asian values' 'movement'. These statements suggested that a sharp contrast – a real divide – existed between 'Asian' and Western values; as a matter of fact, those who made that point also tended to claim that 'Asian values' were not just different from but superior to 'Western values'.

The views represented by these statements were forcefully expressed by a number of prominent Asian politicians, but they were also put forward by some Asian scholars. They were not held by all politicians and all scholars in the region, to be sure: the opposite standpoint has also been put force-fully by many others, the debate being sufficiently 'animated' to occupy the front stage for a number of years. Yet, the notion that 'Asian values' were different from, possibly even superior to, 'Western values' was not put forward in the late decades of the twentieth century only.[1] They were and continue to be the basis of a major debate which belongs to the more general question of the universality of culture, a debate which naturally concerns many other parts of the world besides East and Southeast Asia, as was pointed out in the previous chapter.

The debate has tended so far to be regarded as one for which evidence was sought from sources of a philosophical character or belonging to the realm of cultural and, in particular, religious history. In such a perspective, the ques-tion to answer seemed to be: are there, in the roots of the civilisation of the two regions, reasons to believe that profound differences exist in the values prevailing in these two regions, a point at which the question of the role of Confucianism does arise? Such an approach has the merit of providing an interpretation for the panorama of the values which do prevail: but it is based ultimately on the assumption that the citizens – or at least the large majority of them – do hold these values. To be truly relevant in a social context, a philosophical or cultural historical interpretation of this kind must unquestionably be associated to an investigation designed to ascertain whether, indeed, the citizens of the two regions hold the values – assumed to be vastly different from each other – which they are said to hold. Before attempting to interpret why citizens, in East and Southeast Asia, for instance, hold 'Asian values', that is to say values which are specific to East and Southeast Asian citizens, evidence must be obtained indicating that they do.

The debate on 'Asian values' is particularly relevant to the study of political culture because the values which were discussed in the context of that debate were not concerned so much with straightforward economic or social issues, that is to say with ideology in the way it is usually referred to, but with attitudes, perhaps less political in character, which might be regarded, however, as reflecting 'deeper' aspects of the personality. Thus, in order to examine whether, indeed, 'Asian' values differ profoundly from 'Western' values, one needs obviously to begin by determining, as precisely as possible, what is meant by and what constitutes 'Asian values' if one is to be able, in a subsequent stage, to assess the strength of the evidence suggesting that the citizens of East and Southeast Asia hold these values while the citizens of Western Europe do not. The fact that the present study is based on surveys of eighteen nations in the two regions provides an opportunity to undertake the empirical part of such an inquiry systematically: but this undertaking had to be preceded by an examination of the corpus of ideas which had been subsumed under the general rubric of 'Asian values'.

This chapter is devoted to the first part of the inquiry. To do so, it has to be concerned with four questions. First, the problem of Asian values has to be related to the more general matter of the specificity of values across the world. Second, we need to describe, however briefly, the content of Asian values and consider the extent to which they are said to differ from Western values by those who support these values. Third, we need to move from this description to an operationalisation of these values in the form of questions put to citizens in the countries of the two regions to be able to assess how far the views of these citizens differ in these two regions. Fourth, we need to examine whether the answers to these questions fall into a limited number of separate dimensions and thus can be said to form a syndrome or whether, on the contrary, they constitute discrete elements and thus raise problems about the coherence, in the minds of the citizens, of the notion of 'Asian' or indeed 'Western' values.

I

The question of the specificity of values in East and Southeast Asia

The historical origins of the debate on 'Asian values'

The debate on Asian values has been conducted at two levels. One level is philosophical and concerns the extent to which the traditional values of

East and Southeast Asia, embodied in particular in Confucianism, are both different from and perhaps superior to what is regarded as their opposite, Western values. The other level is socio-economic and political and it relates to the ability of East and Southeast Asia to maintain in their societies a set of principles enabling that society to be well adjusted and efficient, in effect better adjusted and more efficient than the societies of the West.

The two levels have of course many aspects in common, one of which is the refusal to see the West as the ideal to be followed. Behind the claim which is sometimes made of the superiority of Asian values is the desire to affirm the cultural identity of the East and Southeast Asian region, an identity which the West is felt to be crushing by stating that the values which it holds are universal. To quote a Singapore diplomat, Kishore Mahbubani:

> It is vital for Western minds to understand that the efforts by Asians to rediscover Asian values are not only or even primarily a search for political values. They involve, for instance, a desire to reconnect with their historical past after this connection has been ruptured both by colonial rule and the subsequent domination of the globe by a *Western Weltanschauung*.
>
> (*The National Interest*, 1998, 35, quoted in A. Milner, October 2000b, 15)

This point is stressed by Milner who warns against the kind of 'triumphalism' which emerged in some quarters in the West when the financial crisis occurred in 1997, a 'triumphalism' which indeed did not last long, partly because the region as a whole recovered quickly, and partly because, at the same time, the extremely rapid economic growth of China provided further arguments in favour of the 'superiority' of the East over the West. What Milner said at the time was that there was a clear need:

> to understand the 'Asian values' programme within the context of this larger historical alignment, that began in the nineteenth century, [as it] draws attention to the well-established forces that help maintain the direction of change in the Asian region, even at a time of economic reversal.
>
> (October 2000b, 17)

In a similar vein and in an effort to reconcile a variety of standpoints, Chan argues that 'it is not difficult to see why Singaporean leaders are particularly fond of this phrase' (i.e. 'Asian Values') (Chan, 1997, 42). He then mentions three reasons which might have led these leaders and Lee Kuan Yew in particular, to stress the matter, the fact that Singapore is a 'young, small, and multi-racial country', that Singapore, being close to Malaysia, 'cannot afford to build its national identity exclusively on Chinese ethnicity and culture' and, third, the country being small, that it 'might seem unacceptably arrogant to other Asian countries' to export its model as merely that of Singapore and that 'it may be considered more diplomatic to present it as representative of Asia as a whole' (ibid., 42–3).

As a matter of fact, a paradoxical aspect of the emphasis on Asian values is that the West itself insisted on there being a chasm between Eastern and Western civilisations. This viewpoint was put forward, in this case, too, at both the philosophical and socio-economic levels. The stress on the philosophical difference has been very marked from the moment that Europeans went to China and elsewhere in the Far East; but the stress on socio-economic differences is also old. It has thus long been claimed that East Asians were likely to 'beat the West' because of their hard work, their frugality and their ability to handle industrial techniques: such a standpoint has been 'rejuvenated', so to speak, from the 1970s onwards, by all those Western social scientists, economists, sociologists, political scientists, who put forward the view that only by imitating the East, Japan originally, but increasingly other states of East and even Southeast Asia as well, could the West expect to be able to survive the challenge of the East. Such a conclusion implied that the East was different, indeed unique, in that no other region of the globe, as was pointed out in the introductory chapter, had been able to 'take on the West' and not just equate its performance but surpass it.

It is therefore wrong to claim that the debate on Asian values and in particular the question of the specificity of these values and therefore of the lack of universality of values had been an invention of the East. There may have been relatively few Eastern intellectuals putting forward this view before the twentieth century, but some did, mainly from Japan and India, as Milner points out, while the difference between East and West was strongly stressed by Western observers (2000a, 5–6). In the late twentieth century, some Asian intellectuals may then have gone further than Westerners have in this respect, while Western intellectuals may have, as a result of the sheer assertiveness of their Eastern counterparts, adopted a fully universalistic vision of values and, even, for a while, as a result of the financial crisis of the late 1990s, dismissed 'Asian values': 'What the current crisis will end up doing is to puncture the idea of Asian exceptionalism. The laws of economics have not been suspended in Asia', said Fukuyama in 1998 ('Asian Values and the Asian crisis', *Commentary*, 27 February 1998, quoted by Milner (2000a, 3)). What does remain the case is that, on both sides, at one time or another, but very frequently, the specificity of values has been stressed.

The debate on Asian values as part of the general debate on the cultural specificity of values

Before proceeding further, it is important to note that the debate about the specificity of Asian values has to be viewed as part of a general debate about cultural distinctions which may exist among all the regions of the globe. That debate does exist among each of the regions at a variety of levels, but also within each region and in particular at two of these levels, the state/national and the sub-state/national. Whatever claims are made, for instance, by Westerners about the universalistic character of the values which they propound, there are debates about cultural patterns among and within Western countries and these debates are often, to say the least, vigorous. The well-known discussion of the possible impact of Protestantism in fashioning a political culture which is distinct from the Catholic culture is a case in point. Debates of this kind are indeed both well known and endemic among the member-States of the European Union, for instance, as well as within at any rate many, if not all these States with respect to particular areas.[2]

There is no difference in principle between the debate about the specificity of Asian v. Western values and the debate about the specificity of the values of particular 'communities' in a given state/nation or about the specificity of values among different states/nations. It is therefore quite wrong to suggest, as is sometimes claimed, that the East is 'particularistic' while the West is 'universalistic': both are 'particularistic' at different points of time and in different circumstances.

Meanwhile, the debate on the specificity of Asian values or of any other set of values is connected with and can indeed be regarded as being the other side of a debate on globalisation. The debate on the specificity of values at any level, regional, national or sub-national, is related to the debate on globalisation, as the globalisation debate is about the existence of 'one world', from a socio-economic point of view first, but, second, from a cultural point of view. Indeed, the debate on the specificity of cultures does affect the globalisation debate in that, cultures which are intensely specific and lived by the population as intensely specific are unlikely to be markedly receptive to globalisation. That is why, in the last resort, those who insist on the specificity of Asian values alongside those who insist on the specificity of regional, state/national or sub-state/national values are engaged in a debate which relates to and ultimately is about the pros and cons of globalisation.

The debate about the specificity of Asian values is a lively one, not just between Westerners and East and Southeast Asians, but among East and Southeast Asians as well. The discussion is typically focused in this respect on the universality or otherwise of the content of the notions of democracy and of human rights. Many of them stress that there are indeed universal values and that the 'pro-Asian values' standpoint is motivated by political considerations on the part of some leaders. This is not only the case of Professor Sen, who wrote about *Democracy as a universal value* (Sen, 1999, 3–13), from outside the region, but for instance of Margaret Ng, from Hong Kong, who criticises the views of Ambassador Kausikan of Singapore, who argued that Singapore is characterised by a 'Governance

that works' (Kausikan, 1997, 24–33): Dr Ng states that '[i]t is not relevant in this context to ask whether Singapore has a "good government"....
[The] criteria must be universal. They need not be absolute, for democracy can exist in degrees. But they must be universal' (Ng, 1997, 21). More generally, the notion that there are Asian values has not been put forward markedly in Japan, Korea or Taiwan, but it has been advanced, on the other hand, above all by official voices and especially most forcefully in China, Singapore and Malaysia, these being the countries which have been the object of special attacks because of their record in the field of human rights.

There is indeed also some apparent diversity in the ways in which these values manifest themselves, as is indicated by a number of studies which suggest that the question of the cultural unity of the East and Southeast Asian region should not be taken for granted. This is already shown by the fact that, as was just mentioned, not only Japan which manifestly is in a different category since its political, social and economic history has been wholly different from that of the rest of the area, but even Korea and Taiwan have not supported in a significant manner the notion of Asian values, although, as we shall see, there are marked differences between these two countries in terms of attitudes of the population.[3] It is also often claimed, as was already suggested in the previous chapter and as will be examined in detail in Chapters 4 and 5, that, in parallel to what has often been said in Europe about 'cultural' differences which may exist between the North and South or between Protestant and Catholic countries of the region, the 'underlying' values may be different in the 'Chinese area' and in the 'Malay/Indonesian and Thai areas'.

Finally, the notion of the cultural specificity of values is never absolute, even if some of the supporters of this specificity might appear to believe that it is. This is where the position of Professor Chan is particularly realistic.

[W]hether or not there is...a common set of values [between Americans and Asians] is not a critical question from the perspective that I am proposing.... 'Asian values' need not be understood as a set of values entirely distinct from and in opposition to Western values, but simply as those values that many people in Asia would endorse and that could guide them in their search for a political morality.

(ibid., 1997, 42)

Values are 'specific' only up to a point: there are common elements, the real question being how important are the elements which are common and the elements which are not.

In any case, the aim of this study is not to support or oppose the notion of cultural specificity: it is to describe what can be regarded as the content of 'cultures' at the level of the populations of the East and Southeast Asian and Western European regions, to see how profound, even if unfortunately mainly in a cross-sectional manner, are the differences among the cultural values of these populations; it is also to see whether any differences which may be found tend to be at the regional level or at another level. The plane at which the inquiry is conducted in the present chapter is thus not philosophical but empirical; and it is not empirical with respect to what the elites believe, but with respect to what the mass of the population believes. Moreover, while reference is made in the coming section to the view that Asian values are rooted in Confucianism, it is not the object of this chapter nor indeed of this volume in general to examine whether Confucianism can be regarded as the main 'cause' of the support given to Asian values. This chapter is essentially concerned with a description of the ways in which it is claimed that there is a substantial difference in the values of the citizens of the two regions: this was needed to be able to determine the questions which should be asked of respondents, if one were to assess in an accurate manner whether they did or did not hold these values and generally did or did not hold values which differed markedly from those held by Western Europeans.

II

How 'Asian values' have been described in the literature

Confucianism and 'communitarianism' as the bases of Asian values

In order to determine the scope of those attitudes which are referred to as Asian values, one has to therefore first examine what the literature states on the subject. This step is unfortunately somewhat unrewarding, as the supporters of the specificity of Asian values tend to be long on the 'causes' or history of this specificity – religious and/or philosophical – but rather short on what concretely 'Asian values' cover. Much of what is said in this context is relatively vague; it is also in part emotional, possibly because much of it is stated from a defensive position. If the views of populations are to be tested, however, these values have to be given a precise concrete content. In this inquiry, the analysis is centred on 'Asian values' rather than on Western values, as it is on the Asian 'side' rather than on the Western 'side' of the values that controversies about the specificity of 'cultures' in the region have been focussed. It is merely assumed throughout this chapter, however, that 'Western values' are regarded by those who put forward a strong case for Asian values as consisting of standpoints which are opposite to those which are put forward as being those of Asian values, since, were this not to be the case, the claim that Asian values are different and specific to the region would become empty.

Perhaps the point which is most commonly stressed about what is regarded as constituting 'Asian values' is that they emphasise the 'communitarian' character of society, while the societal values of Westerners are regarded as being 'individualistic'. This communitarian aspect is a 'classical' or traditional standpoint: as Yi-Huah Jiang states: 'the ideal regime of Asian leaders can be called communitarian because they frequently refer to the Confucian tradition which they say their people commonly share, while Confucianism is a type of communitarianism' (Jiang, 2000, 9). That author then quotes Russell A. Fox who suggested that 'Confucian theory and practice provides a strong and in many ways unique response to liberalism without fundamentally invalidating those humanistic principles basic to democratic reform' (Fox, 1997, 561).

It is indeed seemingly unanimously claimed that Asian values are rooted in Confucianism. While there appears to be disagreements about how to interpret Confucianism, the fact that Confucianism is at stake does not seem to be in doubt. This is so both among Western and Asian scholars. Thus, while Huntington states that '[a]lmost no scholarly disagreement exists regarding the proposition that traditional Confucianism was either undemocratic or antidemocratic' (Huntington, 1991, 24), Fukuyama endeavours to show 'the ways in which Confucianism is compatible with democracy' (Fukuyama, 1995a, 25). Thus, in a detailed analysis of the relationship between Confucianism and liberal democracy, R.A. Fox carefully examines the pros and cons of the link, one of the key issues being whether Confucianism can be regarded as having given rise to communitarianism. 'The proper question...is not whether Confucius was a communitarian, but in what way classical Confucianism can support a particular style of communitarianism that both is conducive to democratic reform *and* takes account of the ideals and expectations of the people of Confucian Asia' (Fox, 1997, 565). The author then proceeds to refer to three elements 'the relationship between ritual activity and law and order, the importance of historically informed social roles, and the idea of personal cultivation' and to examine 'the relationship between "community-ordering" activity and authority in classical Confucianism' as well as 'how that relationship serves to support many communitarian criticisms to modern liberal politics' (ibid., 571). After a detailed examination of the texts, Fox concludes that 'classical Confucianism lend[s] itself to the communitarian critique of liberalism.... In several ways both practical and theoretical' (ibid., 586), these relating to the idea of immanence, to the acceptance of authoritative rules, rituals and traditions, to the transformative power of social association and public activity and to disinteredness and devotion to the community. Yet, Fox concludes by noting that 'both liberal modernity and Confucianism may be subject to "overly sophisticated exaggerations"' (ibid., 591) and that 'a careful reconstruction of classical Confucian thought supports many communitarian criticisms of liberalism, while rarely challenging those central, humanistic democratic possibilities which make liberal modernity such a powerfully attractive ideology in the first place' (ibid., 592).

Determining the concrete content of the communitarian heritage

The communitarian basis of Asian values was unquestionably strongly used by leaders such as Lee Kuan Yew of Singapore and Mahathir Mohammed of Malaysia in the last decades of the twentieth century. The reason was said to be, as Professor Mab Huang noted (Huang, 2000, 5), that Lee 'was agitated by what he saw happening in America' and, quoting Lee himself: 'As a total system, I find part of it totally unacceptable: guns, drugs, violent crime, vagrancy, unbecoming behaviour in public – in sum, the breakdown of civil society'. In a sharp contrast, Asian values, to quote Chan (1994), 'put great emphasis on communitarian values such as family bondage, communal peace, social harmony, sacrifices for the community and patriotism' (quoted in Huang, 2000, 7, from 'The Asian Challenge to Universal Human Rights: A Philosophical Appraisal', 1994). Yi-Huah Jiang notes:

> on January 9, 1989, four core values were identified by the Singapore government in the presidential address to Parliament – communitarianism, familism, decision-making by consensus, and social and religious harmony.... Communitarianism in the sense of 'community over self' – together with the other three values – should be taught in schools, workplaces, and homes.
>
> (ibid., 2004, 9)

In this context, as indeed in the rest of this volume, the word 'communitarian' is being used as it is used to an extent by those who support the idea of the specificity of Asian values, that is to say by opposition to the use of the word 'individualistic': it does not refer to the deeper philosophical (or religious) meaning which it has in the more specialised literature on the subject.[4]

Yet little effort is typically devoted to being comprehensive and precise about the elements which constitute 'communitarianism'. Milner states, for instance, as a matter of fact in the form of a parenthesis, that Asian values 'usually...include a stress on hard work, saving, order and harmony, communitarianism, family loyalty and a refusal to compartmentalise religion from other spheres of life' (A. Milner, 2000a, 2–3; A. Milner, in G. Segal and D. Goodman, eds, 2000, 56–68). Meanwhile, Chan states that Asian cultures 'put great emphasis on communitarian values such as family bondage, communal peace, social harmony, sacrifices for the community and patriotism' (Chan, 1997, in Mab Huang, 2000, 7).

Yu-Huah Jiang is probably the author who tries most to determine the content of 'Asian values'. He comes up with a list of eight characteristics, namely 'family ties and family duties', 'respect for hierarchy and authority', 'hard work', 'consensus', 'strong commitment to education', 'moral persuasion', 'community' (in the sense that 'the individual should realise that the interests of their nation and state is more important than one's private interests') and 'stress on unity and order' ('too much diversity [being] a threat to society') (Jiang, 2000, 6). Such a list can manifestly serve as a basis for the examination of what Asians and Westerners may or may not have in common.

The question of human rights

Alongside what can be described as the more 'classical' communitarian standpoints which have just been listed, another key debate has been related more specifically to the nature and role of human rights in Asian societies. This debate is somewhat more recent in that it has come to the fore with Westerners criticising increasingly classical viewpoints as negating human rights. There is thus an element of defensiveness in the response of the most traditional supporters of Asian values in that it is a response concerned with rebutting the 'Western' claim that those who support Asian values do not care for human rights. The human rights aspect of the debate took some prominence in the 1990s and in particular in China, when the authorities in that country, and also in Singapore and Malaysia, felt under attack on the grounds that such rights as freedom of expression, of meeting, of association were not being respected. The counter-attack, so to speak, was often couched on grounds that the West was imperialistic and hypocritical. Thus, Mahathir of Malaysia said, Western countries 'threaten sanctions, withdrawal of aid, stoppage of loans, economic and trade boycotts and actual military strikes against those they accuse of violating human rights' (Huang, 2000, 6, from a Mahathir 1994 speech entitled 'Rethinking Human Rights'). Another supporter of 'Asian values', Ying-shi Yu, had claimed that human rights were embedded in the tradition of Confucian culture (ibid., 8). Given the part which the human rights question has played in the debate, an analysis of the extent to which Asian values are adopted by the citizens of various countries of East and Southeast Asia and of Western Europe must therefore also consider, alongside reactions to communitarian values, reactions to rights such as freedom of expression and the right to hold protest meetings.

The question of the compatibility between 'Asian values' and human rights as they are conventionally defined remains somewhat obscure, despite some efforts made by the proponents of Asian values to attempt to accommodate human rights as well. Chan appears to vacillate somewhat on the matter, for instance. He stated in 1994 that Asian states are entitled to 'claim a wide (but surely not arbitrary) margin of appreciation in interpreting the proper scope and limitation of human rights' (quoted by Huang, 2000, 7); three years later, in 1997, the same author said that '[t]he future of Asian countries depends not only on continuing economic growth but, more importantly, on a strong commitment both to human rights and democracy *and* to the revitalisation of Asian traditional values and culture' (Chan, 1997, 46).

As a matter of fact, one form which the rebuttal against the criticisms coming from the West has taken has been to suggest that there are indeed rights in the 'Asian' conception of values, but that emphasis needs to be placed on a different set of such rights. It is stated for instance that Asian cultures do not give so much weight to autonomy and 'put great emphasis on communitarian values such as family bondage, communal peace, social harmony, sacrifices for the community and patriotism' (Huang, 2000, 7, quoting Chan 'the Asian Challenge to Universal Human Rights: A Philosophical Appraisal'). It is also said that Asian values emphasise duties more than rights and that this is why Asian societies are more cohesive than Western ones. This can be viewed as a consequence of the fact that 'Asian values' define, so to speak, a 'communitarian' rather than an 'individualistic' society: in such a communitarian society the emphasis is on the duties rather than on the rights of individuals towards family and state.

Socio-economic standpoints

The fact that Asian values remain at this very general level, and indeed that they emphasise communitarianism, including possibly with respect to human rights as well, means that what is described under the rubric of 'Asian values' does not cover all the societal values, but 'only' what might be described as *basic* societal values, that is to say those values which are related to the structure of power in the society: they are concerned with who the rulers are and how these rulers rule. This field is broad: but it does not constitute the whole field of societal values as these are also concerned with what the rule is about, that is to say with the *policy* goals which are pursued by the society, these goals being at the origin of the decisions which are initiated and implemented by the government. These policy elements have not been the subject of the same kind of debate as the basic societal values: they were probably not deemed to touch as profoundly the nature of the relationship between the citizen and the society.

Yet it does seem unrealistic at this point not to take also into account, alongside the questions specifically relating to the possible existence of an 'Asian values' set of responses on communitarian and human rights matters, some standpoints of a socio-economic character. There is indeed a widespread belief that 'pro-business' views are characteristic of the East and Southeast Asian rapidly developing economies much more than they are of Western societies. Such views about business are likely to have also an impact on some social policy preferences, as for instance about the stress which might be placed on the protection of the environment or on the role of the government with respect to jobs. It seems therefore important to test whether such attitudes prevail among the population as a whole, even if the matter is regarded as being somewhat peripheral to the core of the 'Asian values syndrome'. The analysis of the reactions to these socio-economic standpoints has therefore to take place both jointly and separately.

III

Operationalising Asian values

To draft the questions to be put to interviewees in both regions, one must therefore start from the elements which have been mentioned as being characteristic of 'communitarianism', including references to human rights, as well as to some socio-economic values. From the points made by Yu-Huah Jiang and quoted earlier, one can arrive at a series of concrete matters concerning the position of the individual in the society in general and in the family in particular, while also relating to the process of decision-making.

Along the lines of the list which was provided by Yu-Huah Jiang, seven questions were drafted to inquire into views of citizens about what 'should be' the relationship to the family, to 'hierarchy and authority' (to the government, of course, but also to older people and to the place to be given to women), to consensus in the decision-making process and to the 'community', in the sense of a preference given to the nation over one's private interests. No question relating as such to 'hard work', 'education' or 'moral persuasion' was introduced, as these seemed somewhat vague in a questionnaire which was already relatively long. Meanwhile, the questions which were drafted were expected to provide a good coverage of the reactions to 'Asian values'. To prevent automatic response sets, moreover, these questions were not all placed at the same point in the questionnaire. They were presented also in such a way that the supporters of 'Asian values' were not to give in all cases a positive reply as this might also lead to a response set. The seven questions are the following:

- The government usually knows best how to run the country (Q.306e).
- We should always do what the government wants instead of acting in our own interest (Q.306d).
- Achieving consensus in society is more important than encouraging a lot of individual initiative (Q.412d).
- In decisions older people should be given more influence (Q.412e).
- A women's primary role is at home (Q.412c).
- Public interest should always come before family (Q.412f).
- Individuals should strive mostly for their own good rather than for the good of society (Q.412g).

It was assumed that the 'pro-Asian values' position was represented by agreement in the case of the first five answers and by disagreement in the last two.

To tap the reactions of respondents to human rights as seen from Western eyes, two questions were drawn from among those which have been repeatedly asked in the Michigan election studies.

They are:

- Everyone should have the right to express his opinion even if he or she differs from the majority (Q.208b).
- People should be allowed to organise public meetings to protest against the government (Q.208c).

The second of these two questions could not be asked in China, however, as it was considered too sensitive by the polling organisation in that country. It is therefore possible to find out only to a limited extent what the position of Chinese citizens is in the debate which has opposed, in particular, the Chinese authorities to the Western critics who challenged these authorities in relation to those human rights which are regarded by Westerners as universal and by supporters of Asian values as essentially Western. It was of course assumed that the 'pro-Asian values' position was represented by disagreement in both cases.

Finally, four questions of a socio-economic character were asked to assess to what extent views of respondents in that field were associated with a wholly pro-business position, especially among the East and Southeast Asian rapidly developing economies. These four 'socio-economic' questions are:

- Competition is good because it stimulates people to develop new ideas (Q.306a).
- Society is better off when businesses are free to make as much profit as they can (Q.306g).
- The government should take responsibility for ensuring that everyone either has a job or is provided with adequate social welfare (Q.306b).
- A good environment is more important than economic growth (Q.412b).

In total, thirteen questions (only twelve of which were answered in China) were therefore put to interviewees to obtain a picture of views relating to basic societal values. Seven of these were designed to identify the extent to which these interviewees shared the vision of society embedded in the 'communitarian' syndrome which is regarded as embodying 'Asian values'; two aimed at finding out reactions to the controversial matter of the 'universal' character of human rights; the last four attempted to obtain a vision of attitudes towards the preferred socio-economic framework of society.

IV

Do 'Asian values' appear to constitute a syndrome?

A number of factor analyses were conducted to see whether the answers to these questions appeared related to each other, overall and in terms of those which are specifically concerned with 'communitarian' viewpoints as well as among both regions and in each of the regions. For the purpose of these factor analyses, the answers were recoded by excluding 'don't knows' and by reducing the answers to three only, 'agreement', 'disagreement' and 'neither agreement nor disagreement'. While respondents had been given the opportunity to choose between 'strong' agreement or disagreement and what might be referred to as 'ordinary' agreement or disagreement, the proportion of those who 'strongly' agreed was typically much smaller than the proportion of those who merely agreed, the main exception being with respect to the human rights question on the freedom to express an opinion (Q.208b): Western European respondents were markedly more numerous in 'strongly agreeing' than in merely 'agreeing' (57 v. 35 per cent), while East and Southeast Asian respondents divided 31 to 51 per cent between those who 'strongly agreed' and those who merely 'agreed'. Moreover, those who 'strongly disagreed' were also markedly less numerous in general than those who merely 'disagreed'. It seemed therefore reasonable to consider jointly the two groups of those who agree and, similarly, those who disagree. That recoding was undertaken in part to simplify analyses and to facilitate comparisons; but it was also undertaken as it is surely not at all obvious, in an eighteen-nation survey of this nature, that the distinction between 'agreeing strongly' and 'agreeing' (and between 'disagreeing strongly' and 'disagreeing') has an identical meaning across all the countries and among all the respondents. On the other hand, the meaning given to 'agreement' is likely to be identical across the whole survey, while that given to 'disagreement' is also likely to be identical across the whole survey. It seemed therefore more prudent not to attempt to differentiate between the two types of agreement or of disagreement and to undertake the analysis on the basis of a single categorisation of each standpoint (the category of 'neither agreeing nor disagreeing' being maintained).

There was a second problem, which turned out to be more difficult to settle, as we shall see later, in particular in Chapter 6: this was concerned with the extent to which the factor analyses should be based on the way the questions were presented to the respondents or on the extent to which they were drafted in terms of an agreement or a disagreement with the 'pro-Asian values' position. It seemed ostensibly more appropriate, for a comparable picture of the responses to be provided in the factor analyses, to undertake these analyses on the basis of the 'pro-Asian values' answers in all cases. However, the 'pro-Asian values' answer was the positive answer with respect to some questions and the negative answer with respect to others. If the proportions of the 'pro-Asian values' answers were to be determined, one should use the proportion of respondents who disagreed with the statement presented to them, rather than the proportion of the respondents who agreed with that statement where the negative answer was the one which constituted the 'pro-Asian values' answer. It was not realistic to do so with respect to the socio-economic questions, since, as was noted earlier, these could not

Table 2.1 Factor analyses

All thirteen variables	All eighteen countries				East and Southeast Asia				Western Europe			
	1	2	3	4	1	2	3	4	1	2	3	4
HR												
208b	-447	154	-130	465	-238	-528	-157	-344	126	-067	-673	098
208c	-651	038	-184	205	067	-583	-361	-163	202	-105	-569	-078
COMM												
306e	628	255	184	238	300	570	128	304	796	042	052	065
306d	608	293	211	113	323	573	144	147	750	134	-071	106
412d	104	627	-069	108	637	033	-005	097	186	565	113	-101
412e	112	555	145	083	607	221	160	041	080	538	106	253
412f	-298	548	-027	009	-354	-138	-023	-048	-349	-419	116	-063
412c	076	339	498	-218	179	-014	633	-170	069	501	-188	304
412g	-068	049	-733	-061	-123	-043	-593	075	-094	-135	-046	-757
ECON												
306a	095	-099	067	695	054	106	-094	670	128	-222	508	276
306g	165	-044	655	235	-121	106	593	423	224	-061	058	683
306b	-024	151	-011	593	105	-111	022	655	208	080	512	-106
412b	-278	541	02	-058	446	-266	263	007	-102	536	081	-068
Human rights and 'communitarian' only												
208b	-148	0.738	-203		-134	207	795		063	-119	761	060
208c	164	0.698	-167		213	-331	637		-006	094	790	-117
306e	0.625	617	0.056		657	-034	196		826	099	-013	030
306d	0.594	559	0.139		605	104	264		821	097	068	095
412d	0.605	-187	0.005		586	021	-199		037	715	-062	-012

412e	0.524	−133	0.265	615	236	−003	−020	578	−070	335
412f	−624	−046	−025	−623	−042	077	−237	−586	−101	−078
412c	0.227	−0.035	0.639	100	729	−002	100	313	112	580
412g	009	0.031	−809	102	−700	−001	−042	−133	044	−826

Socio-economic questions only

306a	0.703
306b	0.650
306g	0.611
412b	0.495

Notes
208b Right to express one's opinion
208c Right to organise public protest meetings
306e Government usually knows best
306d Do what government wants
412d Important to achieve consensus
412e Give extra influence to older people
412f Public interest before family
412c Women's primary role in the home
412g Individuals should strive for their own good more than society
306a Competition good
306g Society better if businesses free to make profits
306b Responsibility of government to provide jobs or social welfare
412b Good environment more important than economic growth

be regarded as being directly part of the 'Asian values' syndrome: the answers to these questions were therefore calculated on the basis of the way agreement and disagreement were presented to the interviewees. On the other hand, on four questions, the two human rights questions (Q.208b and c) and two communitarian questions, those concerned with the choice between public interest and family obligations (Q.412f) and with the choice between 'striving for one's own good' and that of society (Q.412g), the proportion of respondents who disagreed with the statement could be regarded as adopting a 'pro-Asian values' line: in the case of these four questions, the respondents who disagreed should therefore be considered to be those who take the 'pro-Asian values' position (Table 2.1).

The number of dimensions at the inter-regional level depending on whether socio-economic questions are or not taken into account with respect to both regions

On the basis of the recoding and of the fact that the emphasis on the 'pro-Asian values' position has led to the reversing the order of agreement and disagreement with respect to four questions, four distinct factors emerge when all thirteen questions are examined jointly and in both regions. The first factor includes the two human rights questions and the two attitudes to the government questions (Q.208b and c and Q.306d and e). The second factor includes the questions on consensus, on the influence to be given to old people, and, but negatively, on placing public interest before family, as well as the socio-economic question on the choice to be made between the environment and economic growth (Q.412d, e, f and b). The third factor includes, but negatively, the question on whether individuals should strive for their own good rather than for the society at large; it includes also in part the question on the position of women in society, as well as the economic question on whether businesses should be allowed to make as much profit as they wish (Q.412g and c and Q.306g). Finally, the fourth factor includes the remaining two economic questions on the role of competition and on the responsibility of the government for jobs (Q.306a and b).

The point which emerges perhaps most strikingly from this distribution is that the replies to the four socio-economic questions, far from being clustered in a separate factor, are divided among three of the four factors. This seems to suggest that the four socio-economic questions do not have any unity. This finding is not only surprising in principle; it is also empirically incorrect as, when the four socio-economic questions are separated from the other nine, the split of the socio-economic questions ceases: the four questions then form one factor only, although the loading on the 'environment' v. economic growth question is lower than on the other three.

Meanwhile, if examined separately from the four socio-economic questions, the nine communitarian and human rights questions become distributed into three factors. The two human rights variables, (which can be described as 'liberalism' variables), form one factor on their own; the two variables concerned with the attitudes to have *vis-à-vis* the government (which can be described as 'government restraint' variables) become linked to the questions on consensus, about the influence to be given to old people, and, but again negatively, about placing public interest before family (these last three can be described as 'decision-making' variables). The third factor relates the question about the role of women in society to, also negatively, the question whether individuals should strive 'for their own good rather than for that of society' (which can be described as 'social relations' variables).[5]

There is little change from this distribution when the seven communitarian questions are examined separately from the replies to the human rights questions, but two factors only then emerge, as could be expected, since two human rights questions did form a separate factor, as we just saw, when these questions are examined jointly with the communitarian questions. The 'decision-making' questions form part of the same factor, while the two 'social relations' questions form the second factor.

Variations in the distribution of factors between the two regions

There are some variations from these distributions when the answers to the two regions are examined separately. On the one hand, when all thirteen questions are taken together, there are four factors in both cases, but the split between these factors is somewhat different. In East and Southeast Asia, both the 'liberalism' questions (which are then negatively loaded) and the 'governmental restraint' questions remain in a single factor; in Western Europe, on the other hand, the two liberalism questions (also negatively loaded) join, somewhat surprisingly, the two socio-economic questions (Q. 306a and b) which form a separate factor both when the two regions are considered jointly and when East and Southeast Asia is considered separately. Meanwhile, the 'decision-making' variables cover broadly the same variables (Q.412d, e and f – this last variable being negatively loaded) in the two regions, except for the fact that, in Western Europe, it includes also the role of women variable (Q.412c), as well as, in both cases, the socio-economic question relating to the choice between the environment and economic growth. The last factor includes the communitarian question concerned with the choice between individuals striving for their own good and the good of the society (Q.412g), negatively loaded, and the economic question dealing with the right of businesses to make as much profit as they wish (Q.306g). At the level of each region, the rather peculiar distribution of the answers to the socio-economic questions is therefore maintained. Once more, but perhaps even more decisively, one finds that the socio-economic questions are distributed somewhat surprisingly among a number of different dimensions.

On the other hand, when the socio-economic questions are considered separately from the other nine, the patterns which emerge in each of the two regions become once more rather similar to those which emerged at the inter-regional level; moreover, the differences between the two regions are also rather limited. The two human rights questions come to form a separate factor in both regions, while the 'social relations' factor includes the same variables on both sides, namely the question concerned with the choice between individuals striving for their own good or that of society, negatively loaded, and the role of women question (Q.412g and c). The only difference between the distribution of the questions in the two regions comes from the fact that the five other communitarian questions constitute a single factor in East and Southeast Asia while the two 'government restraint' questions, on the one hand, and the three 'decision-making' questions, on the other, constitute two separate factors in Western Europe, the question on the choice between the public interest and family obligations being negatively loaded in both regions.

This situation is indeed replicated when the seven communitarian questions are considered separately from the two human rights questions: these questions are distributed between two factors only in East and Southeast Asia and among three factors in Western Europe. Thus, when the seven communitarian questions and the two human rights questions are examined at the level of each region, the only difference in the composition of the factors relates to the fact that the answers to the two government restraint questions are either linked to the questions concerned with decision-making, in East and Southeast Asia, or form two separate factors, in Western Europe. This difference does not suggest, *prima facie* at least, a fundamental contrast between the answers from the two regions with respect to the 'communitarian' questions as a whole. It might indicate, however, that, in Western Europe, but not in East and Southeast Asia, restraining the government is considered as being rather more politically loaded than the questions on 'decision-making'.

There are thus four factors among the human rights and communitarian questions in Western Europe and only three in East and Southeast Asia, but, as the difference between the factor distribution in the two regions results only from a split between the 'government restraint' and the 'decision-making' questions, it seemed appropriate that the four factors of *liberalism, government restraint, decision-making* and *social relations* should be the ones which will be used consistently when attempting to structure the analysis of the relationship among the communitarian and human rights variables, both at the inter-regional level and at levels below the region.

Meanwhile, the four socio-economic questions form a single factor in East and Southeast Asia, as among the eighteen countries, but two factors in Western Europe, the questions on the right of businesses to make as much profit as they wish and the question asking for a choice to be made between the environment and economic growth (Q.306b and Q.412b) constituting a different factor from the other two socio-economic questions (Q.306a and g). This suggests that Western Europeans might be less favourable to business than East and Southeast Asians: while the two more 'classical' economic questions are also pro-business questions, the two questions which form a separate factor in Western Europe are those which tend to limit business, both in terms of what the government should do about jobs and in terms of a choice to be made between the environment and economic growth.

Answers from Western Europe tend thus to fall within one more factor in Western Europe than in East and Southeast Asia; but, when communitarian and human rights questions are analysed separately from the socio-economic questions, differences in the composition of the factors are merely the result of splits within a factor, not genuine variations in the distribution of variables among these factors.[6]

While four factors emerge overall from the combined examination of the answers of the citizens from the eighteen countries of the study, the way in which socio-economic questions divide among these factors appears to indicate that the universe of values to which these questions belong to is rather different from the universe of values to which questions related to human rights and communitarian questions belong. This is shown by the fact that, when socio-economic questions are separated from human rights and communitarian questions, the distribution of the answers to both socio-economic questions and to human rights and communitarian questions becomes appreciably different from what it was originally. It is therefore markedly more realistic to separate these two sets of questions when undertaking the analysis of the data. Once these two sets of questions are separated, four robust factors emerge, not just overall at the level of all eighteen countries, but in each of the two regions examined separately, from the answers to the nine human rights and communitarian questions, while the four socio-economic questions give rise either to one or to two factors. This suggests a degree of similarity between the two regions, together with some differences. Thus, factor analyses help to discover a framework on the basis of which it seems possible to begin to study comparatively the way in which citizens from the eighteen countries covered by this survey react to basic societal values. The analysis of this volume will therefore be conducted on the basis of these dimensions.

* * * * *

The notion of Asian values has emotional appeal; but its content is rather imprecise. To be able to assess whether, as supporters of Asian values – and others – claim, there are major differences in the reactions of citizens in Asia – in this case East and Southeast Asia – from those of citizens of Western Europe with respect to basic societal values, it was necessary to convert this broad conceptualisation into a relatively limited number of survey questions which could be administered to respondents in both East and Southeast Asia and Western Europe. This proved possible.

The following chapters of this book aim at examining in detail the nature of the answers to these questions. Yet, the preliminary assessment which has emerged from the examination of the factor analyses suggests that there may be some differences rather than a sharp contrast in the patterns of values characterising the citizens of two regions. This is because the internal composition of the dimensions which factor analyses help to identify is broadly similar on both sides, both in terms of the questions which are associated to each other and in terms of the direction, positive or negative, of these associations. It does not follow that it is possible to claim, on the basis of this general observation of the structure of the dimensions only, that the views of East and Southeast Asians about socio-political culture are not distant form each other in some, perhaps in many respect from those of Western Europeans: what does seem to follow, however, is that the answers to this question may well be less clear-cut than is often supposed.

3 How opposed are 'basic societal values' in the two regions?

The previous chapter established an empirical framework giving access to the raw material, so to speak, needed to discover the reactions of citizens of the two regions analysed in this study when confronted to questions about 'basic societal values'. That raw material then needs to be interpreted, however. No doubt differences will be found, but also similarities, in the patterns of reactions of citizens: the real problem is to ensure that sensible conclusions are drawn from the combined examination of these similarities and differences, and that both a comprehensive and 'correct' image of the reality emerges at the end of the process. In a nutshell, given that we are unlikely to find differences which are so vast that there is nothing in common between the citizens of the two regions, the question which arises is to decide at what point one can state that 'Asian values' are indeed widespread and at what point, on the contrary, one can state that they are not, even if, no doubt, such a conclusion remains to an extent controversial.

The problem is likely to arise from four types of problems. First, there will be differences between the two regions in the patterns of responses to each specific question: one will have to decide when these differences are large enough to be deemed to constitute evidence that East and Southeast Asians view matters in a truly distinctive manner from Western Europeans. Second, even if one can find a realistic answer at the level of each question, the problem arises as to how to draw an overall conclusion based on the answers to all the questions taken together. Third, the patterns of reactions of citizens to the questions which are posed to them will naturally be different from country to country: these differences must be given due weight as they have an effect on the internal distribution of supporters and opponents of 'Asian values' within each region. Fourth, the reactions of citizens are no doubt, to an extent, linked to the social characteristics of these citizens: differences in these social characteristics have to be considered before a sensible judgement can be passed about the extent of support and opposition to Asian values.

This chapter is thus devoted to an analysis of the respondents' answers to the thirteen questions which were examined in the previous chapter. The aim is to assess the extent to which there are indeed 'regional clusters' on the basis of which one could conclude that some values are specifically 'Asian' or 'European', after having met the four sets of problems which have just been outlined. To do so, the chapter examines successively the mean inter-regional differences with respect to these variables and the intra-regional variations from that mean. If inter-regional differences are large on average and/or if intra-regional variations from the regional mean are small, one will be able to conclude that there is evidence supporting the view that specifically Asian values exist; if, on the other hand, inter-regional differences are small on average and/or if intra-regional variations from the regional mean are large, one will be able to conclude that there is little evidence supporting the view that specifically Asian values exist. Furthermore, the chapter also considers the extent to which the variables which are typically regarded as embodying the values encapsulated in the notion of 'Asian values', are closely related to a number of demographic characteristics as well as to the socio-political knowledge of respondents: if the apparent effect of these relationships is small and/or is common to the two regions, it will follow that these demographic characteristics or that the level of socio-political knowledge do not have any significant effect on the extent to which citizens hold 'Asian values' or not.

I

The overall reactions to 'basic societal' values in the two regions

Let us begin by finding out overall how the views of the respondents of the two regions were distributed with respect to the thirteen questions they were asked to answer. These questions gave respondents the possibility to choose among six types of answers. They could say that they 'strongly agreed', 'agreed', 'neither agreed nor disagreed', 'disagreed', 'strongly disagreed' or that they did not know. These six types of answers divide neatly into two sets. One set of two types of answers provides an impression of the proportion of respondents who were, broadly speaking, uncommitted: these were the 'don't know' and the 'neither agreed nor disagreed' answers. The other set, which includes four types of answers, provided an impression of the manner in which respondents are committed. Let us examine the reactions of respondents to these two sets successively.

Few 'don't knows' but many respondents who 'neither agree nor disagree', especially with respect to the communitarian questions

Formally at least, the answers to all thirteen questions are remarkable in one respect: there are few 'don't knows' in the replies: overall, with respect to eleven questions out of thirteen the proportion of 'don't know' answers is 5 per cent or less; in the other two cases ('the importance of achieving consensus in society' (Q.412d)) and ('society is better off if businesses are free to make as much profit as they can' (Q.306g)) the proportion of 'don't know' answers is, respectively, 7 and 8 per cent. Not surprisingly, given these small proportions, there is almost no difference between the level of 'don't knows' in the two regions: there are tiny differences on eleven questions and a 4 per cent difference on the other two, but in opposite directions. On the question of 'achieving consensus in society' (Q.412d), 'don't know' answers are higher in Europe (10 v. 6 per cent); on the human rights question relating to the right to protest (Q.208c) 'don't know' answers are higher in Asia (6 v. 2 per cent).

Yet this small proportion of 'don't knows' has to be seen in the light of the fact that, for a large majority of these questions, a substantial proportion of respondents also declare that they 'neither agree nor disagree' and thus do not choose. Admittedly, this is in a sense an 'answer': it can even be ranked as intermediate between stating agreement and stating disagreement. Yet because they are also a refusal to take sides, answers of this kind have at least to be related to 'don't know' replies, indeed perhaps because at least some of the respondents felt more comfortable to answer in this way than to declare that they did not know. The reason why this group of answers needs examination is because it is large; in some cases, it is very large indeed.

With respect to ten of the thirteen questions, the proportion of these 'neither agree nor disagree' answers is at least 17 per cent; it is around a quarter in six cases and nearly a third (31 per cent) in one ('individuals should strive most of all for their own good' (Q.412g)). The only three cases in which the proportion of 'neither agree nor disagree' answers is relatively low (8 or 9 per cent) is on the human rights question relating to 'the right to express an opinion' (Q.208b) and on two of the four socio-economic questions ('competition is good' (Q.306a) and 'society is better when businesses are free' (Q.306b)). Thus, if the proportions of 'neither agree nor disagree' are added to the proportions of 'don't knows', the range of 'uncommitted or somewhat uncommitted' respondents is of the order of 10 or 11 per cent in these three cases, about a fifth in two, over a quarter in seven and a over a third (35 per cent) in one.

To put it differently, there are relatively few uncommitted answers (both 'don't know' and 'neither agree nor disagree') (about a tenth) with respect to two of the economic answers but nearly a third (29 per cent) with respect to the other two. There are also few uncommitted answers (also a tenth) with respect to one of the human rights answers (on freedom of speech) while, on the other human rights question which is concerned with the freedom to organise protest meetings, a fifth (21 per cent) of the respondents are uncommitted; there is about the same percentage of uncommitted answers with respect to the question asking for the place of women in society (19 per cent). This leaves six questions, that is to say all but one of those concerned with communitarian matters, with respect to which the proportion of respondents who are uncommitted is between 27 and 36 per cent. On communitarian questions, therefore, the extent to which respondents have an opinion is unquestionably low. It is therefore with respect to the bulk of the communitarian questions that the extent of commitment of respondents is the lowest.

A wide range in the overall distribution of the preferences of respondents

The distribution of the preferences of respondents varies appreciably, as one might have expected, from one question to another. The recalculations undertaken for the analysis were described in some detail in the previous chapter. On the one hand, 'strongly agreed' and 'agreed' answers were recoded under one common answer while the 'strongly disagreed' and 'disagreed' answers were also recoded under a common answer. On the other, the answers were also recoded in order to provide, as 'agreed' answers, the proportions of 'pro-Asian values' in all cases.

As Table 3.1, the proportion of respondents who either agree or disagree, if agreement implies an 'anti-Asian values' position, does vary throughout

Table 3.1 Distribution of 'agree', 'disagree' and 'not deciding' answers to the thirteen 'basic societal value' questions (percentages)

	Agree	Disagree	Difference agree/disagree	DK or NAND	Ratio agree
All eighteen countries					
Freedom of speech (Q.208b)	87	3	84	10	97
Freedom of protest (Q.208c)	60	13	53	21	84
Government knows best (Q.306e)	43	29	14	28	60
Do what – govt wants (Q.306d)	29	42	−13	28	40
Increase influence of old (Q.412e)	56	17	39	27	77
Prefer consensus (Q.412d)	49	16	33	36	77
Women at home (Q.412c)	23	58	−35	19	28
Public v. family (Q.412f)	33	39	−6	28	46
Individual v. society (Q.412g)	28	37	−9	35	43
Competition good (Q.306a)	84	4	80	12	95
Govt resp. for jobs (Q.306b)	85	4	81	11	96
Better if bus. free for profits (Q.306g)	44	27	17	29	62
Environment or growth (Q.412b)	58	13	45	29	82

Table 3.1 Continued

	Agree	Disagree	Difference agree/disagree	DK or NAND	Ratio agree
East and Southeast Asian countries					
Freedom of speech (Q.208b)	82	4	78	14	95
Freedom of protest (Q.208c)	52	21	31	27	71
Government knows best (Q.306e)	56	17	39	27	77
Do what – govt wants (Q.306d)	42	31	11	27	58
Increase influence of old (Q.412e)	58	16	42	26	78
Prefer consensus (Q.412d)	51	14	37	35	78
Women at home (Q.412c)	30	46	−16	24	39
Public v. family (Q.412f)	42	29	13	29	59
Individual v. society (Q.412g)	31	34	−3	35	48
Competition good (Q.306a)	85	4	81	11	95
Govt resp. for jobs (Q.306b)	86	2	84	12	98
Better if bus. free for profits (Q.306g)	52	20	32	28	72
Environment or growth (Q.412b)	58	14	44	28	81
Western European countries					
Freedom of speech (Q.208b)	93	2	91	5	98
Freedom of protest (Q.208c)	78	7	71	15	92
Government knows best (Q.306e)	30	41	−11	29	42
Do what − govt wants (Q.306d)	16	54	−38	30	23
Increase influence of old (Q.412e)	53	17	36	30	76
Prefer consensus (Q.412d)	45	17	28	38	73
Women at home (Q.412c)	16	69	−53	15	19
Public v. family (Q.412f)	24	48	−24	28	33
Individual v. society (Q.412g)	26	39	−13	35	40
Competition good (Q.306a)	85	4	81	11	96
Govt resp. for jobs (Q.306b)	84	5	79	11	94
Better if bus. free for profits (Q.306g)	35	34	1	31	51
Environment or growth (Q.412b)	58	12	46	30	83

the whole range, from the 95 and 96 per cent, respectively, who feel that competition is a good thing (Q.306a) or that it is the responsibility of the government to provide jobs (Q.306b) to the 3 and 18 per cent, respectively, who disagree with the freedom of speech (Q.208b) and the freedom to hold protest meetings (Q.208c). By and large, the support for the four socio-economic standpoints as they are expressed is large – (96, 95, 82 and 62 per cent). The support for 'pro-Asian values' positions on communitarian questions ranges appreciably, from 77 per cent in favour of consensus (Q.412d) or the greater influence to be given to old people (Q.412e), through 54 and 57 per cent, respectively, in favour of the family (Q.412f) and in favour of society rather than of the individual (Q.412g) as well as, respectively, 60 and 40 per cent in favour of the government (Q.306e and d) to a low of 19 per cent in favour of the idea that women's place is at home (Q.412c). The least that can be said is that there is no 'consistency' in the support for and opposition to 'Asian values' positions and in particular that there is manifestly little support for such positions in relation to human rights and to the role of women in society, while there is manifestly strong support for consensus and the increased role of old people. Moreover, both very low and very high overall percentages suggest that there may not be, and at any rate in several cases, a very marked difference in the views of East and Southeast Asians and of Western Europeans, a matter to which we now need to turn, since it is, after all, the key question to examine if the importance of 'Asian values' is to be assessed.

II

The extent of inter-regional differences

Inter-regional differences with respect to 'uncommitted answers' are very small

Let us first consider the case of inter-regional differences among 'uncommitted answers'. We noticed that these differences were small, indeed minuscule, with respect to 'don't know' answers; but, as we also saw, the proportions of 'don't know' answers are small, even very small for the majority of questions. On the other hand, the proportion of uncommitted answers becomes large when those who stated that they 'neither agreed nor disagreed' are added to the 'don't knows'. Yet, even when all the 'uncommitted answers' are taken into account, inter-regional differences remain small: overall, the difference between the two regions is only about two points, despite the fact that, in Japan, the difference is large, as, in that country, the proportion of those who declare, with respect to all thirteen 'basic societal values', that they 'neither agree nor disagree' is 37 per cent with a further 9 per cent who declare that they do not know, a point to which we shall return.[1]

The corresponding proportions for East and Southeast Asia and for the whole sample are, respectively, 20 and 24 per cent.

Overall, in terms of their likelihood to give a 'neither agree nor disagree' answer, Asians are somewhat more likely to do so on the 'human rights' questions (the difference between the two regions is, respectively, 8 and 9 per cent with respect to these two questions). Europeans are more likely to give that type of answer on the 'communitarian' questions, but the difference is 3 per cent or less, except in one case ('the government usually knows best' Q.306e), where it is 6 per cent. Europeans are also more likely to give a 'neither agree nor disagree' answer on two of the socio-economic questions, but the difference is of two points or less. To this very limited extent one can trace some variation in the attitudes of Western Europeans compared to those of East and Southeast Asians. The bulk of the difference does not emerge in relation to what are the 'classical' 'communitarian' questions, since it emerges in the context of the two 'human rights' issues: these are the issues which are viewed in some quarters, as we saw, as an attempt by Westerners to impose their values on Asians.

Differences between the two regions are thus very small overall with respect to the proportion of the respondents from the two regions who have no opinion or who state that they 'neither agree nor disagree' with the proposition which is put to them. Although this anticipates a subsequent more detailed country analysis, it is worth mentioning already that the variations among the countries *within* each region in this respect are larger than the differences *between* the two regions, and that this is so not just in relation to Japan: it seems therefore that there are in both regions cultures of 'fence-sitting respondents' v. cultures of 'decided respondents'. Admittedly, in a more mundane fashion, these systematic differences may also have to do with differences in interviewing cultures among the countries. Given the existence of such a large proportion of respondents who do not choose, this group has to be regarded as constituting a substantial part of the overall picture of value patterns among respondents in Asian and Western countries: these are at least similar in one respect, namely that, by and large, a quarter of them often do not offer a view when confronted with questions relating to 'basic societal values'.

Large but varying overall inter-regional differences with respect to agreement or disagreement about socio-economic, human rights and communitarian questions

The analysis of the substantive replies to the questions asked in the context of the thirteen variables entails examining successively three matters. First, one must discover whether there is or not a big overall difference in the preferences of respondents from the two regions: this is the object of the current section. Second, one must examine the *spread* of the responses given in the countries of each region. Third, one must see whether the preferences expressed in each region are close to the mean for that region or whether there is a substantial *overlap* between the preferences expressed by respondents in the countries of one region and the preferences expressed by respondents in the countries of the other: these matters will be considered in subsequent sections. Whether, or to what extent one can refer to a similar or a different 'basic societal value system' in Western Europe and in East and Southeast Asia depends on the answers to these sets of questions.

Even if one merely considers the overall proportions in the two regions and in contrast to what we just noticed at the level of 'uncommitted answers', inter-regional differences do appear to exist with respect to committed answers. There is a gap between the average answers in the two regions and it has a systematic character. First, on five of the seven communitarian questions, the average response given by those who agree minus those who disagree with the statement proposed in East and Southeast Asia is more in the direction of an 'Asian values position' than the average response given in the Western European countries. There are thus proportionately more respondents from East and Southeast Asia than from Western Europe who believe (1) that 'in decisions older people should be given more influence' (Q.412e) (2) that 'a women's primary role is at home' (Q.412c) (3) that 'achieving consensus in society is more important than encouraging a lot of individual initiative' (Q.412d) and, perhaps above all (4) that 'the government usually knows best how to run the country' (Q.306e) and (5) that 'we should always do what the government wants instead of acting in our own interest' (Q.306d).

On the other hand, East and southeast Asian respondents take less of a 'pro-Asian values' position on two communitarian questions, those on whether the 'public interest should always come before family' (Q.412f) and that 'individuals should strive mostly for their own good rather than for the good of society' (Q.412g). In these two cases, it is rather surprising that Western European respondents should be more likely than East and Southeast Asian respondents to take what seems ostensibly to be a 'communitarian' rather than an individualistic line.

On the other hand and not altogether surprisingly, on both human rights questions, even on the question related to the freedom of expression, the responses given by East and Southeast Asian respondents, also calculated on the basis of the difference between those who agree with the statement proposed and those who disagree with it, are on average more 'pro-Asian values' positions than those of Western European respondents. Meanwhile, the views of respondents from both regions are very similar to each other on three of the socio-economic questions. There is a difference on only one of them, that which is concerned with the right of businesses to make as much profit as they wish (Q.306g): respondents from East and Southeast Asia are markedly more positively inclined on this matter than respondents from Western Europe.

There are thus differences between the two sides: yet the distance between the average responses from these two sides is not uniformly large and indeed varies appreciably. It is tiny to small with respect to five of the thirteen questions (from 0 to 13 points), not very large (20 to 25 points) with respect to two questions, but substantial for the last six (between 31 and 50 points). The five questions for which that distance is small includes, not surprisingly, the three of the socio-economic questions which have just been mentioned as resulting in very similar types of answers (Q.306a, b and 412b), the human rights question relating to the freedom of speech (Q.208b), as well as one of the two communitarian questions on which more Western European respondents adopted a more 'pro-Asian values' position than East and Southeast Asian respondents (Q.412g, which asks whether 'individuals should strive mostly for their own good rather than for the good of society'). The two questions on which the distance between the two sides is not very large concern the extent of influence to be given to old people (Q.412e) and the importance to be given to consensus (Q.412d). The six questions for which there is a large distance include the fourth socio-economic question, the one dealing with the right of businesses to make as much profit as they wish (Q.306g), the human rights question concerned with the right to hold protest meetings (Q.208c) and four of the communitarian questions, that concerned with the choice between family and public interest (Q.412f) – but, in this case, East and Southeast Asian respondents, as we saw, adopted less of a 'pro-Asian values' position than Western Europeans – the question concerned with the position of women in society (Q.412c) and, above all, the two questions concerned with the attitudes which citizens should have *vis-à-vis* the government (Q.306d and e) (Figure 3.1).

The overall evaluation of these inter-regional differences has therefore to be mixed. On the one hand, there is a clear indication that the 'Asian values' syndrome has resonance in East and Southeast Asia both with respect to the majority of the communitarian questions and to one of the human rights questions. On the other hand, even at the level of averages, the gap is not as large nor is it as uniformly widespread as to suggest that we are confronted here with two 'civilisations'. As Figure 3.1 shows, there is no case in which one sees the East and Southeast Asian countries clustered at one end of the range and the European countries at the other: even where the gap is largest, it is never more than a quarter of the possible maximum, whether in relation to 'communitarian' values and to human rights values, let alone to standpoints on economics and social matters. As a matter of fact, even on the two questions relating to the attitudes *vis-à-vis* the government, on which the gap is highest and reaches a quarter of the maximum, the answers given by the Westerners are not diametrically opposed to those of East and Southeast Asians. Yet these are questions which can be regarded as highly sensitive to Western ears, since they suggest that the government is somehow endowed with an aura of knowledge which fits with

Agree minus disagree

Right to express an opinion (208b)

AV
PHIL INDON
MAL SK
SING THAI
TW JA CH

−90	−70	−50	−30	−10	0	10	30	50	70	90

E D F,IRL
S AV I, P
GR
GB

Liberalism

Organise protest meetings (208c)

SING TW MAL INDON   AV   THAI PHIL JA   SK

−90	−70	−50	−30	−10	0	10	30	50	70	90

F
E D GB IRL P
S GR
AV

Government usually knows best (306e)

JA   SK   AV INDON SING
THAI CH PHIL TW MAL

−90	−70	−50	−30	−10	0	10	30	50	70	90

GB D   E   IRL   GR EP
S
AV

Governmental restraint
We should do what government wants (306d)

JA   THAI   SK   AV SING   CH PHIL
INDON   MAL TW

−90	−70	−50	−30	−10	0	10	30	50	70	90

D GB   S F   P IRL   GR
AV

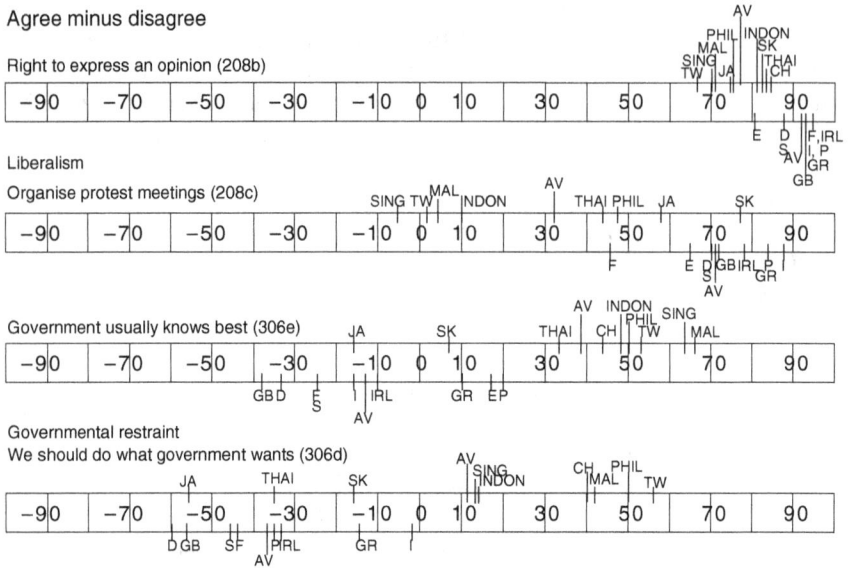

Figure 3.1 Spread of answers to human rights, communitarian and socio-economic questions, divided between the two regions by country.

difficulty with the 'critical' views which Westerners are expected to have. Meanwhile, it is 'only' as high as a fifth on the equally sensitive issue, but this time in parts of East and Southeast Asia at least, of the right to organise protest meetings, though it should be remembered that the question was not asked in China. Perhaps one should also be surprised that the gap is only about a fifth with respect to the place of women. On the other hand, it is perhaps not surprising that East and Southeast Asians should be more prepared than Western Europeans to allow businesses to be free to make as much profit as they wish.

It is surprising, on the other hand, that the distance should be small with respect to the preference to be given to the environment, given that East and Southeast Asians are typically regarded as being more 'pro-business' than Western Europeans. It is also surprising that the distance should be relatively small with respect to the notion that older people should have greater influence and to the place to be given to consensus: these are views which are said to be typically 'Asian' rather than 'European' or 'Western'. The fact that the distance is small surely indicates that, whatever difference there may be between the two sides on some of the elements of the syndrome of 'communitarian' values, it does not apply to all of the elements, while views about freedom of expression appear to be shared to a very substantial extent by Asians and not be in any way a monopoly of the Westerners. The combined examination of these similarities and differences does therefore show that, while differences exist between the two sides, it surely cannot be claimed with justification that 'Asian' values are universally distinct from 'European' values, even on an inter-regional basis.

* * * * *

III

Intra-regional differences: the extent of country spread and of overlap between the two regions

The difference between the means for the two regions as an indicator of the extent to which distinct 'cultural patterns' exist

We examined so far what was referred to as the distance between the regional means of the positions of respondents on the thirteen variables which are analysed here, these positions being based, as was indicated earlier, on the difference between the proportion of those who agree and the proportion of those who disagree with the 'pro-Asian values' position. If these means are very distant from each other in relation to a particular variable, there is an apparent difference, at any rate between the two regions as a whole, in the stance taken by respondents in these regions. If these means are not distant in relation to another variable, on the contrary, the difference in the stance taken by the respondents of the two regions taken as a whole with respect to that variable is not substantial. As we saw, that distance is low or even non-existent in relation to five variables, still rather small in relation to a further two and substantial in relation to six, while, in two of the thirteen cases, the position of East and Southeast Asian respondents is even less 'pro-Asian values' than that of Western Europeans. In the cases of the six variables about which the position is reversed or a small distance is recorded, it is clearly not permissible to argue that anything resembling a truly 'Asian' viewpoint distinct from a truly 'European' viewpoint does exist. There is a case for arguing that there are a genuinely 'Asian' viewpoint and a genuinely 'European' viewpoint in relation to five variables, on the other hand, three communitarian, one dealing with human rights and one concerned with a socio-economic question. However, as was noted earlier, even these large distances are only at most a quarter of and in several cases substantially less than what the maximum distance could be.

The distance between the means recorded on each of the thirteen variables at the level of the region as a whole does not tell the whole story, however. For values to be regarded as distinctly 'Asian' or 'European', it is not sufficient that the responses given by the countries of the two regions should display substantial average differences: these responses also have to be close to the average for the region. Regional averages can disguise a wide *spread* between a marked agreement and a marked disagreement with the propositions to which interviewees have to react: if there is such a wide spread, it becomes impossible to refer to a common set of values shared by the respondents of the countries concerned. The spread or concentration of the countries' responses constitutes therefore an element in what can be regarded as the extent of *cohesion* of the citizens of the countries of each region.

A further element also needs to be taken into account: for value patterns to be specific to one region, there must be a limited *overlap* between the responses given by the citizens of one region and those given by the citizens of the other. The greater such an overlap in the responses given to a particular question, the less it becomes possible to refer to an 'Asian' or a 'European' set of values, since these values are in effect shared by the respondents of a substantial number of countries of the two regions. Before acknowledging that there is a strong case for arguing that attitudes to the basic societal values are different in the two regions, one must therefore look at the spread of the country answers with respect to each of the questions and at the overlap between the country answers of the two regions.

The generally wide spread in the responses of interviewees in the countries of the two regions

The answers given by respondents of the countries of each of the two regions tend in general to be widely spread. The spread is wide on both sides, but, on communitarian questions – on which it is widest – it is appreciably wider on the Asian side (76 points) than on the European side (53 points), while it is about the same, but not on the same questions, on socio-economic matters. A spread of such a magnitude means that, *on average*, in Asia, the difference between those who agree with the proposition put to them and those who disagree with it ranges from, for instance, +40 points at one extreme (that is to say that, in one country, respondents divide 70 to 30 *for* the proposition), −36 points at the other extreme (that is to say that, in one country, respondents divide 68 to 32 *against* the proposition). In Europe, equivalent figures would be, *again on average*, for instance, 70 to 30 *for* and 30 to 13 *against*. Such a spread shows that there are major divisions of opinion among the respondents of the countries of each region: value patterns which are so diverse within a region cannot therefore be described as being 'common' to the region (Table 3.2). The existence of a common regional political culture is therefore at stake.

The responses given by interviewees from the East and Southeast Asian countries to the thirteen questions are, except in one case, markedly more concentrated in Western Europe than in East and Southeast Asia. Indeed, in East and Southeast Asia, one finds two questions with respect to which the spread is 14 or 15 points, one for which it is 27 points, one for which it is 41 points, one for which it is 57 points, two for which it is 63 or 64 points,

Table 3.2 Intra-regional differences: spread (in percentage points from −100 to +100)

	Nine Asian	Nine European	All eighteen countries
Communitarian values			
Always do what government wants (306d)	112	57	116
Government usually knows best (306e)	79	57	103
Women's role at home (412c)	106	51	117
Consensus more important(412d)	63	58	68
Older people more influence (412e)	77	51	77
Public interest before family (412f)	111	126	133
Individuals strive mostly for own good (412g)	57	39	70
Average	86	60	98
Human rights values			
Right to express opinion (208 b)	15	15	26
Allowed to organise protest meetings (208c)	84	43	96
Average	50	29	61
Economic values			
Competition good (306a)	41	21	42
Responsibility of government for jobs (306b)	14	36	36
Businesses free to make profits (306g)	64	54	91
Environment more important than growth (412b)	27	64	64
Average	37	44	58

three for which it is between 77 and 84 points and three for which it is between 106 and 111 points. In Western Europe, on the other hand, the spread is between 51 and 58 points on six questions, being smaller on five questions and larger on two, but one of these being 126 points! Among East and Southeast Asian countries, the three questions, all communitarian, for which the range of country answers is over 100 points relate to whether citizens should do what the government wants them to do (Q.306d), whether public interest should come before the family (Q.412f) and whether the women's place was at home (Q.412c). It is clear that, on those three questions, little agreement exists among Asian citizens as to what the 'right' answer should be. On doing 'what the government wants people to do', very surprisingly, given the way politics has developed in the two countries, Taiwanese citizens *agree* by a majority of 55 points over those who disagree and Philippine citizens by a majority of 50 points[2]; their reaction is in sharp contrast with the views of Japanese citizens who *disagree* also by a majority of 55 points and Thai citizens by a majority of 37 points. On putting the public interest before the family, Indonesians agree by a majority of 58 points and Taiwanese by a majority of 37 points, but the Japanese citizens disagree by a majority of 55 points and the Philippine citizens by a majority of 11 points. On the place of women being at home, Korean citizens agree by a majority of 38 points and Philippine citizens by a tiny majority of 3 points, while Chinese citizens disagree by a majority of 67 points and Thai citizens by a majority of 44 points.

Although the responses of Western European interviewees are less spread out, that spread is far from insignificant since it is 50 points or more in the majority of cases. The question with respect to which the spread is 126 points relates to whether 'the public interest should come before family obligations' (Q.412f), the difference between supporters and opponents of the proposition being markedly in favour of the supporters among French respondents (51 points) and to a substantially lesser extent among Greek respondents (16 points), while that difference was markedly against the proposition among Swedish respondents (75 points), British respondents (63 points) and Irish respondents (55 points). The position of the French respondents goes a long way towards explaining why the overall position of respondents from Western Europe with respect to that question is more 'pro-Asian values' than that of East and Southeast Asian respondents. In both regions, therefore, one finds only one example among communitarian questions – the same one – of a genuine concentration of answers around the average and this case corresponds to a near unanimous agreement with the proposition that there should be freedom of expression (Q.208b). The other cases are characterised by at least a fairly large spread of country responses on both sides of the average.

The substantial overlap in the responses of interviewees of the countries of the two regions with respect to 'basic societal' values

The spread is therefore wide, but there can be also more or less overlap, if the positions of the countries of the two regions with respect to the variables are, so to speak, more or less 'intertwined'. The more countries overlap each other in this way in the context of a particular variable, the less one can speak of a specifically 'Asian' or 'European' position. As a matter of fact, in contrast with spread, overlap is slightly greater on the Western European 'side', where it is on average for all thirteen variables of 6.0 countries out of a maximum of nine countries, than on the East and Southeast Asian 'side', where it is on average of 5.6 countries also out a maximum of nine. The extent of overlap ranges from a minimum of one country on the European side and of two countries on the East and Southeast Asian side (for one question on each 'side') to the absolute maximum of nine countries in one case on the Western European 'side' and of two cases (both on economic matters) on the East and Southeast Asian side. There was also an overlap of eight countries in one case on the East and Southeast Asian side and in three cases on the Western European side (Table 3.3).

Table 3.3 Intra-regional differences: overlap (number of countries)

	Nine Asian countries	Nine European countries
Communitarian values		
Always do what government wants (306d)	3	8
Government usually knows best (306e)	2	4
Women's role at home (412c)	4	8
Consensus more important (412d)	6	8
Older people more influence (412e)	6	9
Public interest before family (412 f)	8	7
Individuals strive mostly for own good (412g)	7	6
Average	5.0	7.0
Human Rights values		
Right to express opinion (208b)	4	1
Allowed to organise protest meetings (208c)	4	7
Average	4.0	4.0
Economic values		
Competition good (306a)	8	8
Responsibility of government for jobs (306b)	9	5
Society better off if business free for profits (306g)	4	4
Environment more important than growth (412b)	9	6
Average	7.5	5.7
Overall average	5.7	6.2

The smallest amount of overlap is found, among East and Southeast Asian countries, on the question whether 'the government usually knows best', the two countries overlapping with the Western European side being Japan and Korea, both of which score low with respect to the proposition. The smallest amount of overlap is found, among Western European countries, on the question about the freedom to express an opinion. The fact that the overlap is small on these two questions indicates that there is here a degree of cultural 'distinctiveness'. The absolute maximum amount of overlap is reached on the Western European side in response to the question whether older citizens should be given more influence in decision-making and, on the East and Southeast Asian side, on competition and on employment rights. The cases in which there was an overlap of eight countries related to whether 'the public interest should come before family obligations' on the Asian side, the role of women, the role of consensus and whether one should do what the government wants on the Western European side. Thus, as with respect to the fact that country replies are typically widely spread out, it is difficult to conclude, given the existence of such an overlap, that, overall, a given pattern of responses is truly typical of one region and therefore that 'Asian' values are intrinsically distinct from 'European' values. For this reason as well, the existence of a 'common regional political culture' is manifestly in question.

Another way of examining the extent to which East and Southeast Asian responses differ or not from Western European responses consists in examining the results of the cluster analysis, not on average, but with respect to each of the thirteen questions analysed in this chapter. This more detailed analysis shows that substantial differences exist among the answers to the seven questions dealing with 'communitarian' values, between the answers to the two human rights questions and between the answers to the four questions dealing with economic matters. If one considers the 'primary' linkages which emerge, those which relate the countries to each other directly and immediately, the picture becomes rather blurred. On the one hand, in 37 per cent of the cases, these linkages bring together countries of one region only, but, on the other, in 47 per cent of the cases, similar linkages occur between countries of the two regions, and in the majority of these (32 per cent of the total sample) these groupings relate about the same number of countries in both regions. In the remaining 16 per cent of the cases, countries do not relate to any other country at the level of primary links, but, interestingly, this is appreciably more the case among East and Southeast Asian respondents than among Western European respondents (12 per cent against 4 per cent overall). To some extent at least, the Western European group of countries appears therefore to be somewhat more compact than the East and Southeast Asian group (Tables 3.4 and 3.5).

A gradation in the extent to which there is cultural distinctiveness

It is therefore not permissible to argue that Asians and Europeans are 'poles apart' with respect to the basic societal values they hold, whether with respect to 'communitarian' matters, with respect to human rights or with respect to socio-economic questions. There are too few cases of a substantial difference between the average position of the two sides; there is too

Table 3.4 First-level linkages between countries

	Groupings including countries of one region only			Groupings including countries of both regions		Countries not grouped at all	
	WE	AS	Total	Unequal in numbers	Equal in numbers	WE	AS
All thirteen questions							
N	33	36	69	30	89	14	31
%	14	15	30	13	38	6	13
Human rights and communitarian only							
N	33	27	60	24	51	7	19
%	20	17	37	15	32	4	12

Table 3.5 First-level linkages between countries by answer

	Groupings including countries of one region only			Groupings including countries of both regions		Countries not grouped at all	
	WE	AS	Total	Unequal in numbers	Equal in numbers	WE	AS
HR							
208b	5	8	13	0	2	0	3
208c	3	0	3	8	3	1	2
(not China)							
Communitarian							
306d	5	5	10	0	5	1	2
306e	8	8	16	0	0	1	1
412c	4	1	5	7	3	0	3
412d	0	0	0	0	14	2	2
412e	4	3	7	5	4	0	2
412f	2	2	4	0	11	1	2
412g	2	0	2	4	9	1	2
Economic							
306a	0	2	2	0	15	0	1
306b	0	2	2	6	6	3	1
306g	0	5	5	0	6	1	6
412b	0	0	0	0	11	3	4
Total	33	36	69	30	89	14	31

Notes
208b Right to express one's opinion
208c Right to organise public protest meetings
306d Do what government wants
306e Government usually knows best
412c Women's primary role in the home
412d Important to achieve consensus
412e Give extra influence to older people
412f Public interest before family
412g Individuals should strive for their own good more than society
306a Competition good
306b Responsibility of government to provide jobs or social welfare
306g Society better if businesses free to make profits
412b Good environment more important than economic growth

much spread in the reactions of citizens of the various countries concerned; and there is too much overlap between the reactions of citizens of the countries of one region and the other.

Yet it would equally be wrong to claim that there is no difference whatsoever between the values held in the two regions. As we noted earlier, Western Europeans tend to be more negative than Asians on the 'communitarian' questions and more positive than East and Southeast Asians on the two human rights questions; the picture is less clear-cut with respect to economic questions. We cannot of course know, given that this analysis is cross-sectional, whether changes are taking place and whether, for instance, East and Southeast Asians are now more prepared to endorse human rights standpoints than they did earlier: as of the beginning of the third millennium, however, more than a residuum of difference between the two regions unquestionably exists.

There is unquestionably a gradation in the extent to which a difference exists between the respondents of the two sides. On socio-economic matters, differences are rather small and they are in particular less marked than might have been expected on the choice between growth and the environment or on the freedom to be given to business to make as much profit as it wishes.

The seven 'communitarian' questions can be divided into two groups. On four questions respondents from the two sides do not react very differently or Western Europeans hold a more 'pro-Asian values' position than East and Southeast Asians: these are the questions on the role to be given to consensus (Q.412d), on the role to be given to old people (Q.412e), on whether 'individuals should strive most for their own good' (Q.412g) and on the choice to be made between public interest and family obligations (Q.412f). It is with respect to the other three communitarian questions, and in particular with respect to the two questions relating to the attitude which citizens should have *vis-à-vis* the government, as well as, though to a lesser extent, with respect to the human rights question dealing with the right to hold protest meetings that a genuine difference among the standpoints of the two sides does occur, even if it is not as marked as it could be – and possibly should be – to justify the conclusion that there is a major distinctiveness in political culture. On the two questions which relate to the attitudes citizens should have *vis-à-vis* the government, in particular, the distance between the regional averages is the largest of all the questions; there is some overlap, but in one case, it is limited and in the other not very large. The spread is rather large in both cases, however. If there are questions which do justify the view that 'Asian values' exist among the populations of East and Southeast Asia, these are the questions: East and Southeast Asians are, on balance, more prepared than Western Europeans to believe that the government knows best and that it should (therefore?) be obeyed.

It is worth noting that these questions do cover the part of Asian values which politicians such as Lee Kuan Yew and Mahathir Mohammad are probably instrumentally most concerned with; as a matter of fact, Singaporean and Malaysian respondents are among those who take the line that one should 'always do what the governments wants' rather strongly, but they are accompanied, not just by the Chinese respondents, but by the Taiwanese, Indonesian and Philippine respondents: once more, Taiwan and the Philippines react in a manner which appears inconsistent with voting patterns in these two countries, but which may have to do, as we noted earlier, with a feeling of unease about what can be regarded as instability. The only countries of East and Southeast Asia in which the respondents are lukewarm to the idea are Korea and Thailand while that attitude is wholly rejected by Japanese respondents. A similar view, only more marked even, concerns the question as to whether 'the government usually knows best how to run the country'. Yet, if 56 per cent of the East and Southeast Asians agree with the view that 'the government usually knows best', 30 per cent of the Western European respondents also think the same way. The question will be examined in further chapters, however, as it relates directly to the matter of the existence of a 'common regional political culture'.

The inter-regional patterns of answers to two human rights questions are distinct. There is only a marginal difference between the two sides on the right to express an opinion, but the difference is substantial with respect to the right 'to organise public meetings in order to protest'. Admittedly, there is a majority globally in both regions in favour of this right, but not in Singapore, and the majority in favour is very slim in Malaysia and, here again, in Taiwan; meanwhile, the question was not asked in China. Thus, while 52 per cent agreed in East and Southeast Asia and 21 per cent disagreed, 78 per cent agreed in Western Europe and only 7 per cent disagreed, France being, curiously perhaps, the only country of the Western European group in which the proportion of those who disagreed was truly significant (20 per cent). Yet, because of the fact that the distance between the averages is medium rather than large, because there is a substantial spread and a sizeable amount of overlap, the answers to that question are more comparable to those of the second group of 'communitarian' answers. There is simply no evidence that human rights are rejected *en bloc* by East and Southeast Asian respondents, even if one were to consider on its own the responses to the more sensitive question of the right to protest. Overall, therefore, 'communitarianism' may be more marked in East and Southeast Asia, while human rights are more supported in Western Europe (socio-economic differences being rather blurred): there is no true syndrome of 'Asian values', however. At best there is some tendency, with respect for the authority of the state being, in a somewhat uneasy and limited manner, at the apex of that tendency.

IV

'Basic societal' value patterns, demographic characteristics and knowledge of politics

Value patterns cannot be expected to emerge exclusively as a consequence of the cultural context: they are likely to depend in part on the social structure. This is true in the West: it seems difficult to believe that this should not be the case in others parts of the world, in East and Southeast Asia in particular. To examine the possible impact of such factors, gender, education, age, religious practice, occupation, living standards and the distinction between public and private sector employees have been related to the findings about 'communitarian' values, views on human rights and socio-economic standpoints which have been explored in this chapter. A number of recodes have been undertaken in order to reduce to three or at most four the number of categories in the variables which are being used: details of the recoding are given in Appendix III. In order to tap the knowledge of the respondents, there was a choice between two variables, a variable asking who are the permanent members of the UN Security Council and another asking about the name of the foreign minister of the country of that respondent: the second of these two variables appeared to constitute a better indicator.

In order to assess whether there was an apparent difference in the relationship between these background variables and responses in the two regions, separate cross-tabulations were undertaken among the two groups of nine countries. Cross-tabulations between the responses to the knowledge variable and those to the demographic variables were carried out, primarily to discover whether some of these were intercorrelated. There appeared to be a relationship between knowledge and education, age and gender. The relationship between knowledge and living standards was not clear for the Asian countries, while that between knowledge and religious practice was not apparent for the European countries. The demographic variables and the knowledge variable were then cross-tabulated with the thirteen value variables which have been analysed in the course of this chapter.

The general aim of the analysis is to find out to what extent the responses of the interviewees in the two regions appear to vary in relation to the demographic background and the knowledge of these interviewees. There is also a more specific aim: if respondents seems to react differently in the two regions when background variables intervene, there may be a degree of regional specificity in the behaviour of these respondents; if, on the contrary, the intervention of the background variables result in respondents reacting in the same manner in the two regions, there would seem to be rather little support for the notion that the values of respondents are markedly different in the two regions.

Very little regional specificity is introduced as a result of the intervention of background variables

The effect of the intervention of the background variables described earlier is examined for all thirteen questions being analysed here: this is assessed in practice by examining whether there are variations in the proportion of the respondents stating that they agree, whether strongly or not, with the statement which is made.

Reactions of Asian and European respondents to each cross-tabulation between each of the background variables and each of the value variables were classified under the same four *rubrics*, namely 'no apparent relationship', 'similar type of apparent relationship on both "regional sides"', 'no apparent relationship on one "regional side" but an apparent relationship on the other' and 'apparent relationships going in opposite directions'. With seven demographic variables and one knowledge variable being related to thirteen values questions, the total number of these relationships was 104.

There were few cases in which 'contradictory movements' among respondents of the two regions between two sides were registered (8 or 7 per cent) and in which a movement occurred in one region but not in the other (18 or 17 per cent). In thirty-six cases (34 per cent) there was no movement on either 'side' – but the majority of these cases came from the answers to economic questions – and in forty-two (40 per cent) there was some movement, but in the same direction on both 'sides' (Table 3.6). Thus, in three-quarters of the cases, the apparent effect of the background variables was to touch both sides in the same way, whether to affect the value patterns or not to affect them at all. In a little under a fifth of the cases, there was what might be described as 'half-divergence', since one side moved and the other did not. Only in under 10 per cent of the cases was there true divergence, as the movements were in opposite directions: interestingly, none of these cases occurred with respect to the two human rights questions. There is therefore very little support for a view which might be put forward, namely that the lack of specificity of 'Asian' and 'European' values may result in part from the fact that the responses of interviewees are affected diversely by the background variables to which they are subjected (Table 3.6).

Let us examine the distribution of the cases in which there was 'half-divergence' and those where there was 'full divergence'. Seven of these twenty-six cases are related to age while living standards and knowledge each provide four cases of a relationship with the pattern of values. It is not possible to determine, however, whether the apparently significant part

Table 3.6 Type of relationship between background variables and societal values among Asian and European countries (number of cases)

	No movement either 'side'	Same type of movement both 'sides'	Half-divergent	Fully divergent	Total
Religious practice	4	6	1	2	13
Education	2	8	1	2	13
Age	2	4	4	3	13
Gender	4	7	2	0	13
Living standards	2	7	4	0	13
Occupation	11	0	2	0	13
Public–private distinction	9	3	1	0	13
Name foreign minister	2	7	3	1	13
Total	36	42	18	8	104

played by age constitutes evidence of over time changes in the value patterns of respondents. Yet there may still be some support for the view, which was for instance put forward about Taiwan, that substantial changes in value patterns have taken place in recent years and that these changes have reduced regional 'specificity' (Parrish and Chang, 1996, 27–41).

On the other hand, age appears to play a markedly more limited part in relation to the cases in which the relationship is exercised in the same direction in the two regions: there were only four cases out of forty-two where some relationship could be traced. Meanwhile, among these forty-two cases, education, gender, religiosity, living standards and the knowledge of the name of the foreign minister played a part in between six and eight cases: but, as these and indeed the other variables, which played a more limited part, appeared to have a similar effect on the value variables, the result is not to lead to one region *becoming* closer to or more distant from the other. Any regional specificity which might have existed earlier is therefore neither reduced nor increased. It follows that the conclusions which were reached earlier in this chapter are not modified in any significant manner by the introduction of these background variables.

Moreover, the relationships between the background variables and the value variables are rarely strong. The most outstanding examples are two cases relating to education (concerning the role of old people in decision-making and whether the government 'knows best') and one case relating to age, interestingly enough, concerning the influence which old people should have in public decision-making. The relationships between the background variables and the human rights variables are weak, perhaps because the support for the propositions presented to the respondents is large. Most of the apparent relationships, both those in which there is commonality in the direction of the relationship and those in which there is divergence, are fairly weak. The weakest relationship is provided by the distinction between public and private sector employment, which, perhaps not surprisingly, appears to have no relationship at all with basic societal values in nine out of the thirteen variables analysed here. Above all, the occupational background had very little effect. Only in two cases (and in one of these marginally) is there a difference in the reactions of non-manual and manual workers: these were found in both cases in Western Europe, while the reactions were in the same manner with respect to all thirteen variables in East and Southeast Asia.

* * * * *

The main aim of this chapter was to consider whether there was substantial evidence among the bulk of the population to warrant the conclusion that the 'basic societal values' of citizens differ markedly in East and Southeast Asia from what these are in Western Europe. The examination of the evidence shows that this is the case only to a limited extent: the overall differences between the two regions are not sufficiently marked to support the view that there is a sharp distinction. Moreover, as we shall examine in greater detail in the next two chapters, there seem to be doubts as to whether a common regional political culture exists in either East and Southeast Asia or in Western Europe.

Whether this state of affairs is recent or not is impossible to determine on the basis of the cross-sectional evidence on which the present study is based: all that can be stated is that the examination of the background demographic variables suggests that any such impact may not be as large as might have been supposed. Whatever evolution may have taken place in the course of the second half of the twentieth century in the two regions, however, there is evidence showing that, on average, some differences exist in the political cultures of the two regions: but these differences are not large enough to allow for the conclusion that the countries of East and Southeast Asia hold 'Asian values' which are pitched against the 'Western values' of Western European countries.

4 A common political culture in Western Europe?

So much literature has been written to demonstrate either that the Europeans feel part of a common Western political culture or, on the contrary, that there are vast differences between the various segments of the European population on the subject of the political culture that it seems almost preposterous to attempt to clarify the matter. There is something bordering on schizophrenia in the reactions of Europeans on this question, or, at any rate, of the members of the elite, European or even non-European, who write on the subject. How many times has one pointed out that the British often relish to say that they 'go to Europe' when they cross the Channel? How many times has one pointed out that 'Northerners' – Scandinavians, Dutch, British of course – either make fun or show deep worry about the attitudes of the 'Latins'? Thus, in a referendum which took place at the end of the 1990s in Denmark, a 'no' vote was advocated by some on the grounds that the condition of women was simply too 'old-fashioned' in Italy or elsewhere in the South to be acceptable to the 'modern' Danes: the majority of Danish voters were not swayed, but the fact that the point was made suggests that the question of a 'common political culture' is wide open across Western Europe, without going as far as extending the frame of reference to Western culture in general.

Admittedly, in Western Europe at least, in contrast to East and Southeast Asia, sample surveys might be expected to have tested the opinions of citizens on the matter of political culture. They might be expected to have explored these matters to such an extent that the debates about the presence or absence of a 'common political culture' would no longer seem necessary, except in so far as surveys might regularly monitor with precision changes taking place on the matter. Of course, surveys are conducted frequently in Western Europe: yet questions relating to political culture are rarely asked. To begin with, most surveys are national, and the wording of questions is often such that it is difficult to compare the answers given to surveys conducted in one country to those given to surveys conducted in another. Moreover, by far the largest proportion of these surveys is devoted either to electoral behaviour or to policy matters of a topical character, not to 'deeper' problems of political culture. This is indeed also true of the one series which is Europe-wide – or at least European Union-wide – the

Eurobarometer series. Uniform information is provided across the European Union; but the questions are directed towards obtaining reactions to problems and policies closely related to European integration.

Justifiable or not, there is therefore little if any attempt to examine in depth the 'basic societal values' held by European citizens: it is therefore not possible to obtain from surveys a precise picture of the political culture of these citizens; nor, as a result, is it possible to find out whether that culture is common across Europe or whether there are massive differences among the various nations or groups of nations.

The present study is therefore not merely valuable because it makes it possible to compare the basic societal attitudes of Western Europeans to those of East and Southeast Asians, but because it also gives an opportunity to explore the extent to which the attitudes of Western Europeans on these matters are broadly similar or, on the contrary, diverse. One can discover, moreover, whether or not any such diversity leads to the clustering of sub-groups of nations, in particular though not necessarily exclusively, along geographical lines.

This chapter thus examines the way in which the respondents from the nine Western European countries interviewed in this study distributed their answers to the questions put to them with respect to their basic societal values. Before undertaking this analysis, however, the chapter needs to look at the state of the debate about the presence or absence of a common European or of a common Western political culture and in particular about the factors which might have impeded the development of a common culture. This debate has had a long history: it has known major fluctuations rather than shown a tendency to move on an ascending linear path. The aim of this chapter is thus to examine Western political culture in Europe from two standpoints. On the one hand, it looks at the reasons which have been typically put forward to account for the fragmentation of the Western European political culture. On the other, it assesses the extent to which European citizens appear close to or distant from holding a common political culture. By analysing the factors which, in the eyes of the elites, rendered difficult the emergence of a common Western European political culture and by comparing these difficulties to the attitudes which prevail currently among European citizens, one can discover how far the divisions which were felt to exist in the past may be in the process of being currently overcome or whether, on the contrary, at least some of the factors which were felt to be significant continue to play a major part.

I

The debate about a common Western European culture

When did Europe began to be conceived as a 'common culture area'? Probably not as long ago as one might be inclined to believe and seemingly not before the later part of the seventeenth century. A number of reasons prevented such a vision from emerging previously. Earlier, Rome had brought together and led for centuries a common 'civilisation' in a substantial part of what is commonly referred to as Western Europe, but that civilisation had been centred on the Mediterranean: to the North of the Roman empire there were 'barbarians'; indeed, the proof that they were truly 'barbarians' was provided by what happened repeatedly from the second century AD, when 'hordes' eventually destroyed the Western part of the empire.

In a sense, the Arabs contributed indirectly to creating a first, but temporary, common vision of (Western) Europe, since they broke (seemingly for ever) the unity of the Mediterranean area by conquering the Southern shores of that sea and going as far as entering Spain and even making their way into 'Gaul'. If, henceforth, there was to be some semblance of unity it could only be by linking the remnants of the Roman Empire which were north of the Mediterranean together with that part of Europe in which the 'barbarians' had settled. The papacy and Charles the Great were involved in such a unification process, but the dream lasted for a very short period, as the sons of Charles split the empire; the further fragmentation of the area then became unstoppable. Indeed, at the time, as had been the case before Rome took over the leadership of the European 'world', first militarily and then culturally, it was Greece and generally the Orient which were viewed as the centre of civilisation. With the collapse of the Roman part of the empire under the weight of the 'barbarians', the Orient became once more and remained for centuries the centre of European civilisation. If Italy was regarded up to the late nineteenth century as a 'geographical expression only', this was even truer of Western Europe from the ninth to the sixteenth centuries. There was simply no 'Western' culture.

However, during that time and while the Orient was gradually losing its prestige, parts of its territory and eventually its very existence with the fall of Constantinople, a number of monarchs in the Western part of Western Europe, especially those of England, France, Spain and Portugal, were increasing their power, both internally and externally though the Portuguese king turned his back to Europe to be concerned exclusively with the rest of the world – Africa, America, even Asia. Italy played a part in 'civilising' these monarchs, although at the cost of most of its territory becoming for centuries a virtual colony of a variety of countries. Monarchs came to Italy with their armies to learn about civilisation: Italy was thus to play *vis-à-vis* the rest of (Western) Europe the part which Greece had played for the Romans over 1500 years earlier: one could go there to learn about being 'civilised' and bring back what one could, but the political power was not there.

The strengthening of the power of the states in the Western part of Western Europe had a further consequence. The fragmentation of political units in Europe's centre, not just in Italy, but also in Germany, turned, especially in the seventeenth century, that part of the continent into a battleground for the forces allied to the 'Western' monarchs, the French and Spanish kings in particular, but also the Swedish king, who, having transformed his regime into a strong absolute monarchy, actively participated in many of these wars.

Meanwhile, the theological and political difficulties periodically experienced throughout the 'Middle Ages' by the Catholic Church and by the papacy in particular culminated in the sixteenth century by what were to be the first successful 'heresies', those of the various forms of protestantism. In the name of religion, whether sincerely or not, Europe was torn apart: there was clearly no common Western European political culture at the end of the sixteenth century.

It was only a century later, from the later part of the seventeenth century, that the concept of a Western European cultural area began to emerge, almost for the first time. As Segal states:

> from the late seventeenth century on, in the context of New World plantations that relied on unfree labour of 'Africans', peoples who had previously thought of themselves as being of diverse class and national origin were rendered into a singular race identified as 'European'.
>
> (ibid., 1991, 171)

In reality, the emergence of this European feeling occurred more by accident than by design and more for practical than for theoretical reasons, despite the fact that the change was due in large part to 'intellectuals', soon to be known as 'philosophers', whose numbers had grown substantially from the second half of the seventeenth century. This development was rather surprising, as these intellectuals played a major part even in the context of absolute monarchies and in particular in France, although they were naturally better protected in such little centres of 'free thinking' as the United Provinces and parts of Switzerland, as well as in England, where absolutism had not prevailed, despite the repeated efforts of the Tudor and Stuart kings. Basically, the 'philosophers' came to discuss and question the grounds for the 'absolutist' character of monarchies and the grounds for the role of the (catholic) church in society: the place of the individual in society was therefore the key element of the 'common political culture' which was developing.

The philosophers were not silenced, quite the contrary, although agents of the monarchies naturally engaged in cat-and-mouse operations against them more than once in the course of the eighteenth century. The prestige of French literature under the 'Sun-King' in the second half of the seventeenth century resulted in the predominance of the French language: this led to the predominance of French 'culture' throughout the eighteenth century all over the continent and in turn resulted in a great demand for French 'philosophers', including on the part of the most authoritarian monarchs, however inconsistent it may have been of these monarchs to have invited and extolled the virtues of these 'philosophers'. The movement of ideas and of persons which was the consequence of this process led to the emergence, probably for the first time, of a (Western) European (lay) intellectual elite. The impact on the bulk of the population was probably negligible, indeed almost non-existent; but the *idea* of (Western) Europe constituting a common cultural area had been born.

The history of the idea of the European culture becomes infinitely more complex from the end of the eighteenth century, the French revolution having transformed into nationalism what were previously somewhat latent feelings of revulsion against the 'colonial' activities of the major absolutist monarchies; but nationalism not only did break – or at any rate slowed down markedly – any move towards a common political culture in Western Europe but it also for the first time led the people (or at least substantial segments of the people) to participate in the process of shaping Europe's political culture(s). Yet the fragmentation of the culture which nationalism brought about was only one of the factors which had contributed to preventing a common political culture from emerging. Alongside nationalism and its rise from a 'colonial' legacy in the heart of the continent, four other elements have played a major part – the climate, religion, the industrial revolution and socialisation at the national level coupled with and embodied in administrative centralisation. Except for the last one, these elements have tended to reinforce each other and to contribute to a feeling (true or false) that the political culture of Western Europe was divided into two broad groups.

Western European culture divided by its climate: an eighteenth century belief

Probably the first time the question of the presence or absence of a Western political culture came to be examined was by those who claimed that climate made some Europeans different from others. This occurred almost at the very moment that a common political culture was being forged, we noted by accident, as a result of the spread of common reflections about the state of European societies in relation both to the role of the government and to that of the church.

Climate was viewed as a crucial element in that it was argued that the cold made it easier for citizens to react whereas the heat led people to be more passive: in such circumstances, a common political culture was unlikely to develop and the 'North' was bound to be different from the 'South'. One of the first prominent writers who brought this theme to light was Montesquieu towards the middle of the eighteenth century in *The Spirit of Laws*, first published in 1748. Montesquieu was not part, strictly speaking, of the group of 'philosophers': he had an 'independent' mind; he was a practising lawyer. His aim was to propound straightforward and clear political reforms by means of institutions, in the way Locke had done half a century before; but he was also someone who might be labelled at present a political sociologist in that he paid much attention to the environment in which institutions developed. Hence the importance given to climate, among other 'influences on mankind': 'Mankind are influenced by various causes: by the climate, by the religion, by the laws, by the maxims of government, by precedent, morals, and customs; whence is formed a general spirit of nations' (Montesquieu, 1878 edn, Vol. I, 316). His conclusions resulted from what he felt were his empirical observations of the way people behaved in various parts of the world, 'civilised' or not. Climate was an ingredient which fashioned human behaviour, and it was foolish not to pay attention to it. Montesquieu goes into the matter in book XIV, entitled *Of laws in relation to the nature of the climate*, and subsequent volumes. Book XIV being in the second section of this Book, entitled 'Of the Difference of Men in different climates', he writes:

> People are therefore [because of the physical effect of the cold on the 'external extremities of the body'] more vigorous in cold climates. This superiority of strength must produce various effects; for instance, a greater boldness, that is, more courage; a greater sense of superiority; a greater opinion of security. The inhabitants of warm countries are, like old men, timorous; the people in cold countries are, like young men, brave.
>
> (ibid., 238–9)

Much of this applies to differences between very hot climates, such as those of Asia, and temperate regions, but the idea of the importance of climates is general.

The notion that climate played a part was widely shared in the course of the eighteenth century: as the century progressed, idyllic visions of parts of the world (mainly the islands of the Pacific) in which people lived free and well came to be almost commonplace. The notion that climate could play a part in the 'civilised' world, which Montesquieu had put forward, was not taken up by the 'mainstream' philosophers of the period, however, possibly because such a view would not have fitted with the general goal of concentrating on questioning government and church since it also meant questioning characteristics of the 'people'. Thus the prominent writer who took up the idea again, Madame de Stael, was also to mention it later during the Napoleonic period. She indicated, for instance, that things were different in Germany from elsewhere in Europe in part as a result of the climate: 'These observations must no doubt be modified as a result of the climate' (Stael, 1813, Vol. 1, 2).

The idea has not died out. If admittedly in a rather diffuse manner, the notion that climate has a significant effect on Western European culture in particular and on political culture in general continues to play some part, however linked that idea may be to other elements which divide that culture.

As a matter of fact, climate being by its very nature geographical in character, it is difficult to resist the conclusion that the idea that climate affects political values has had the indirect effect of embedding, more forcefully than might otherwise have been the case, political culture divisions in a geographical context. It is true that at least three of the four other elements which have been widely recognised as playing a part in the fragmentation of Western political culture have been embedded in geography; but this was by accident and not as a result of the nature of the element itself. This is not so with climate and one wonders therefore to what extent climate, having been chronologically the first element which was recognised as contributing to divide Western culture, has not in effect tended to structure the discourse about that division beyond what might have been the case, had it not been regarded as a significant element in the debate.

From colonial to national

It may not altogether be a mainstream interpretation to regard colonialism as a key feature of Western Europe, except probably in the case of Ireland; it is possibly even less of a mainstream interpretation to view nationalism as a development of colonialism. Yet among the first colonies which Western European powers created were European areas, indeed Western European areas, the example par excellence being Italy, although the same could be said to an extent of parts of Southern France (indeed, to an extent, colonisation occurred there earlier than in Italy)[1]; Germany was more a case of occupation, periodic occupation, rather than colonisation, although aspects of what occurred during periods of occupation resembled the protectorate form of nineteenth century European colonisation in the Third World.

As was pointed out earlier, Italy became an object of colonisation for the same reason as Greece had been when the Romans decided to enter that territory: Italy was richer and more 'civilised': other Europeans, principally from the North, wanted to benefit by plundering the goods and copying the manners. The consequences of this mode of behaviour on the Italian 'mentality' have often been noted. Barzini stated for instance:

> The ancient habit of disobedience or flexible selective obedience may be also due to the fact that, with but a few glorious exceptions, Italian provinces had been conquered and governed by foreigners or dominated by their influence since the fall of the Roman empire.
>
> (ibid., 1984, 179)

He continues:

> This was one of the reasons why most Italians preferred to go on relying, for the conduct of their lives and the solution of problems, as they still do, on their own ancient private way, which inevitably robbed public institutions of their validity.
>
> (ibid.)

The effect on social and political life was later analysed rigorously by Putnam who sharply distinguished the modes of behaviour of North and South, while Barzini's comments applied more generally, on the basis of a systematic empirical examination which enabled him to conclude: 'For the last ten centuries, the North and the South have followed contrasting approaches to the dilemmas of collective action that afflict all societies' (Putnam, 1993, 181). What can be found in Southern Italy, where the colonisation period was longest, since a Spaniard elite ran the 'Kingdom of the Two Sicilies' into the nineteenth century, is a reaction to the state which is not altogether different from what can be found in those parts of Latin America where nineteenth century immigrants from Europe have been relatively rare and where the key ethnic distinction is between the 'indigenous' population and the descendents of the Spanish 'conquistadores'. Admittedly, there are not two ethnic groups in Southern Italy, but those who represent the state are viewed as if they were alien to the 'culture' of the area.

It is not by accident that nationalism should have taken over a large part of that 'Mitteleuropa' which for centuries had not had the opportunity to govern itself or at least to govern itself fully independently and without interference from other powers. The Napoleonic episode served as a catalyst, since it showed to many the way to go forward. This was because, as in Italy, Napoleon was the first to create an embryonic unitary state on the basis of the kind of protectorate arrangements which were to lead to demands for independence from Europe, a century later or even less, in many parts of the Third World. This was because, as in Germany in particular, the Napoleonic invasion was in a sense the 'last drop' after a repeated, indeed incessant, entry of French troops in German territory during the previous 200 years. France was also nationalistic, of course, but in the way the United States has been, that is to say on the basis of an affirmation of its 'manifest destiny'; only much later, after her defeat in 1870, and even more after her collapse in 1940, did France experience the nationalism of the vanquished: indeed, that nationalism has led France to be, ever since the European Union was set up, the most outstanding supporter – indeed possibly the only real supporter – of a Europe which should go it alone for fear of possible 'contamination' of its culture by American culture.

A colonial (or protected) past, first, and a nationalistic line, second, tended to distinguish the characteristics of the political culture of 'Mitteleuropa' from the characteristics of the political culture of Northwestern Europe, if not of the whole of Western Europe. France was partly associated with the Northwest, but only partly; Spain and Portugal for a period almost disappeared from Europe, not because of a colonial past but because these two countries, Portugal in particular, had become 'fat' as a result of what they had absorbed from the colonies they had created: they were unable to 'move' when these colonies became independent, and almost vegetated for a century or more.

Not surprisingly, the result of these sharp distinctions led to the emergence of the commonly held view that the culture, including the political culture of the South of Europe and possibly of 'Mitteleuropa' in general, at least until Germany was to become a major industrial power, was profoundly different from that of Western and especially Northwestern Europe. The prevailing notion among Northern European elites was that, perhaps, after much effort, the South and Centre would take on the principles which the West, and in particular Britain, had developed: but, for the time being, one could not expect anything 'good' to happen in the rest of Europe. Western European political culture was thus divided into what would have to be called a 'progressive' and a 'decadent' part, the value judgements attached to the division being indeed part of the division itself, as it gave those who were progressive a sense of (moral) superiority. It was to be the function of the 'progressives' to 'educate' gradually the 'decadents', a mission which the Piedmontese arrogated to themselves when Italy was united in the 1860s, with, as has been pointed out ever since, almost no effect. The division of Italy into two political cultures was, in a smaller way, an image of the division of Western Europe into two fundamentally distinct political cultures, though there were also subdivisions of each of the two groups and in particular of the 'decadent' group.

Religion and the belief in the Protestant ethic

While climate and colonisation-cum-nationalism are not perhaps typically regarded as either causes or symbols of the division of Western European political culture, religion certainly is. This has been stated by many generations both before and since Weber wrote his famous *The Protestant Ethic and the Spirit of Capitalism* (new edn, 1976), which has admittedly been strongly criticised by large numbers of authors.[2] Weber does proceed to attempt to 'understand the connection between the fundamental religious ideas of ascetic Protestantism and its maxims for everyday economic conduct' by 'examin[ing] with especial care such writings as have evidently been derived from ministerial practice' (ibid., 155). He adds further: 'The emphasis on the ascetic importance of a fixed calling provided an ethical justification of the modern specialised division of labour. In a similar way the providential interpretation of profit-making justified the activities of the business man' (ibid., 163).

The case is well known: protestant Europe is characterised by a spirit of enterprise, Catholic Europe is not. It is perhaps not very important to determine what the root causes of this phenomenon are: Weber sees it as being largely due to the doctrine of predestination which characterises Protestantism in its Calvinistic form. Why predestination should have had the consequences which Weber attributes to it is not really clear, though one can understand that Catholicism should not, on the other hand, push people to be entrepreneurial: redemption will occur for Catholics if they live a moral life, not if they are concerned with wordly activities.[3] What is perhaps even more difficult to understand in the context of Weber's thesis is, on the one hand, the fact that in the Renaissance, Catholic Italy and the Catholic Low Countries should have been very entrepreneurial before Protestantism emerged; nor is it clear why, as distinct from Scotland, England, which did not embrace the Calvinistic doctrine, should also have been entrepreneurial, though it might be argued that the truly entrepreneurial part of England was to be the North, and the North was often non-conformist as well as Anglican.

While the specifically theological reasons which led Protestants to be entrepreneurial may not be entirely convincing, it does remain apparently true that there has been more entrepreneurship, on the average, in Protestant countries than in Catholic countries. Indeed, it has often been pointed out that the 'Revocation of the Edict of Nantes' by Louis XIV of France in 1685 led to a massive emigration of 'huguenots', the French (Calvinist) Protestants who could no longer practise their faith openly. This massive emigration does seem to have benefitted several countries (England, the United Provinces, some German states) and hence perhaps explains part of the entrepreneurial character of Southern England at least, while contributing to the relative lack of French economic progress for generations.

Unquestionably, episodes such as the emigration of the 'huguenots' seem precisely to confirm the difference between Protestant and Catholic 'political culture' and therefore to emphasise the cultural division of Western Europe. As with colonial modes of behaviour, but only even more so, the geographical aspect of that division is paramount. Ireland is exceptional in this respect: the Republic is the one Catholic country north of the 52nd parallel. As a matter of fact, those parts of Germany and the Netherlands which are Catholic are South of that parallel. Moreover, France remained Catholic, including in its Northern parts, these being somewhat to the South even of Belgium: during the religious wars of the second half of the sixteenth century, the kings of France, with different degrees of fervour, supported the Catholic cause. Meanwhile, what is now Belgium and the Southern part of what is now the Netherlands were under Spanish domination.

The division between Catholic and Protestant Western Europe is thus a North–South division. The fact that this should be the case has clearly to do, first and foremost, with the distance from Rome and the papacy: the counter-reform had simply less clout the further one moved North. Moreover, the decision to choose a religion was scarcely in the hands of the citizens but was entirely in the hands of the monarchical rulers, not just in Lutheran Germany (cujus regio, ejus religio), but also elsewhere. The only case which appears on the surface to be special is that of France, but it is not in reality: the decision to give the huguenots the right to practice their faith in an otherwise Catholic country was taken by the king who issued the 'Edict of Nantes', Henri IV, who had himself been a Protestant and had only converted to the Catholic faith to be able to receive the French crown – 'Paris is worth a mass'. It is therefore not surprising that the religious division should have a geographical and indeed a North–South character: but this state of affairs reinforced the North–South 'cleavage', which had emerged as a result of climatic considerations as well as of colonialism, at any rate in Italy.

The industrial revolution and its effect on the North–South divide

Weber's analysis of the 'Protestant ethic' was designed to link that ethic to the 'rise of capitalism': the German sociologist wrote over a hundred years after the industrial revolution had begun. If Protestantism was the cause of capitalism, by and large, and if Protestantism was essentially from the North of Europe, the same effect would seem to take place as a result of capitalism.

Admittedly, capitalism in the strict sense of the word had begun and had begun in areas which were not Protestant, specifically in Italy, at the time of the Renaissance. What is at stake is therefore not so much capitalism as such and in particular its financial version, but industrialisation which orig-inated and was at first primarily geographically circumscribed in the North. Thus the industrial revolution began in England in the eighteenth century and gradually progressed, by capillarity, so to speak, to areas close to England, such as Northern France, Belgium and the Netherlands, Germany, particularly in its Western part. It extended later further South, again by capillarity: but the process was slow and, as a matter of fact, it was not before the late nineteenth century and even the early twentieth century that it started to make a real impact on Italy, except to an extent in Northern Italy. In Spain, apart from Catalonia and the Basque country, and in Portugal, the effects of industrialisation remained marginal – as in the Third World subsequently – before the twentieth century.

The fact that the industrial revolution began in England, developed first in the Northwest of Europe and only slowly extended, and to an extent par-tially, to the South is, of course, well known. It is also well known that the social and political consequences of the industrial revolution were immense. Where the industrial revolution took profound roots, the structure of society was simply transformed: the agricultural labour force declined, although not as rapidly on the Continent, even in its Northern part, as in Britain; the urban proletariat grew and so did a new 'white collar' middle class. Where the industrial revolution took roots, living conditions also changed dramatically, with social services being set up and education being extended to the whole population. As a result, and for perhaps half a century at least, the South of Europe became, even more than as a result of a climate which was too 'favourable', of the hangover of colonialism where it had been marked and of the effect of Catholicism, more culturally distant from the North. Sample surveys of public opinion did not exist before First World War: had such surveys been possible then, it is difficult to believe that they would not have indicated a sharp cleavage between the citizens of the two areas. Although we cannot know with assurance that this was the case, there seems little doubt that there was no 'common political culture' among the citizens of Western Europe in the early years of the twentieth century. The differential development of industrialisation between North and South was too sharp and, by way of consequence, the differential development of 'new classes' was too marked: it could be expected that these 'new classes' would have had profoundly different sets of political attitudes from those which they replaced. Above all, perhaps, the marked differences in the way of life of citizens must have affected attitudes deeply in the North, while the South was remaining little affected, relatively speaking at least, as the changes which were taking place there remained limited.

The situation altered markedly in the course of the second half of the twentieth century: industrialisation progressed in the South and, there, too, perhaps even more importantly, the way of life began to resemble the way of life in the North: indeed, Britain seemed in many ways to be left behind, at any rate from the 1960s to the 1980s, in the process of socio-economic development which characterised the rest of Western Europe. Yet it would seem a priori surprising if a residual differential effect on political culture were not to be found among citizens in a region in which deep social changes occurred in the late nineteenth century in some countries and in the second half of the twentieth century in others.

The shaping of national political cultures, in particular through political socialisation and administrative centralisation

The factors analysed so far suggest that the political culture of the citizens of Western Europe was unlikely to have been uniform and that, on the contrary, the region might have been divided principally on a North–South basis. On the other hand, the cultural distance between the countries concerned may have been reduced in the last decades of the twentieth century. This might be, in the first place, as a result of the spread of industrialisation. Moreover, the effect of the Protestant–Catholic distinction may not be as large as it once was in view of the general decline in religious practice and in formal religious appartenance. The other two factors which were discussed earlier, the role of climate and the feelings of 'colonial' inferiority, may also have declined in importance in the areas concerned, with technical progress rendering citizens less affected by climate while time and economic progress was gradually wiping out the psychological effects of the feelings of socio-political 'refusal to be involved' stemming from a dependent past. On these grounds it seems at least possible, if not likely, that Western Europe might be moving since the end of the twentieth century towards a more uniform political culture than almost at any time in the past: its citizens had never previously participated in the feelings of 'Europeanness' which were shared at the time by at least part of the elites of the eighteenth century.

Yet, while the key North–South division in the political culture of Western Europeans may be on the decline, one further source of division may not, and that source may lead to distinctions which are more complex and more numerous than the factors analysed so far. That source is political socialisation both in general and by virtue of the effect it has had on citizens through administrative centralisation. Such developments are likely to lead to differences on a national, not on a sub-regional basis.

Socialisation, directly or through administrative centralisation, may well influence and to a substantial extent even shape the political culture of citizens since, as was pointed out in the introductory chapter, Western European states, being strong institutions, are able to have an effect on the daily life of citizens. There are some variations from country to country in this respect, admittedly: Italy and Greece, as well as perhaps Portugal, are limited exceptions, but only limited exceptions, to what is otherwise the rule. To say that the state is strong means that, by and large, the state is able to make a marked impact on a whole series of arrangements, although, in Germany, Spain and even more Belgium, this impact is reduced, not because the state is not strong in these countries, but because sub-units of that state administration have taken over from the state a number (but not all) of its powers.

These centralising characteristics take essentially the form of setting up *uniform* arrangements and *uniform* modes of behaviour for the administrative agencies and even for various aspects of political life. Thus health, welfare and social security provisions tend to be national; education is organised on a national basis. Thus such intensely political matters as electoral systems tend to be national; local government structure and activities are organised nationally. Progress may have occurred in the 'Europeanisation' process in the European Union, but, apart from the emergence of a common currency, there are no visible signs of that 'Europeanisation' in the ways in which the citizens are confronted with 'the authorities'.

It would be surprising, to say the least, were it to be the case that these national idiosyncrasies did not leave traces on the ways in which citizens relate to political and social life. Admittedly, the characteristic elements of administrative centralisation are more likely to affect specific practices than to touch on the social philosophies which are at the root of the political culture; but some of these practices have unquestionably an impact on the way in which, for instance, citizens view the role of the government, since what is regarded as the government may very well include administrative structures as well as political bodies. It has often been remarked that the development of the European Union is rendered difficult by the 'weight' of member-states which have had, in a number of cases, a long and prestigious existence. As Hofstede notes:

> The integration of national markets in the European Community increases the number of cross-national ventures among member countries. EC countries, from Denmark to Portugal, differ primarily on the diagonal, from small power distance, weak uncertainty avoidance to large power distance, strong uncertainty avoidance. But on this diagonal the differences among them are very considerable, and about as large as could be found anywhere in the world. Intra-EC cooperation is therefore rife with cultural problems; the EC can be considered the biggest laboratory of intercultural cooperation of today's world.
>
> (ibid., 1997, 145)

There is therefore a *prima facie* case for suggesting that Western European citizens are unlikely to share a truly common political culture, although differences may have come to be smaller at the beginning of the twenty-first century than they were earlier, a point which, unfortunately, seems, to say the least, most difficult to substantiate. What can be elucidated, however, is the extent to which there are cultural differences among Western European countries at the beginning of the twenty-first century and, at least within limits, how large these differences are and with respect to which aspects of political culture they are particularly salient. It is therefore to these differences which we now need to turn on the basis of the evidence provided by the dataset which has begun to be analysed in the previous chapter.

II

The 'shape' of the citizens' political culture(s) in Western Europe

An obvious advantage stemming from the use of the same *data set* to examine both differences between East and Southeast Asian countries and Western European countries and differences among Western European countries is the opportunity for comparisons which is provided as a result. There is a major theoretical problem, however, namely that the underlying structure of the analysis may also be diverse as one moves from the inter-regional analysis between East and West to an intra-regional analysis among the countries of the West. The distinction between East and West has been based, as was argued in Chapter 2, on the notion that it was essential to test whether the standpoints of the citizens of the two regions differed on the question of 'Asian values' based on communitarianism (together with somewhat similar values held with respect to human rights and with a number of attitudes, on a somewhat distinct 'register', to socio-economic questions). We found that the inter-regional distinction did occur to an extent, but only to an extent.

The literature relating to Western Europe does state that there are differences among Western Europeans and indeed that these differences are systematic; in particular, it seems that climate, perhaps religion, levels of industrialisation, especially earlier, as well as possibly some remnants of a colonial or semi-colonial past suggest that there might be in particular a North–South division within the cultural patterns prevailing in Western European countries. What the literature does not suggest, however, is whether the differences which are referred to conform to the distinction made earlier between 'communitarianism' and, so to speak, 'non-communitarianism' or, if one wishes, between a communitarian posture and an individualistic posture with respect to basic societal values.

To be able to claim that the distinction made earlier at the inter-regional level also applies at the intra-regional level, there must therefore be grounds for suggesting that the same distinction is likely to be valid at both these levels. These grounds could be that the distinction between 'communitarianism' and 'non-communitarianism' or between a communitarian posture and an individualistic posture with respect to basic societal values is so universal that it is in effect the only one which can exist in human societies. The overall history of the development of human societies does indeed seem to provide some support for that proposition, to be sure: there seems to be less individualism in societies which are not politically, socially and economically advanced; yet not only does such a standpoint assume the kind of linear 'progression' characterising modernisation theory and entailing the further point that Western societies are necessarily 'better' than other societies; but also, while there may be some justification for that proposition among societies at both extremes, namely when one contrasts truly primitive societies to contemporary societies, such a justification seems to evaporate when complex societies are being compared on the basis of a variety of factors, and in particular, alongside economic development, geography, religion or the incidence of forms of colonial rule.

There is yet another and more fruitful ground for adopting the proposition at the intra-regional level, however. What is at stake is not so much to discover whether, in the abstract and in a definitive manner, there is a profound contrast between, for instance, North and South in Western Europe; what is at stake is more realistically to determine whether the notion of 'individualism', which is so often said to characterise Western values, does indeed characterise to the same extent Northern and Southern Europe; to put it differently, it may well be that there is a large variety of cultural differences between sub-regions of Western Europe and in particular between North and South: but what is being sought here is merely whether these sub-regions differ in terms of the extent to which they are 'individualistic' in their approach to basic societal values. It is on the basis of that second and more limited type of hypothesis that intra-regional differences within Western Europe are being examined here.

As a matter of fact, to be precise, what is specifically being examined is whether there are differences in the sub-regions of Western Europe with respect to the extent that the citizens in these sub-regions hold 'pro-Asian values' positions, the notion being, as was pointed out in Chapter 2, that what was being examined here was the extent to which 'pro-Asian values' positions were being adopted, but on the basis of the assumption that, given that 'Asian values' are opposed to 'Western values', the 'communitarianism' which characterises Asian values is opposed to the 'individualism' which characterises the West and Western Europe in particular.

On this basis, it becomes also permissible to conduct the analysis of Western European political culture, as in the previous chapter, on the basis of a composite figure obtained by deducting the proportion of respondents disagreeing with each statement from the proportion of respondents agreeing with that statement, but on the understanding that, whenever appropriate, the signs, so to speak, will be changed, so that what emerges is the proportion of respondents who agree with 'pro-Asian values' positions as against the proportion of respondents who disagree with these positions. Conclusions drawn about the extent to which a 'common' or a 'divided' political culture exists in Western Europe and about the shape of the 'division' will thus be based on the manner in which the responses of interviewees are distributed on the scale between full agreement and full disagreement calculated in this manner to 'pro-' and 'anti-communitarian' positions, the responses to human rights and to socio-economic questions being treated in the same manner at the intra-regional level as they are at the inter-regional level.

As in the previous chapter when examining the extent to which responses varied between the two regions under analysis, the analysis is conducted here on the basis of the consideration of both the *spread* of these responses in each of the two 'sub-regions' and the extent of *overlap* between countries belonging to one of the 'sub-regions' with countries belonging to the other 'sub-region'. The extent to which the answers from the various countries are *spread* out on the scale indicates whether respondents from the countries of the region hold values which are close to each other or distant from each other. Thus the answers of the respondents from the countries of the North of Europe could all be closely grouped together while those of the respondents from the countries of the South could also be grouped together. If, on the other hand, the spread is large among the countries belonging to a particular 'sub-region', it is not permissible to claim that the countries belonging to that 'sub-region' are truly associated, at any rate with respect to the value under consideration. Each country in the 'sub-region' would have, with respect to that value, basic societal values of its own. Second, if there is substantial *overlap* between the responses from countries belonging to different 'sub-regions', for instance between countries belonging to Northern and countries belonging to Southern Europe, with respect to a particular value, it is not permissible to claim, with respect to that value, that the attitudes of the respondents truly divide into the 'sub-regions' under consideration.

So far, we discussed intra-regional differences within Western Europe as if these were based exclusively on a North–South distinction: the literature examined earlier in this chapter does indeed suggest that such a distinction is likely to be important. Yet it cannot be postulated that the North–South distinction is the only one which needs to be examined or, at least and perhaps more accurately, it is not certain that the North–South distinction may not have to an extent to be modified. This may occur, for instance, if the Catholic–Protestant divide is truly critical and therefore needs to be taken into account; but this divide is only in part geographical, as was indicated earlier, given in particular that the Republic of Ireland is both a Northern and a Catholic country. It seems *prima facie* sensible to begin by assessing the extent to which a North–South division does exist – that is to say, in effect, a division between Britain, Ireland, Germany and Sweden, on the one hand, and, on the other, Portugal, Spain, Italy and Greece, with France being expected to be an intermediate case, although, as much of the political, social and economic decision-making takes place in the capital, in the French case in particular, the country's culture is probably more 'Northern' than 'Southern' in character. Adjustments may well have to be made subsequently to see whether a different division might be more fruitful, on the understanding that the search is limited to an examination of the division between sub-regions with respect to 'communitarian' or 'pro-Asian values' positions and differing positions from this point of view.

Fragments, but only fragments of a common Western European political culture

The evidence from the answers given to the questionnaire strongly suggests that the Western Europeans do not have a truly common political culture with respect to basic societal values as they have been examined here. Out of the thirteen questions designed to tap attitudes to 'communitarian', human rights and socio-economic values, only in two cases is the spread of the answers really small (15 and 21 points respectively). In another three, it is significant (36 to 43 points). It is substantial in another seven (between 51 and 64 points) and very large in one case (127 points). Moreover, the two questions where the spread is smallest relate to views about freedom of expression and about competition, both of which are supported by very large majorities. It was pointed out in the previous chapter that these were among the questions about which there was least difference between Western European and East and Southeast Asian respondents. Thus the fact that there are very similar Western European attitudes on these two matters cannot be regarded as surprising: given that this study covers only Western European and East and Southeast Asian respondents, it cannot be concluded that the reactions to these two questions are nearly identical all over the world; but it can at least be concluded that the reactions to be found among the large majority of Western Europeans on these two matters are not characteristic of Western Europeans only (Figure 4.1).

Agree minus disagree

Right to express an opinion (208b)

-90 -70 -50 -30 -10 0 10 30 50 70 90

Liberalism

Organise protest meetings (208c)

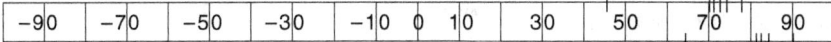

-90 -70 -50 -30 -10 0 10 30 50 70 90

Government usually knows best (306c) AV

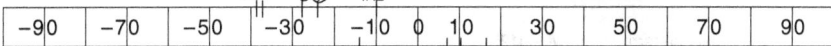

-90 -70 -50 -30 -10 0 10 30 50 70 90

Governmental restraint

We should do what government wants (306d)

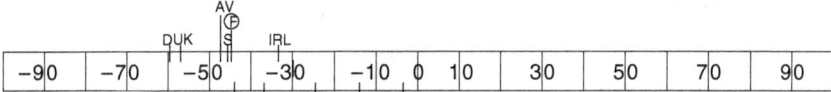

-90 -70 -50 -30 -10 0 10 30 50 70 90

Agree minus disagree

Consensus better than a lot of institutional initiative (412d)

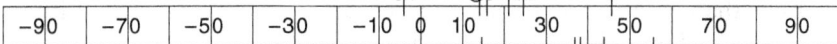

-90 -70 -50 -30 -10 0 10 30 50 70 90

Decision

Older people more influence (412e)

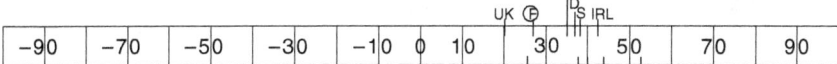

-90 -70 -50 -30 -10 0 10 30 50 70 90

Making

Public interest before family (412f)

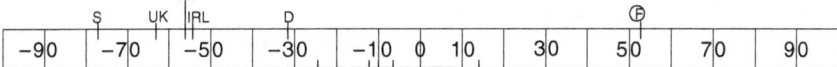

-90 -70 -50 -30 -10 0 10 30 50 70 90

Woman's place at home (412c)

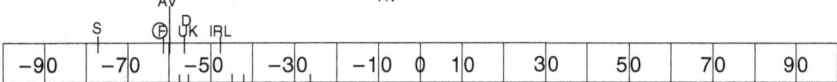

-90 -70 -50 -30 -10 0 10 30 50 70 90

Social relations

Individual for own good rather than society's (412g)

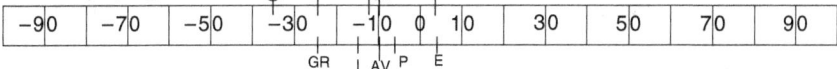

-90 -70 -50 -30 -10 0 10 30 50 70 90

Figure 4.1 Spread of answers to human rights, communitarian and socio-economic questions, divided between northern and southern Western Europe by country (*continued*).

Agree minus disagree

Socio economic standpoint
Competition good (306a)

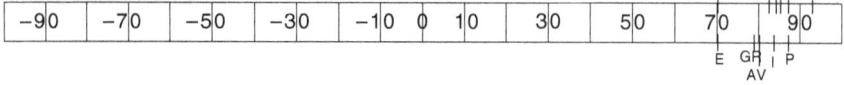

Government responsible for jobs (306b)

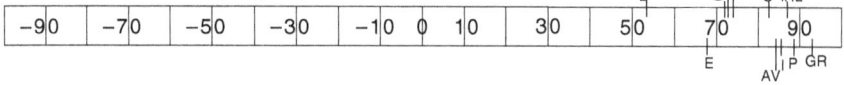

Society better if profits free (306g)

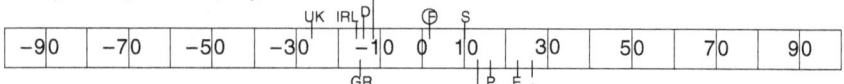

Goode environment preferred to growth (412b)

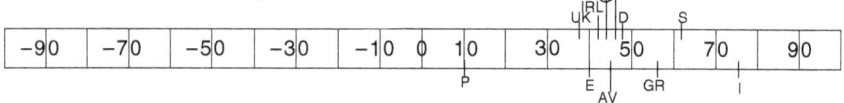

Figure 4.1 (Continued).

Broadly speaking, moreover, the spread of attitudes among Western Europeans is larger with respect to communitarian issues (60 points on average) than with respect to human rights and to socio-economic attitudes (on average 29 and 44 points respectively). This suggests that there is less controversy among Western Europeans on these last two types of standpoints than on 'communitarian' values. Yet the 'communitarian' values can be regarded as being concerned in a more fundamental way with the beliefs of individuals about their relationship to society: Western Europeans should therefore be closer to each other on these matters than on others if they were to hold a really common pattern of values.

Indeed, the detailed variations in attitudes with respect to 'communitarian' values among Western Europeans are a further indication of the extent to which the very existence of a common Western European culture is in question. To begin with, it is somewhat surprising, in the context of Western Europe at least, that one of the communitarian questions about which these variations are smallest should be the one concerned with the choice to be made between the individual and society (Q.412g): the spread is of 39 points, *and* a substantial majority is in favour of the proposition. On this question, the majority in favour of the 'pro-Asian values' position is 13 per cent; 39 per cent of the Western European respondents agree with the view that society should come first against 26 per cent who hold the opposite view. There are, on the other hand, appreciably larger variations in the attitudes of Western European respondents over the position which women should have in society. Large majorities do believe that the place of women is 'not in the home'; but there is a 51 point difference between the countries which are located at the two extremes of the range, Sweden and Spain.

More importantly perhaps, there are large variations from one Western European country to the other with respect to three questions. The gap is large, at 57 points, with respect to (1) whether 'it is more important to achieve consensus than to encourage a lot of individual initiative' (Q.412d), (2) whether 'government usually knows best' (Q.306e) and (3) whether 'we should always do what the government wants' (Q.306d). On the role of the government, for instance, the balance between those who agree with the view that one should follow the government and those who disagree is sharply negative (between 30 and 40 per cent) in some countries, while in others, it is positive, though not as strongly, at between 10 and 20 per cent. It cannot therefore justifiably be claimed that on that issue (or indeed on any of the others in that group) a 'common' viewpoint exists among Western European respondents.

Variations are therefore large in the average attitudes of respondents to the questions designed to assess basic societal values in the nine Western European countries which are studied here. These variations are substantial on many questions; they are large enough with respect to six of the communitarian questions for one to have to conclude that there is no common political culture across the region. What there are, are fragments of a common culture, with respect to human rights in particular, as, on that subject, there is identity of views or close to being identity of views. Views are also relatively similar on two of the socio-economic standpoints: on the questions which relate to the way in which power should be distributed in society, however, views of Western Europeans are typically not just different but truly distinct.

The North–South division constitutes an element but not an overwhelming one in accounting for variations among patterns of political culture in Western Europe

Yet, if there is no genuinely common Western European political culture, the existence of a sharp divide between a Northern and a Southern political culture is also in question. For the respondents' answers to suggest that such a divide is fundamental, the answers from the two relevant sets of countries would have both not to be spread out and not to overlap (or scarcely to overlap). The existence of a North–South divide depends therefore on there being sharp variations of attitudes between the respondents of Britain, Ireland, Germany and Sweden, on the one hand, and the respondents of Italy, Spain, Portugal and Greece, on the other. France has to be excluded from that comparison in the first instance, as that country might be expected to be an intermediate case given its geographical position: it can be reintroduced at the end of the analysis, if the distinction between the two groups is found to be valid, to see whether the country fits into one or the other of these groups, whether its respondents indeed hold intermediate positions or whether its attitudes are idiosyncratic.

When the relevant eight countries of the region are analysed into two separate groups, however, it emerges that the North–South distinction does not 'explain' the bulk of the variations. Only with respect to one question, that which asks whether 'the public interest should come before family obligations' (Q.412f) is there a marked division between Northern and Southern respondents. Yet, in this case, the answers are spread so widely that, while there may be little overlap, there is no clustering. The answers from the Northern countries range, all positively in terms of the 'pro-Asian values' position, from almost 80 points (Sweden) to a little under 30 points (Germany), while the answers from the Southern countries range from a little under 20 points (Italy) to nearly −20 points (Greece). France is even more negative at slightly over −50 points! It seems therefore unreasonable to claim that a 'Northern' point of view is pitted against a 'Southern' point of view on that issue.

Yet this is the only question for which there is no overlap at all between the answers from the 'Northern' and those from the 'Southern' countries. On three other questions, there is a 'limited' overlap, admittedly, an overlap which is due to Ireland in two cases, as if that country behaved more like a 'Southern' than a 'Northern' country. These two questions relate to the part which respondents are prepared to see the government play: in both cases, three of the four 'Northern' countries (and, as a matter of fact, France as well) have a more 'negative' attitude about what that role of the government should be than the four 'Southern' countries and Ireland. However, the distance separating the countries in each group and in particular in the 'Southern' group is such that there is no 'cluster'. Asked whether 'the government knows best how to run a country' (Q.306e), the Italians are negative by a margin of nearly 20 points, while the other three 'Southern' countries are positive by a margin of between 10 and 20 points: one cannot reasonably conclude that respondents from these countries have a common attitude on that subject. Asked whether 'we should always do what the government wants' (Q.306d), all four Southern countries are negative, but the Italians are almost evenly divided while the other three countries are negative by a margin of about 40 points: one cannot reasonably conclude in this case either that respondents from these four countries hold the same values. The third question on which there is only a limited overlap between Northern and Southern countries concerns businesses and profits (Q.306g): a majority of respondents from three of the four Northern countries (Sweden being the exception) and from Greece are against giving businesses complete freedom over profits, while the other three Southern countries are in favour of granting that freedom to businesses by large majorities.

Meanwhile, on the remaining nine questions, there is not so much an overlap as a genuine intermixing of 'Northern' and 'Southern' countries. This is so, of course, of the human rights question relating to the freedom of expression; but this is also true of the other human rights question, although the spread of responses from the 'Southern' countries is, there too, greater than that of those from the 'Northern' countries. This is true of the question relating to the influence which older people 'should' have in decision-making, where (again most surprisingly if one believes in the distinction between North and South in Europe) there is little average difference between these two groups although the South believes slightly more (at +41 points) in what that influence should be than the North (at +34.5 points), and Ireland tends to behave, here again, in the same way as the Southern countries at +42 points. This is true of the question asking whether 'a woman's primary role is in the home', where the views of respondents from Southern Europe are spread between under −20 points and almost −60 points (and where Ireland, once more, is the Northern country which is closest to the Southern countries by being the least negative). This is true, finally of the question relating to consensus and of the question asking whether 'individuals should strive for their own good' (Q.412g), where there is almost no way in the first of these cases and no way at all in the second to distinguish between the reactions of the Northern and the Southern countries. On three of the socio-economic questions, moreover, the overlap is also substantial. The ground on which to suggest that a North–South division exists is thus very thin indeed.

A Catholic–Protestant Europe distinction?

As we just saw, however, on four 'communitarian' questions, Irish respondents were found close to the respondents from the Southern countries: their answers were most 'like' those of the respondents of the Southern countries. Since Ireland is a Catholic country, it might therefore seem reasonable to hypothesise that, rather than a North–South divide, the 'truer' divide is that between Catholic country and Protestant (or, in the case of Germany and even Britain, mixed Protestant–Catholic) country. As a matter of fact, we noted in the previous section that Ireland was the only Catholic country which was geographically Northern.

Such an interpretation is truly satisfactory for the answers to one question only, however, that which asked whether 'the government knows best how to run a country' (Q.306d), where there is indeed a gap of over 30 points between the response given by Irish respondents and the response given by the Northern country closest to Ireland, in this case Sweden, and while the Italian response is much closer to that given by Sweden than to that given by Ireland. In the other three cases where Ireland is somewhat closer to the Southern average (on the influence of older people, on the role of women, and even on doing what the government wants, respectively,

Q.412e, Q.412c and Q.306e), the difference between the Irish responses and the responses from the other Northern countries is small; on the last of these questions, the difference between the Irish and the Swedish response is slightly over 10 points, but so is the distance between the Swedish response and that of Britain. It is not possible to draw any conclusion from the responses to the two human rights questions, partly because they are bunched very closely and partly because, as was noted earlier, there is no Northern or Southern pattern. Nor is it possible to draw any meaningful conclusion from the responses to the socio-economic questions: Ireland is in the middle of both the Northern and the Southern groups on two questions, while on a third (on competition, Q.306a) it is as distant from the Northern as from the Southern group. On the other hand, with respect to the last three 'communitarian' questions (on choosing the public interest rather than the family, on individuals striving for their own good and on consensus, respectively Q.412f, Q.412g and Q.412d), Ireland is no more Southern than the other Northern countries. While it is thus perhaps the case that a Catholic–Protestant divide fits the responses given to the questions relating to basic societal values a little better than a North–South divide, this is only to a very limited extent and in a context in which the North–South divide scarcely seems to matter at all.

Do some countries have an idiosyncratic reaction to basic societal attitudes? The cases of France and, indeed, of other countries

A further difficulty which arises if one substitutes a Catholic–Protestant division for the North–South divide comes from the case of France. It is true that France is somewhat peculiar among Catholic countries in that many of its citizens have had for generations strong anti-clerical sentiments, although these have ostensibly largely abated. Yet France does remain culturally Catholic, at least in the sense that it is not Protestant: but it is not possible to place France, even in a very limited manner, among the Southern or the Catholic countries. As a matter of fact, if it is to be placed at all, it must be with the Northern countries, since, with respect to five of the nine questions, French respondents are with the respondents of Northern countries and not with those of the South (indeed appreciably less so than Irish respondents).

Four questions remain, one of which is not relevant in this case: this is the human rights questions about the freedom of expression (Q.208b) about which, as we saw, responses are bunched very closely to each other. The remaining three questions lead to answers which are rather puzzling. This is so especially of the question as to whether the public interest should be preferred to the family (Q.412f), but also, to a lesser extent, of the question asking whether individuals should 'strive most for their own good' (Q.412g) and of the human rights question relating to the right to organise public meetings against the government (Q.208c). In all three cases the answers of French respondents are apparently idiosyncratic. Thus the decision not to include France in the division between Northern and Southern countries has to be made partly on geographical grounds since the country is intermediate between North and South; but it is made partly on these grounds only because three of the answers, and in particular two of these, cannot be classified as belonging either to North or South or to Catholic or Protestant countries.

One of these three answers, that which relates to the question whether individuals should 'strive most for their own good' (Q.412g), can indeed be considered as being simply a little more positive towards the 'pro-Asian values' position than the answers coming from the four Northern countries: but it is also more positive towards that position than the answers coming from the four Southern countries, since we noted that, on this question, there was no difference at all between North and South; this renders the position of French respondents on this question rather peculiar. Yet, in the other two cases, the pattern of French responses is even more peculiar. French respondents are the ones, as was noted earlier, who are most 'lukewarm' about allowing citizens to organise public meetings against the government – and 20 points separate French respondents from the respondents of the country nearest to them, Spain. French respondents are also the only ones who are strongly in favour of suggesting that public interest should come before family obligations: the difference is of almost 40 points between them and the respondents of the nearest country, in this case Greece.

It is rather presumptuous to hazard a general interpretation of these findings as they seem to be, ostensibly at least, particular. Indeed, other findings which have been examined so far are also particular. It is equally hazardous to classify them, whether on the basis of the notion of a common political culture or on the basis of the notion of a North–South division in Western European political culture, that division being in turn based either or both on the Protestant–Catholic cleavage and on the distinction between old and recent socio-economic development. For instance, one might be tempted to believe that Italy is the 'least Southern' of the Southern countries, given the level of industrialisation of that country since the 1950s (and before) and given the income per head which the country has achieved for its citizens. Italy is indeed closest, among the Southern countries, to the average position of respondents of the Northern countries with respect to three 'communitarian' questions ('preferring the public interest to that of the family', the role to be given to consensus, and 'whether the government knows best' – respectively, Q.412f, d and Q.306e). On the other hand, Italian respondents are more distant from Northern countries than the respondents of other Southern countries in answering the question as to whether one should do 'what the government wants' and the question as to whether businesses should be free to make profits. They hold a middle position among Southern countries on three 'communitarian' questions, those concerned with the role to be given to older people, with the part that women should play and as to whether individuals should 'strive for their own good rather than for the good of society'; they also hold a middle position on the question of social welfare. To this extent, therefore, Italian respondents can be viewed as 'idiosyncratic' as well; but there are also cases in which respondents in other countries could be regarded as 'idiosyncratic' in view of their reactions to specific matters.

* * * * *

In the previous chapter, we found that the East–West divide accounted for a part, but only a limited one, of the variations from state to state among the respondents of the eighteen countries of this study. We therefore naturally explored the possible impact of the strongly expressed distinctions which have been typically put forward to account for attitudinal differences among Western Europeans with respect to views about 'communitarianism', as well as human rights and some broad socio-economic standpoints. These distinctions, which have become 'classical', tend to link religious background and aspects of socio-economic developments to what is basically a geographical divide. Yet, in the Western European context, these distinctions account only, as do the distinctions between East and West, for a limited part of the variations which are registered from state to state in attitudes to 'basic societal values'. These variations from state to state emerge as substantial: they need therefore ostensibly to be closely examined.

Before doing so, however, we must first discover whether large sub-regional distinctions are found within East and Southeast Asia with respect to the attitudes of citizens to 'communitarian' values, as well as to human rights and to some socio-economic standpoints. We must discover in particular whether the sub-regional distinctions which are found in that region in this way account for a truly substantial proportion of the variations in attitudes among the respondents of the countries concerned. If this were to be the case, the contrast would indeed be sharp between the two regions, as, in one region, one would find no strong basis for a 'sub-regional' divide, while such a basis would exist in the other region. If, on the contrary and as in Western Europe, such a crucial 'sub-regional' division cannot be found in East and Southeast Asia either, there would then be no alternative but to examine closely the attitudes to basic societal values at the level of individual states. The first task is therefore at this point to examine whether, in East and Southeast Asia, a well-defined 'sub-regional' divide among groups of countries appears to categorise the attitudes of large numbers of respondents with respect to the 'communitarian' and other standpoints which have been examined so far: this is the object Chapter 5.

5 A common political culture in East and Southeast Asia?

As was pointed out in preceding chapters and especially in Chapter 2, a number of prominent politicians and academics from East and Southeast Asia propounded the notion that there were commonly-held 'Asian values' across the region (Koh, 1993; Kausikan, 1997; Goodman, White and Kwon, 1998; Kelly and Reid, 1998; Bell and Bauer, 1999; Mahbubani, 2002). Admittedly, in Chapter 3, we found little evidence to sustain the view, at the level of the citizenry at large, that the basic societal values of East and Southeast Asians were profoundly different from those of Western Europeans: this does not mean, however, that the citizens of East and Southeast Asia do not hold values in common. It may well be, even if the basic societal values held in the two regions are not as sharply distinct as is often believed, that the same values are broadly shared among East and Southeast Asians. Yet this view is challenged, as we also saw, by those scholars, both from Asia and from the West who claim that, far from being based on a single political culture, East and Southeast Asia has long been divided into a number of cultural areas. We need at this point to examine the matter more closely, as was done in the previous chapter with respect to Western Europe, and examine, first, whether there are indeed strong grounds for suggesting that a 'common' political culture prevails among the citizens of the nine countries analysed here, but also see, second, what profound distinctions indicate that there may not be one but on the contrary several 'sub-regional' cultural groupings among these countries.

Ostensibly at least, the study of political culture in East and Southeast Asia is hampered by the fact that, in contrast to Western Europe, surveys of attitudes of citizens across the region as a whole had not been conducted so far: the only country in which this type of investigation has taken place repeatedly is Japan, while in Korea, Taiwan and the Philippines there have occasionally been empirical studies of popular attitudes, in particular in the *World Values Surveys* and in Hofstede's work. Admittedly, as was pointed out in Chapter 4, the surveys undertaken in Western Europe have rarely if ever explored political culture in a fully comparative manner: the problem of the presence or absence of a 'common political culture' in that region had therefore not been systematically tackled. As a result, the gap between the extent of empirical knowledge about the political culture of Western European citizens and about the political culture of East and Southeast Asian citizens is not as wide as might have been expected.

However, in the case of East and Southeast Asia, and this time more so than in Western Europe, views about the extent to which a common political culture exists in the region have often been expressed forcefully, as could be seen by some of the statements quoted in Chapter 2. It is therefore essential to examine particularly closely whether there is indeed evidence suggesting that the political culture of the citizens of the nine countries of East and Southeast Asia analysed here is broadly similar. Only when that question has been explored and only if it then appears that the answer is negative will it become permissible to proceed to consider the ways in which and the extent to which political culture is divided in the region and whether one can even refer to 'sub-regional' cultural areas in East and Southeast Asia.

This chapter is thus concerned with the way in which the respondents from the nine East and Southeast Asian countries which were interviewed in this study distributed their answers to the questions put to them with respect to their basic societal values. To be undertaken satisfactorily, however, the examination of current attitudes among the broad mass of citizens must be related to the historical and socio-political context in which these attitudes have come to emerge, as was indeed done with respect to Western Europe in the previous chapter. The first section of this chapter looks therefore at the extent to which it seems permissible to refer to the presence of a common Asian or at least common East and Southeast Asian political culture. To the extent that differences appear to be such among the countries of the region that it seems more realistic to view the political culture as rather fragmented, the nature of and the grounds for such a fragmentation have to be considered. The second section of the chapter, as does the second section of the previous chapter on the Western European region, then assesses the extent to which the attitudes of the citizens of East and Southeast Asia with respect to communitarianism, human rights and socio-economic standpoints appear close to or distant from constituting a common political culture. If these attitudes are not clustered in such a way as to result in a common political culture, the evidence for possible 'sub-regional' cultural distinctions will be examined. The diverse conclusions drawn from the history of the societies as well as from statements made in particular by politicians about East and Southeast Asian political culture will thus be confronted with the views which, at any rate currently, citizens of the area hold about basic societal values.

I

*The debate about a common East and
Southeast Asian culture*

*The case for a common socio-political culture in
East and Southeast Asia*

Two major authors have spread the idea that there may be a common East
and Southeast Asian culture (Kelly and Reid, 1998). One is Montaigne,
who wrote in one of his writings that in Asia there is only one person
(presumably an autocrat) who is free. Following him was Hegel, who wrote
similarly on Asian freedom. From Hegel many Westerners came to believe,
somewhat unconsciously, that Asia had a common culture of no freedom
except for one person. This led to the idea of Oriental power entertained by
Wittfogel in *Oriental Despotism* (1980), who argued that the need for
hydro-agricultural work concentrated power into the hands of an autocrat.
These and other ideas focusing on the Asian concentration of power and
thus lack of freedom have been popular in the minds of many Westerners
including Karl Marx and Max Weber, two towering figures of modern
Western social science. In this respect, Karl Marx became famous for asserting that in Asia capitalism was hampered by this autocratic tradition and
that its development was much slower than in the West. Max Weber
also believed that a number of cultural-cum-legal-cum-institutional factors
prevented Asia from producing a more rational mind not so different from
his spirit of capitalism derived from the ethic of Protestantism.

It is thus a small surprise to some that these major figures of the West
entertained these and other beliefs about a common Asian culture without
there being much empirical investigation on the subject even into the nineteenth and twentieth centuries and that the idea has deeply influenced the
thinking of social science even today. Only with a path-breaking work by
Lucian W. Pye, *Asian Power and Politics* (1985), was that tradition broken,
as he most convincingly argued that there is no common Asian culture and
that there are many political cultures in Asia that await a full and serious
empirical examination. Pye himself presented an expertly drawn picture of
many political cultures of Asia, East, Southeast and South, largely based on
his own interviews with political elites and academic specialists of East,
Southeast and South Asia as well as wide-ranging works on various aspects
of political cultures of Asia. Two points need to be made in relation to Pye's
path-breaking work, however. First, despite a major emphasis placed on the
importance of examining political cultures of each and every major kind in
Asia, Pye comes up, after a detailed analysis, with the general picture that
there may be a common emphasis on authority and a need to restrain freedom in the light of the community one belongs to. Second, Pye's work is not

based on a systematic empirical survey of political cultures: it follows the tradition of Westerners such as Ruth Benedict, who conducted an outstanding study on the minds of Japanese in wartime during the Second World War (1946). Before and after Pye, a few empirical works focused on individual countries. They include those of Benedict Anderson (1991), Richard Solomon (1971), Bradley Richardson (1974), Samuel Popkin (1979), James Scott (1976) and Mary White (1987), to name but a few; but most of these works are not systematic from a comparative standpoint, despite the fact that they are empirical and penetrating.

As was pointed out in Chapter 1, the idea that there should be common values in Asia, and in particular in East and Southeast Asia, was taken up very strongly by a number of politicians, perhaps the most prominent of whom was Lee Kuan Yew, the Singaporean leader and indeed founder of the country. Lee Kuan Yew's views were systematised in his work, published in 2000, *From Third World to First: The Singapore Story 1965–2000*. He pre-empted the ideological vacuum of the immediate post-Cold War period by putting forward the argument about 'Asian values', boldly stating that, with American-style democracy being introduced, chaos would ensue in Asia. If one looks at two kinds of statistics, one on the frequency of executions in Singapore and the other on the number of prisoners in the United States, one might well be persuaded by Lee Kuan Yew. The Singapore figure of capital punishment was 200 in 2003, as reported by the NGO focusing on freedom and human rights, *Amnesty International*, while the American figure of prisoners is 1.2 million. Lee Kuan Yew argues that unless freedom is restrained to an extent to maintain order and stability in a community, neither freedom nor democracy can be established. To maintain order and stability strong punishments must be consistently applied to disturbers and violators of law and order. The figure of 200 capital punishments per year in Singapore may be large: yet it fits with the profile Lee Kuan Yew envisages for Singapore and in general for Asia. Two further points can be made in relation to Asia. First, whereas capital punishment is unconstitutional in many countries of the world, only two countries in Asia uphold a constitution which makes capital punishment unconstitutional, that is Cambodia and East Timor, two countries recently born of the United Nations' supervision of their free elections and democratisation. Second, crime-rate figures in Asia are the lowest of all the regions of the world. Whether the pervasive practice of capital punishment and the low regional crime rate might be related or not is not a question which can be pursued in this volume. The point here is simply to state that for Lee Kuan Yew the picture portrayed here does not conflict with his 'Asian values' argument. The American figure of prisoners, 1.2 million, fits nicely with his image. Indeed, American-style freedom requires the holding up of as many as 1.2 million in prisons, he would argue.

At the core of that 'Asian values' argument lies, as we saw, the tradition of the 'communitarian' spirit. The argument is related to two elements, one leading to order and stability and the other to prosperity. The notion is that, if 'communitarianism' is maintained, crime is reduced and stability ensues. Self-restraint would result in reduced crime rates and more order and stability. Meanwhile, unless order and stability are maintained, costs and risks associated with business transactions are bound to go up, and the economy ceases to develop rapidly and it may even decline. Thus, by fostering order and stability as well as by bringing about business and prosperity, the 'Asian values' argument, according to its proponents, is the polar opposite of the kind of libertarianism put forward for instance by Nozick (1977). To constrain freedom to an extent for the collective good does indeed benefit the population as a whole. To regulate conduct to an extent for the good of the whole population would be beneficial to all.

Can the view that there is a common East and Southeast Asian socio-political culture be sustained?

The arguments presented by Lee Kuan Yew have had considerable influence. Their weakness is not necessarily born out by findings of a systematic empirical comparative dataset, admittedly, but they need to be considered in the light of such findings. Comparative survey datasets are now beginning to emerge, in particular those of Inglehart (1997) and of Hofstede (1980) which were examined in some detail in Chapter 1, although, as was pointed out in that chapter, neither of these authors undertook a comparative analysis of a substantial number of Asian states, even if Hofstede's coverage is somewhat more extensive and touches on Southeast Asia as well as East Asia. Significant differences emerge among the countries concerned, some of these differences being stressed by Milner, whose work was referred to in Chapter 2 and who points out that there is a 'range of perspectives operating within the Asian region' (Milner, October 2000b, 14). The case of the Philippines is unquestionably special, even if, when he was President, Estrada stressed the Asian character of his country (ibid., 15–16). A systematic analysis of modes of behaviour of Thai and Indonesian businessmen did show that they displayed substantial differences from the modes of behaviour of their Chinese or Malaysian counterparts (Milner and Quilty, 1997). At a minimum, these findings strongly indicate that a study of variations in cultural patterns within East and Southeast Asia needs to be undertaken, both at the level of the intellectual discourse and at the level of empirical findings among the citizens.

Indeed, as in the case of Western Europe, there are seemingly strong geographical and historical grounds for suggesting that major differences are likely to exist among the countries of the region. Indeed, the widely held view that, following Japan, the countries of East and Southeast Asia would follow the same development path (the 'flying geese' image) more than suggested that there were profound differences between the countries of the region. Moreover, that image also suggested, indirectly at least, that these differences might well lead to 'sub-regional' groupings.

These sub-regional groupings could be considered on the basis of six characteristics. First, climate could be expected to play a part in cultural distinctions among the countries of the area: if the distinction had some validity in Western Europe, it is difficult to see why it would not have also some validity in East and Southeast Asia as well, indeed more validity even, given the fact that the region ranges across more latitudes than does Western Europe. Second, the possible impact on political culture of the island character of several of the countries needs to be examined, given that it is often claimed that the political culture of island states is somewhat peculiar. Third, some of the countries were colonies, while others were not, and they were colonies of different countries as well as for varying amounts of time: such developments cannot be regarded as having had no effect on social and political culture. Fourth, as in Western Europe but only more so, the area is strongly divided in terms of the prevailing religions, from a variety of Buddhist traditions in some countries to Muslim or Christian dominance in others, these religious differences being to a substantial extent associated to ethnic differences. Fifth, again as in Western Europe, the extent to which the region has industrialised and become economically developed does vary truly extensively, indeed again more so than in the case of Western Europe. Finally, sixth, the question of the normative base of the political system of the countries of the region does arise, since liberalism and democracy have come gradually but also, in a number of cases, still only partially. Overall, while these factors may combine in a different way among the countries of the region, it appears none the less to be believed by some that, as in Western Europe, the main cultural division is between North and South, that is to say between East Asia in the narrow sense and Southeast Asia. Perhaps it is not by accident that the countries of Southeast Asia formed a political organisation first among themselves (ASEAN) and only subsequently associated to it three countries of East Asia, indeed to an extent partially. It seems therefore important to assess whether these six grounds for distinctiveness among the countries of the region can be regarded as combining to lead either to no division at all or to a dichotomous division between North and South.

Does climate play a part in forging the socio-political culture in East and Southeast Asia?

The arguments given in Western Europe with respect to the possible effect of climate would appear to be applicable to East and Southeast Asia, the general notion being that citizens from cold climates are likely to be more active than those from warmer climates. The question of the possible validity of this argument does not need to be rehearsed. Two points only need to be made here. One is that such an argument can be regarded as providing a natural, geographical basis for the division of the region into two sub-regions. The second is that China obviously straddles between North and

South, but that, as in the case of France in Western Europe, most public decision-making in that country has always tended to take place in the North (in part as a result of invasions): hence the feeling that it might be justified to label China a 'Northern' rather than a 'Southern' country or at least as occupying an intermediate position.

Two types of island countries

Another geographical distinction can be made in East and Southeast Asia: this concerns the fact that five of the countries analysed here are islands (Japan, Taiwan, the Philippines, Singapore and Indonesia, while a sixth, Malaysia, has a partial island alongside a peninsular character). China, on the contrary, is a huge land mass, while South Korea and Thailand are continental but have also a peninsular character. It is widely believed that islands have a more idiosyncratic type of socio-political culture, as they are likely to be less influenced by neighbouring countries than nations which are separated from their neighbours by a land border only.

Yet these five island countries of East and Southeast Asia are of two quite distinct types. The states of Taiwan and Singapore are constituted, by and large, of one island and only one; the geographical configuration of the Japanese archipelago is not very different, in that the country is composed of four main islands which are close to each other and among which communications are easy and unproblematic. Despite its size, Japan is 'compact', almost as compact as Korea and Taiwan. On the other hand, the other two island countries, the Philippines and Indonesia, are not just archipelagos: they constitute constellations of a multitude of islands, many, if not most, of which are very distant from each other. As a result, one would expect both these countries to be culturally less united with consequences for the political and administrative structure. As a matter of fact, it is most probable that colonisation from the West, however differently organised and different culturally they may have been, played an important part in both cases in bringing these geographical 'constellations' into single political entities.

The large impact of colonisation

Thus geography is not the only factor which resulted in shaping the socio-political characteristics of island states: these states were also affected by the impact of other countries. Much more than in Western Europe, colonisation has clearly been a major element in the way a majority of states of the region developed. China, Japan and Thailand were the only countries analysed here never to have been colonies; the other six were dependent on Japan in two cases, Korea and Taiwan, in another two on Britain, Malaysia and Singapore, and in one each on the Netherlands (Indonesia) and Spain, first and for several centuries, only to be followed by the United States as a result of the Cuban War (the Philippines). Thus East Asia remained outside direct Western European control, even if there were manifestations of Western influence, in particular in Japan and in China; admittedly, there was for a while Western colonisation in Taiwan as well when, as Formosa, it was ruled by Portugal. However, Japanese occupation of both Taiwan and Korea respectively from 1895 and 1908 to 1945 had the effect, by partly insulating these two countries from the West, of ensuring that the path of their development would follow a 'Japanese' rather than a Western model.

The South of the region was on the contrary under direct Western control, except for Thailand (then Siam) which, being squeezed between Malaya and Burma, under British rule, and Indochina, under French rule, succeeded in remaining politically independent but was under considerable pressure from both sides: hence the rather close links between Thailand and Japan which have been indeed maintained throughout the second half of the twentieth century. Colonial rule did on the contrary extend to what was then Malaya, to Singapore, to Indonesia and to the Philippines. Having been colonies of Western countries, these countries were as a result dependent on and obliged to follow in part Western characteristics, to the extent, for instance, that, unlike the countries of East Asia, they abandoned the local script in favour of the Latin alphabet (while independent Thailand did not). Moreover, the forms of government adopted by these countries after they gained independence in the 1940s and 1950s followed to an extent the model of the 'mother country': thus the parliamentary system was introduced in Malaysia, Singapore and Indonesia (in the last case, for a few years only), while the presidential system was adopted in the Philippines, partly under American influence, but, interestingly, in parallel to what the other ex-Spanish colonies of South America had done early in the nineteenth century. There is thus a degree of 'Westernisation' of these countries although reactions to Western influence have also been forceful or at least ambivalent, indeed more so than in East Asia: Mahathir Mohammad of Malaysia and Lee Kuan Yew of Singapore have been those leaders of the region who stressed most forcefully the distinctiveness and indeed superiority of 'Asian values' while East Asian leaders did not. This has occurred although the links and exchanges between Britain and Malaysia or Singapore and even between Indonesia and the Netherlands have continued to be strong.

Religious and ethnic differences

As has been repeatedly pointed out in the course of the previous chapters, Confucianism is typically regarded as being at the origin of the 'Asian values' syndrome, although it is essentially Chinese and East Asian only. Confucianism is not a religion, however, but it has had an often difficult, though also close relationship to Buddhism. In parallel, Buddhism, having originated in India, came to prevail in Burma and Thailand but mostly further North, especially in China and, consequently, in Taiwan as well as, but in a different form, in Korea and Japan. Meanwhile, in the bulk of Southeast Asia, the spread of Buddhism has depended on the presence of significant Chinese communities, in particular in Malaysia and Singapore. Southeast Asia is dominated by Muslims in Malaysia and Indonesia, and Christian, indeed Catholic, (as well as Muslim) in the Philippines. Thus, in terms of the nature of the religions which do prevail, East Asia is more specifically the home of truly Asian religions, while, in much of Southeast Asia, the predominant religions come from further West. These religious differences are associated to a substantial extent to ethnic differences, especially in Southeast Asia, where the division between the ethnically Chinese and the ethnically Malay population is large and has been to a substantial extent at the root of political divisions. Moreover, while most Philippinos are Catholic, they are ethnically and linguistically close to Indonesians and are part of what might be described broadly as a 'Malay' group.

The presence of a number of distinct religions in the area does not appear to have had the same divisive consequence in East and Southeast Asia, however, as did the opposition among the Christian churches in Western Europe. This may have been the result of the nature of Buddhism, as is shown for instance by the fact that in Japan, Shintoism and Buddhism appear rather mixed.

> The division of spiritual labour [in Japan] tells us something not only about the fluid character of religious identities but about one of the primary functions of Buddhism in contemporary society. If Buddhism often seems marginal to public life, it remains central to private life through its role in the care and commemoration of the family dead.
>
> (Buswell, 2004, Vol. 1, 384–5)

The influence of Buddhism may have had the effect of ensuring that religion has been widely regarded as being indeed a more private affair in East and Southeast Asia than in Europe. It is remarkable that the presence of a substantial minority of Christians in Korea did not lead to socio-political divisions in that country, in contrast to what has occurred in many parts of Europe. As a matter of fact, religious violence has tended to flare outside the predominantly Buddhist area, to an extent on ethnic rather than on religious grounds in Malaysia in the 1970s and, more recently, where Muslims and Catholics have been confronting each other, to a limited extent in Indonesia and on a major scale in the South of the Philippines.

Industrialisation and socio-economic development

If the division between North and South does not lead to truly clear-cut distinctions with respect to the prevailing religions, the process of industrialisation and of socio-economic development seems to have done so. As in

Western Europe, but perhaps even more markedly, this process began in the North, both in Japan and on the continent, and extended, but appreciably later, to the South. It is indeed to account for the way industrial development and what is conventionally described as economic modernisation occurred that the image of the 'flying geese' has been drawn.

Japan remains by far the most industrialised and the most economically developed of all the countries of the region: the model of the 'flying geese' does indeed reflect the fact that we are confronted here with a hierarchy and not with a dichotomy, Korea and Taiwan in East Asia, but also Singapore in Southeast Asia, having developed markedly more and somewhat earlier than the bulk of Southeast Asia as well as, for a long time, China. Perhaps above all and in contrast to Western Europe, the Southeast Asian states and to a large extent China can be described as being still 'dependent' economies: to develop, they have had to rely on capital and know-how from abroad, in particular from Japan, partly from Taiwan and Korea, as well as from outside the region. This is why, at least to an extent, one can now distinguish between Japan, Korea and Taiwan, together with Singapore, on the one hand, and the bulk of Southeast Asia as well as, in this case, China, though the massive economic progress of China in the last years of the twentieth century and the first years of the twenty-first renders somewhat uncertain the location of that country in what might be described as the second category.

The spread of liberal democracy in the region

Although this is not normally done, the image of the 'flying geese' should also be regarded as applying to the spread from North to South of pluralistic political values, given the extent to which liberal democracy is gradually playing a greater part in the life of the countries of the region. Here too, Japan is unique in the area in having had constitutional government before the end of the nineteenth century and having been fully liberal-democratic immediately after Second World War. Admittedly, also soon after Second World War, two of the newly independent countries of Southeast Asia, Indonesia and the Philippines, did become liberal democracies, but this was only for a few years in the case of Indonesia, while, in the case of the Philippines, behind the façade of a presidential system which appeared to be functioning regularly, at least up to 1973, the system was profoundly oligarchical – as in many parts of Latin America in the nineteenth century and beyond – and not truly democratic. Thus only from the 1980s did liberal democracy come to emerge strongly in four countries of the region outside Japan, Korea, Taiwan, Thailand and the Philippines; the fall of Suharto then resulted in Indonesia joining that group in the late 1990s with the first truly open presidential election having taken place in the country in 2004 only. On the other hand, liberal democracy is far from having been by then fully implemented in Malaysia and Singapore, as severe restrictive arrangements continued to operate in both countries, especially in connection with electoral processes, while China's move towards a pluralistic polity remains, to say the least, rather limited.

The notion of extending the idea of the 'flying geese' to the political domain seems therefore to correspond closely to what occurred in the region during the last decades of the twentieth century. Yet, while such an extension makes it likely that the socio-political culture of the region will be affected, the extent and speed of the effect on the citizens' socio-political culture remains unknown. Although a similar conclusion is valid with respect to the impact of industrialisation on the socio-political culture, there is a double complication in the context of the possible link between the introduction of liberal-democratic institutions and the nature of the socio-political culture. First, the direction of the influence, if such influence exists, is not clear: that influence is probably reciprocal, as it could be that the introduction of liberal-democratic political institutions precedes the emergence of strong support among citizens for such institutions, with the result that there might be dissonance between the two elements. Second, the introduction of liberal-democratic institutions typically takes place at a particular moment, perhaps rather suddenly even, with the result that support for these institutions may not have had time to be strong. This contrasts with any attitudinal changes which may occur as a result of economic development, since economic development, even if it is rapid, always takes place over a substantial period.

The six factors described here have a different character. Two of them are the product of underlying geographical characteristics, although the boundaries of island states are 'man-made', so to speak, as they may well have been different and these islands could have been incorporated in a larger continental polity. Two of the factors, colonisation and religious affiliation, are part of a historical legacy, on the other hand, and that legacy is distinct from the current nature of political life in these countries. The last two, economic change and political change, on the contrary, are not just the product of recent developments in the case of most polities: the role which these factors can be expected to have in influencing citizens' attitudes does not result so much from the past as from what is occurring at present.

Overall, given the complexity of these factors and, therefore, given that these will tend to affect citizens in markedly different ways, the basis on which to claim justifiably that the countries of East and Southeast Asia are likely to have a common political culture appears rather thin. Yet what the nature may be of any broad cultural distinctions within the region is not immediately apparent either. The case for a North–South division is strong in some respects, but there always seems to be at least a country from one of the two potential 'sub-regions' which is more closely associated with the countries of the other 'sub-region'. Only detailed examination of the reactions of citizens can provide the evidence required to conclude how far socio-political culture is divided in East and Southeast Asia and if so in what ways.

The 'shape' of the citizens' socio-political culture(s) in East and Southeast Asia

Unlike with respect to the examination of intra-regional attitudes to basic societal values among Western European countries, there is no need, with respect to East and Southeast Asian countries, to discuss whether one should or not base the analysis on the responses to the same questions as the ones asked of respondents in order to determine the extent to which attitudes differed between the two regions. The inter-regional analysis has been based on the notion that it was essential to test whether the standpoints of the citizens of the two regions differed on the question of 'Asian values' based on communitarianism (together with somewhat similar values held with respect to human rights and with a number of attitudes, on a somewhat distinct 'register', to socio-economic questions): to analyse how far respondents from within East and Southeast Asia differ among each other on the extent to which they adopt communitarian values seems therefore not only permissible but logical. What is attempted by the intra-regional analysis within East and Southeast Asia is merely to see how far and to what extent positions on 'Asian values' are shared across the countries of the region.

Analysing the attitudes of respondents to basic societal values

The analysis of political culture in East and Southeast Asia must naturally be undertaken in this chapter on the same basis and with the same method as the one adopted in Chapter 3 to assess whether the political culture of East and Southeast Asians differs profoundly from that of Western Europeans and in the previous chapter to assess whether there is a common political culture among Western Europeans. We saw in these two chapters that it was only partially possible to distinguish between the values of East and Southeast Asians and those of Western Europeans and that it was only partially possible to distinguish between the values of Western Europeans on the basis of 'sub-regional' distinctions. We might therefore not be altogether surprised to discover that there is also a lack of clarity and even to an extent confusion as one attempts to characterise the 'shape', so to speak, which emerges from the examination of the values held by the citizens of the various countries of East and Southeast Asia.

The study is also conducted here on the basis of the composite figure obtained by deducting the proportion of respondents disagreeing with 'pro-Asian values' statements presented to them from the proportion of respondents agreeing with these statements. Conclusions drawn about the extent to which a 'common' or a 'divided' political culture exists in East and Southeast Asia and about the shape of the 'division' are thus based on the manner in which the responses of interviewees are distributed on the scale between full agreement and full disagreement. To examine the extent to which responses varied between the two regions under analysis here and within the Western European region, we needed to look at both the *spread* of these responses across the region and the extent to which, if the countries are to be grouped into 'sub-regions', the responses from the countries belonging to one of the 'sub-regions' did *overlap* with responses in countries in another. The same points apply when examining the distribution of the answers in East and Southeast Asia. The extent to which the answers from the various countries are *spread* out on the scale indicates whether respondents from the countries of the region hold values which are close to each other or distant from each other. For instance, the answers of the respondents from the countries of what might be described as an East Asian 'sub-region' could all be closely grouped together while those of the respondents from the countries of a Southeast Asian 'sub-region' could also be closely grouped together. If, on the other hand, the spread is large among the countries belonging to a particular 'sub-region', it is not permissible to claim that the countries belonging to that 'sub-region' are truly associated, at any rate with respect to the question under consideration. Each country in the sub-region would then have, with respect to that question, basic societal values of its own. Second, if there is substantial *overlap* between the responses from countries belonging to different sub-regions, for instance between countries belonging to one 'sub-region' and countries belonging to another, with respect to a particular question, it is not permissible to claim, with respect to that question, that the attitudes of the respondents truly divide into the sub-regions under consideration.

The extent to which one can or cannot refer to a common political culture in East and Southeast Asia emerges from the examination of the position of the various countries with respect to all thirteen questions which have been examined throughout this volume. If the overall spread among the nine countries of the region is small but the overlap is extensive, there is indeed a common political culture, as one cannot discover more than traces of 'sub-regional cultures'. If the spread is somewhat larger, there can still be a common East and Southeast Asian political culture, but that culture appears to be undermined to an extent by sub-cultures. This is particularly so if, in such a case, there is no or very little overlap among the countries of the 'sub-regions' which have been defined. If the spread is larger, one is confronted, not just with sub-cultures, but with truly different cultures. If the extent of overlap is very small, the countries belonging to each culture form a genuine group; if, on the other hand, there is overlap, the region is composed of sets of diverse national cultures.

Very limited traces of a common political culture in East and Southeast Asia

The evidence from the answers given by respondents suggests that the citizens of East and Southeast Asia do not have a truly common political culture. Among the thirteen questions designed to tap attitudes to the human rights, communitarian and socio-economic values which are analysed here, out of a maximum possible spread of the answers of 200 points, only in two cases is that spread really small (14 and 15 points, respectively) and in another case relatively small (27 points). The spread is significant in a fourth case (41 points) and becomes substantial in another three (between 57 and 64 points). It is large in three cases (between 77 and 84 points) and indeed very large in the last three cases (between 106 and 112 points). On the basis of such findings, it is clearly not permissible to conclude that there is unity in the attitudes of East and Southeast Asian respondents with respect to the thirteen basic societal values examined here. As a matter of fact, the spread is appreciably larger in the East and Southeast Asian region than it is in the Western European region (66 points as against 50 points on average).

Moreover, the two questions where the spread is smallest are rather peculiar in character. They relate to views about freedom of expression (Q.208b) and about the responsibility of governments for jobs (Q.306b), both of these questions being supported by very large majorities across the board not just in East and Southeast Asia but in Western Europe as well, with the single exception of Germany with respect to the responsibility of governments for jobs (Q.306b). It was pointed out in Chapter 3 that these two questions were among those about which there was least difference between Western European and East and Southeast Asian respondents: thus the fact that there are very similar attitudes among East and Southeast Asian respondents on these two issues cannot be regarded as surprising. Admittedly, given that this study covers only Western European and East and Southeast Asian respondents, it cannot be concluded that the reactions to these two questions would be nearly identical all over the world; but it can at least be noted that the reactions to be found among the large majority of East and Southeast Asians on these two matters are not characteristic of East and Southeast Asians only.

It was found in the previous chapter that the spread of attitudes among Western Europeans was larger with respect to communitarian issues than with respect to human rights and to socio-economic attitudes: the same is true in East and Southeast Asia, where the spread with respect to communitarian issues is 87 points on average while being 50 and 37 points with respect to human rights and to socio-economic questions respectively. This suggests that, as in Western Europe, there is less controversy in East and Southeast Asia on these last two types of standpoints than on communitarian questions. Yet communitarian values can be regarded as being concerned in a fundamental way with the beliefs of individuals about their relationship to society: if there was a truly commonly held socio-political culture in the region, one might have expected that answers would be closer to each other on communitarian matters than on others. As this is not the case, the notion that, in East and Southeast Asia, respondents hold a really common pattern of values is further undermined, for the same reasons as it was found, in the previous chapter, to be undermined in Western Europe.

Indeed, the detailed variations in attitudes with respect to communitarian values among East and Southeast Asian respondents are a further indication of the extent to which the very existence of a common East and Southeast Asian political culture is in question. The spread of the difference between positive and negative replies is never below 57 points out of 200 and it is among communitarian questions that the spread can be over 100 points, that is to say that, at one extreme, the difference may be 50 per cent in favour and, at the other extreme, 50 per cent against the policy suggested. The three questions which fall in this category are whether one should always do what the government wants (Q.306d), what the role of women should be (Q.412c) and whether one should prefer the family to society (Q.412f). It is surely not permissible to conclude that the citizens of East and Southeast Asian countries have a common political culture on the basis of such a record.

Admittedly, in the case of five of these seven communitarian questions, the spread is rendered wider because of the reactions of Japanese respondents. Given that Japan was the first country of the area to industrialise and to adopt modes of political and economic behaviour resembling closely those of Western European countries, it might be felt that the attitudes of Japanese respondents would differ markedly from those of other East and Southeast Asian countries. There is indeed some difference, but it is not sufficient enough to account for the absence of a common culture across the region: while the average spread among all nine countries is 87 points, it is still 69 points if Japan is excluded, substantially above the 60-point spread among Western European countries and surely large in its own right. As a matter of fact, Japanese respondents are not those who hold a position at the end of the range on either of the human rights questions; they hold such a position on two of the four socio-economic questions, especially on competition – they are more likely to be against competition – and to a more limited extent on the role of the government about jobs: the spread among the other eight countries of the region on socio-economic questions is 29 points as against 37 when Japan is not included – not a vast difference. Thus, even if we were to consider Japan to be a 'special' case, a point to which we shall return, the spread of the reactions of respondents in the region, whether Japan is or is not included, is not small enough, except on three questions on which agreement is in any case widespread in the two regions, to suggest that there is a common political culture. What there are, are not even 'fragments' of a common culture, as in Western Europe, but only 'traces' of such a culture with respect to some of the socio-economic questions and with respect to freedom of speech.

Does the evidence from the nine countries of the region suggest that they belong to two clearly defined cultural groups?

Given that the respondents of the nine countries of East and Southeast Asia analysed here do not hold the same basic societal values in roughly the same proportions and given that, as a result, one has to conclude that there is no common political culture in the region, one must begin to look for evidence in the survey suggesting that there might be recognisable patterns of sub-regional cultures. The geographical, historical, socio-economic and political background summarised in the previous section provides a basis for hypotheses as to what the distribution of citizens' attitudes might be with respect to the attitudes of citizens to these basic societal values. To be par-simonious, however, one can begin by examining how far the region may justifiably be divided into two broad cultural groups defined on geograph-ical lines and thus corresponding to East Asia and to Southeast Asia, albeit by making some 'adjustments' essentially designed to add Singapore and China to the East Asia 'sub-region', while leaving Malaysia and Thailand, correctly geographically, but less so on cultural grounds, in the Southeast Asia sub-region. The two sub-regions might therefore be described more correctly as being 'mostly' Buddhist and Chinese, on the one hand, and, on the other, 'mostly' Malay. For the respondents' answers to suggest that such a divide is fundamental, the answers from the two relevant sets of countries would have both not to be spread out and not to overlap (or scarcely to overlap). The existence of a 'mostly Chinese-mostly Malay' divide depends therefore on there being a sharp contrast in the attitudes of respondents of Japan, Korea, China, Taiwan and Singapore, on the one hand, and the respondents of Malaysia, Indonesia, Thailand and the Philippines, on the other.

Such a sharp contrast does not exist, however. Quite the contrary, when the nine countries of the region are divided in this way, only with respect to one question, that which relates to the role of consensus (Q.412d), is there no overlap at all between the respondents from these two groups. The respondents from the 'Chinese' cultural area are markedly less in favour of consensus than those from the 'Malay' cultural area, although the opposi-tion to consensus is smaller in Singapore, whose respondents divide almost in the same way as the respondents from the Philippines. Yet attitudes to consensus are not necessarily the consequence of a cultural similarity but may well be merely due to the practical point that the closeness of Singaporeans to the broad 'Malay' cultural area in this respect is indicative of what is likely to be at least one of the reasons for the reactions of the two groups of countries on the issue of consensus: the countries belonging to the broad 'Malay' cultural area are all, to some degree at least, constrained to be multi-cultural. Singapore is simply similar on this matter to the countries of the 'Malay' cultural area. Not only Malaysians, but at least Indonesians and Thais, if not Philippinos to the same extent, are confronted with pow-erful, even when they are not large, Chinese communities which they have to take into account and agree with on many points. The fact that there is a clear divide between the respondents from the two country groupings with respect to consensus must thus be regarded to a substantial extent as the practical consequence of the condition in which the countries of the two cultural areas find themselves. Meanwhile, one finds a marked spread in the reactions of respondents within both the 'Chinese' and 'Malay' sub-regions with respect to the other questions. The way in which the respondents from the East and Southeast Asian countries divide is presented graphically in Figure 5.1.

However, in order to find out whether there is any ground at all to support the idea of a North–South division in East and Southeast Asia, one might concentrate the analysis on those among the nine countries which appear most likely to fit such a division. This means considering five countries only, Japan, South Korea and Taiwan, on the one hand, and Indonesia and the Philippines, on the other. Despite the very large difference in wealth and general socio-economic development between Japan and both Korea and Taiwan and despite the fact that Korea and Taiwan became liberal democracies much later than Japan, these three countries have much in common: they are 'naturally' centralised countries; Korea and Taiwan displayed an ability to industrialise on the basis of their own capital resources and are gradually coming closer to Japan in terms of the development of their economy; they are part, together with Japan, of the Buddhist cultural area, even if the differences are substantial from one country to the other, but on the understanding that Buddhism allows for more 'syncretism' than, for instance, the Muslim or Christian religions. Japan was never a colony, admittedly, while Korea and Taiwan were, but these were colonies of Japan: this is likely to have reinforced similarities between these three states, even if memories of colonisation have meant that feelings towards Japan have not been especially tender in Korea in the course of the second half of the twentieth century.

Conversely, Indonesia and the Philippines are, as we noted, both constellations of islands in need of being brought together, somewhat forcefully, to form a single nation: colonisation from the West did have such an effect, even if the Western power was not the same in both countries. Neither country falls within the Buddhist orbit, though they differ by being Muslim in one case, mainly Catholic in the other. Colonial experience may or may not have been responsible for the serious political difficulties which these two states had to face, more so Indonesia, admittedly, than the Philippines: liberal democracy has been hampered in both cases, although the return to pluralism has taken place, admittedly later, in Indonesia. Meanwhile, economic development is in both cases rather slow and is vastly dependent on foreign capital.

There does therefore appear to be enough of a *prima facie* contrast between these two groups of countries to suggest that there might be here a distinction between two forms of socio-political culture. On the other hand, the other four countries cannot be located as closely within this dichotomous division. First, if Singapore is to be attached to a cultural group, it is has to be to that of East Asia, not to that of Southeast Asia. Yet it remains distinct from the East Asian group in that it was a colony from

Agree minus disagree

Right to express an opinion (208b)

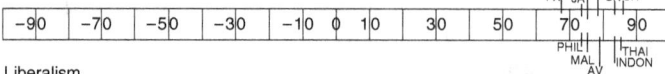

AV SING TW JA SK CH
−90 −70 −50 −30 −10 0 10 30 50 70 90
PHIL MAL INDON THAI AV

Liberalism
Organise protest meetings (208c)

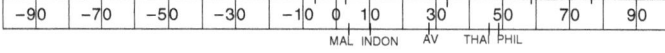

SING TW   AV   JA   SK
−90 −70 −50 −30 −10 0 10 30 50 70 90
MAL INDON   AV   THAI PHIL

Government usually knows best (306c)

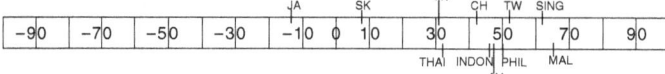

JA   SK   AV   CH TW SING
−90 −70 −50 −30 −10 0 10 30 50 70 90
THAI INDON PHIL MAL AV

Governmental restraint
We should do what government wants (306d)

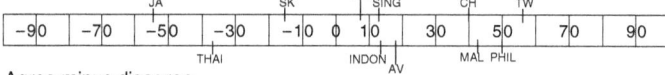

AV
JA   SK   SING   CH   TW
−90 −70 −50 −30 −10 0 10 30 50 70 90
THAI   INDON AV   MAL PHIL

Agree minus disagree

Consensus better than a lot of institutional
initiative (412d)

AV
JA SK CH TW   SING
−90 −70 −50 −30 −10 0 10 30 50 70 90
PHIL THAI MAL INDON AV

Decision
Older people more influence (412e)

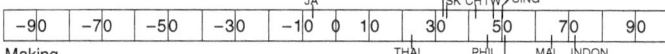

AV
JA   SK CH TW SING
−90 −70 −50 −30 −10 0 10 30 50 70 90
THAI   PHIL   MAL INDON AV

Making
Public interest before family (412f)

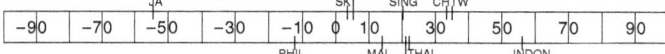

AV
JA   SK SING CH TW
−90 −70 −50 −30 −10 0 10 30 50 70 90
PHIL   MAL THAI   INDON
AV

Woman's place at home (412c)

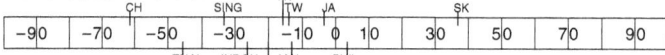

AV
CH   SING   TW JA   SK
−90 −70 −50 −30 −10 0 10 30 50 70 90
THAI INDON MAL PHIL AV

Social relations
Individual for own good rather than
society's (412g)

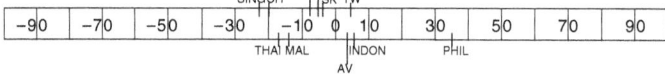

AV JA
SING CH   SK TW
−90 −70 −50 −30 −10 0 10 30 50 70 90
THAI MAL INDON PHIL AV

Agree minus disagree

Socio economic standpoint
Competition good (306a)

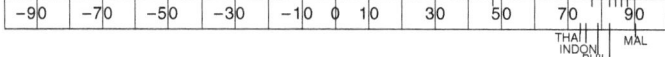

AV TW CH
SK SING
JA
−90 −70 −50 −30 −10 0 10 30 50 70 90
THAI INDON PHIL MAL AV

Government responsible for jobs (306b)

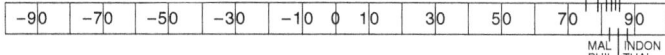

AV
SING TW SK JA CH
−90 −70 −50 −30 −10 0 10 30 50 70 90
MAL INDON PHIL THAI AV

Society better if profits free (306g)

TW   CH JA   AV SING SK
−90 −70 −50 −30 −10 0 10 30 50 70 90
INDON PHIL THAI MAL AV

Good environment preferred to growth (412b)

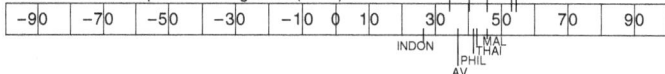

AV SING AV JA TW CH SK
−90 −70 −50 −30 −10 0 10 30 50 70 90
INDON MAL THAI PHIL AV

Figure 5.1 Spread of answers to human rights, communitarian and socio-economic
questions, divided between East and Southeast Asia by country.

Britain and that it has far from achieved so far a decisive move towards a pluralistic political system. Second, Malaysia is culturally in part close to Indonesia, but it is also culturally deeply divided as a result of the presence of a large Chinese minority, this division being perhaps partly at the origin of the political restrictions to some of the freedoms which have been in force in the country for a generation. Malaysia is also a smaller and more 'compact' state than either Indonesia or the Philippines, despite the fact that it is federal, unlike the two big island nations, and includes much of the Northwestern part of Borneo. Third and fourth, neither Thailand nor China can easily be located within one or the other of the two 'cultural' groups which have been defined earlier. Thailand is close to other Southeast Asian countries on economic grounds, but not on other grounds; China appears almost impossible to place in one or the other of the two regions. While East and Southeast Asia appears therefore to 'house' more than one socio-political culture, the basis of the division does not appear to emerge easily from the past development of the countries concerned.

Yet, even if one restricts the comparison to the five countries which were mentioned earlier, the *prima facie* impression that the attitudes might be similar does not coincide with the empirical evidence. There are only two questions where there is a clear divide between these countries, the question on consensus (Q.412d) and the question asking as to whether 'one should choose one's own good or that of the society' (Q.412g): this is surely not enough. Thus, whether on the basis of five countries only, let alone on the basis of all nine countries, there is scarcely any support for the view that the basic societal values of citizens of East and Southeast Asia divide into two cultural sub-regions. There are, admittedly, some variations from question to question in the nature and extent of the mix between the countries of the two sub-regions. If one leaves aside, not merely the question on consensus, but the two questions where the spread is very small across all countries, that which relates to the freedom of expression (Q.208b) (15 points) and that relating to the role of the government with respect to jobs (Q.306b) (14 points), some differences emerge, but they are sufficiently large to be described as separate patterns: they are not merely slight tendencies. First, in two cases, there is what might be referred to as a 'slide', with a mix in the middle, and one or two countries of each group at polar opposites: these are the questions on the choice between family and society (Q.412f) and on the choice between the individual and the public interest (Q.412g). Second, in three cases, there is a mix at one end, but one or two countries of one sub-region at the other end: these are the questions on when to obey the government (Q.306d), the question asking whether the government knows best (Q.306e) and, but much less markedly, the question on competition (Q.306a). Third, in two cases, the 'Malay' group of countries is entirely in the middle while the 'Chinese' group of countries is spread out: these are the question on the right to demonstrate (Q.208c) – to which, as has been pointed out, Chinese respondents were not given the opportunity to answer – and the question on the part which women should play (Q.412c). Fourth, there is a complete mix or 'confusion' in three cases: these are the questions on the part which old people should play (Q.412e), on the choice between growth and the environment (Q.412b) and on the extent to which businesses should make profits (Q.306g). While there are thus degrees in the extent to which the countries are mixed with respect to their attitudes to basic societal values, the mix is substantial: there is therefore no *prima facie* ground for suggesting a distinction of the countries of the East and Southeast Asian region into a 'Chinese' and a 'Malay' cultural sub-region.

Do the attitudes of Japanese respondents suggest that they should not be included in the 'Chinese' cultural area?

We noted already that the attitudes of Japanese respondents differed substantially from those of respondents of other countries of the region and contributed therefore to increasing the spread of the reactions of the respondents of the area. That spread remains none the less so large, especially on communitarian questions, that it was not permissible to conclude that the absence of a common culture in the region could be said to be due to the fact that Japan was part of the group. *Prima facie*, admittedly, the exclusion of Japan from the 'Chinese' cultural area countries appears to have a significant effect in rendering that area more 'compact'. If one leaves aside the two questions on which the spread is very small overall, the question on freedom of expression (Q.208b) and the question on the role of government on jobs (Q.306b), the exclusion of Japan from the 'Chinese' cultural area makes a difference in seven of the eleven remaining questions; in four of these seven, the difference is substantial: these are the question asking about when to obey the government (Q.306d), the question as to whether the government knows best (Q.306e), the question relating to the choice between the family and society (Q.412f) and the question on competition (Q.306a). Moreover, only in relation to the role of women (Q.412c) does the spread of the answers among the respondents of the 'Chinese' cultural area remain very large (106 points) even when Japan is not included. Interestingly, however, the spread does not change with respect to the right to hold protest meetings (Q.208c).

   Yet, even if Japanese respondents are not included, the spread of answers among respondents in the four other countries of the 'Chinese' cultural area remains large (41 points on average): it is indeed marginally larger than among the four countries of the 'Malay' cultural area. Thus, while Japanese respondents differ in substantial ways from the respondents of the other countries of the 'Chinese' cultural area, especially in terms of attitudes to the role of the government and to the role of competition, the answers of the respondents of the other four countries of the 'Chinese' cultural area remain too spread out to be said to form a single sub-regional culture. Moreover, the extent of overlap between the countries of the 'Chinese' and 'Malay' cultural areas is not significantly altered if Japan is not included.

*Are the attitudes of the respondents from
semi-authoritarian countries significantly different
from those of the liberal-democratic countries?*

One question remains, however: do respondents from the semi-authoritarian countries differ sharply in their reactions to basic societal values from the respondents of the liberal-democratic countries? At least four of the thirteen questions examined here could be regarded as likely to raise serious problems in the semi-authoritarian countries of the area; indeed, the question relating to the right to organise protest meetings (Q.208c) was not asked in China at all. It may be that the respondents did react in an idiosyncratic manner to these 'problematic' questions, either because of some worry about the extent to which their views might become known or because political socialisation is such that these respondents are likely to be more favourable to the government than where the regime is liberal-democratic.

The fully liberal-democratic countries are Japan, South Korea, Taiwan, the Philippines and Thailand; China, Singapore and Malaysia are not, although, admittedly, to a varying extent; the case of Indonesia was less clear-cut at the time the survey was conducted (end of 2000), since the first fully open parliamentary election after the fall of Suharto had taken place only in that year. Yet the survey is based on attitudes of respondents most of whom would have lived all their life under a regime which was not liberal: traces of this authoritarianism are likely to have remained – if it is indeed the case that attitudes are shaped to an extent by the regime under which citizens live. As a matter of fact, comments of a somewhat similar character have to be made in relation to four of the five 'liberal' countries: in effect, apart from Japan, the regime was authoritarian in these countries for substantial periods up to the 1980s, even the late 1980s. This is indeed why we described the liberalisation of the region as having followed a pattern not dissimilar to that which was followed by economic development, that is to say on a 'flying geese' model. Given that the case of Indonesia is the most borderline, with respect to that country, the data needs to be examined in two ways, one including Indonesia and the other excluding it from the group of the semi-authoritarian countries.

If all thirteen questions are examined together, the spread of the answers to the thirteen questions is markedly larger among the liberal-democratic countries than among the semi-authoritarian countries (58 points against 29); the spread is reduced to 45 points among the other four liberal-democratic countries if Japan is not included, but a substantial gap does remain: even these four liberal-democratic countries thus do not constitute a cohesive group. There is, moreover, a marked amount of overlap among the two groups of countries: as a matter of fact, there is not even one question on which there is not some overlap: indeed the question on consensus gives rise to the greatest mix between the liberal-democratic and the semi-authoritarian countries. Yet, although there are variations in the extent to which the two groups are 'mixed', overall, that mix is somewhat less pronounced, perhaps somewhat surprisingly, than when the countries are divided into a 'Chinese' and a 'Malay' sub-regional grouping.

Given that the distinction is between liberal-democratic and at least somewhat authoritarian regimes, it was to be expected that the contrast – that is to say a small spread in each sub-group and a limited overlap between the two sub-groups – would be sharpest in reply to the two human rights questions (Q.208b and c) and to the two questions relating to the attitudes of citizens *vis-à-vis* the government (Q.306d and e). This is indeed the case in terms of overlap: the 'mix' is less marked with respect to these four questions than with respect to seven of the nine others; but the spread is substantial, especially among liberal-democratic countries, except with respect to the question relating to the freedom of expression (Q.208b) where the spread is in any case small overall among all countries. Indeed, the spread remains high on all these questions even if Japan is not included with the other liberal-democratic countries, although there is then some reduction of the spread at least on the two questions relating to the attitudes of citizens *vis-à-vis* the government (Q.306d and e) (from 79 to 58 points in the case of Q.306e and from 112 to 92 points in the case of Q.306d). Yet one would have expected that the liberal-democratic countries would have had a more 'compact' type of reaction with respect to these four questions: in reality, only four of the five liberal-democratic countries have a 'compact' reaction with respect to the right to organise protest meetings (Q.208c) and only three of the five countries have a 'compact' reaction with respect to the two questions relating to the attitudes of citizens *vis-à-vis* the government (Q.306d and e).

Taiwan constitutes the exception in all three cases and the Philippines in two of them. On the right to organise protest meetings (Q.208c), Taiwanese respondents are close to the Singaporeans and Malaysians (while the Chinese were not asked the question); Taiwanese and Philippino respondents are also close to Singaporeans and Malaysians on the question whether the government knows best (Q.306e), while Taiwanese respondents are the most 'illiberal' of all respondents on whether one should always obey the government (Q.306d), more than Philippinos, Malaysians and Chinese. Such attitudes on the part of Taiwanese and of Philippino respondents on these questions are clearly in sharp contrast with the character of the regime, a contrast which was already apparent in Chapter 3.[1] Thus, on three of these questions, Japanese and Taiwanese respondents occupy the two extreme opposite positions, with Taiwanese respondents being close to respondents from Malaysia on two 'communitarian' questions (Q.412c and e) and on competition (Q.306a). Taiwanese respondents and to an extent Philippino respondents account therefore in part for the large spread of the answers to these questions. This is so in part only, however, as South Koreans and Thais are also distant from each other on the right to organise protest demonstrations (Q.208c) and on the two questions concerned with the attitudes citizens should have *vis-à-vis* the government

(Q.306d and e). Yet the attitudes of Taiwanese and Philippino respondents are those which differ most from those of the respondents of the other three liberal-democratic countries. Moreover, the attitudes of respondents from the liberal-democratic countries of the region are spread out, not merely with respect to issues which are directly related to liberal problems, but more broadly: such a 'stretching' does not occur to the same extent among the authoritarian countries.

Meanwhile, the reactions of Indonesian respondents are not markedly different from those of the respondents from China, Singapore or Malaysia: the spread is reduced only by three points, from 29 to 26, when Indonesia is not included in the group. It cannot be demonstrated that the limited character of this difference is due to the fact that, as was hypothesised earlier, the long period of authoritarian rule had a durable impact on the views of the average Indonesian citizen. What emerges, however, is that attitudes of Indonesian respondents resemble in many cases the attitudes of respondents from the authoritarian countries, although it is intermediate between the two groups on the human rights questions (Q.208b and c) and on the two questions concerned with the way in which citizens should react *vis-à-vis* the government (Q.306d and e).

There is therefore only limited evidence suggesting that the distinction between liberal-democratic and authoritarian rule might constitute a basis for a sub-regional division. First, the clustering is not markedly greater than in terms of the division between respondents from countries belonging to the 'Chinese' cultural area and those belonging to the 'Malay' cultural area. Second, while the authoritarian sub-regional grouping is relatively compact, the liberal-democratic sub-regional 'grouping' is not, partly because Japanese respondents are more liberal than the respondents of the other countries and partly because Taiwanese and to an extent Philippino respondents are less liberal and therefore fairly close to the respondents of the authoritarian countries. Third, the question does remain as to why respondents from the authoritarian countries are somewhat close to each other in terms of their attitudes, even if this similarity must not be exaggerated. The reasons may be diverse and in particular may be connected to the fact that the respondents' answers are affected to an extent by the character of the society in the country to which they belong. The matter will therefore need to be investigated further.[2]

* * * * *

In Chapter 3, we found that the East–West divide accounted for a part, but only a limited part, of the variations from state to state among the respondents of the eighteen countries of this study. We therefore naturally explored the possible impact of the strongly expressed distinction which has often been put forward to account for attitudinal differences among East and Southeast Asian citizens, the distinction between a 'Chinese' and a 'Malay' cultural background. That distinction is in some ways 'classical', as the North–South divide among Western European countries. Yet, as in the Western European context, that 'classical' distinction seemingly accounts only, as do the overall distinctions between the Eastern and the Western region, for a limited part of the variations which are registered from state to state in attitudes to 'basic societal values'. Meanwhile, an ideological divide relating to the liberal-democratic or authoritarian character of the polity turned out to have some explanatory potential; but it has only some explanatory potential. This potential is more marked with respect to the 'authoritarian' countries than with respect to the liberal-democratic countries, perhaps because of the character of the earlier regime in the countries concerned and of the timing of the move towards liberal democracy.

We noted at the end of the previous chapter that Western Europe and East and Southeast Asia would be in marked contrast to each other if intra-regional variations did account for a large proportion of the variations in attitudes among the respondents of the countries of East and Southeast Asia. This would have meant that, in one region, there would be a strong basis for a 'sub-regional' divide, but not in the other: this is clearly not the case. As was suggested at the end of Chapter 3, there is therefore no alternative but to examine attitudes to basic societal values at a lower level, that is to say at the level of the individual states.

6 Political culture at the level of individual states

As Chapter 3 showed, there are differences, but on the average no sharp contrast, between respondents from East and Southeast Asia and respondents from Western Europe in terms of attitudes to basic societal values. As Chapters 4 and 5 then showed, no clear signs suggest that average variations, within 'sub-regions', in geographical conditions, in culture and in particular in religious practices, in economic and social development, constitute, despite what is often thought to be the case, major sources of intra-regional distinctions in attitudes to basic societal values either among respondents from Western Europe or among respondents from East and Southeast Asia. These sets of rather negative findings strongly indicate, therefore, that one should not expect to discover simple and straightforward 'explanations' of variations in basic societal values, either in general or, in the particular case of this study, at the level of regions or sub-regions in either East and Southeast Asia or Western Europe.

If regional differences or clearly recognisable cleavages within each region do not seem to provide more than a partial explanation for the differences which exist – and these do exist – in the basic societal values of citizens, the most obvious next move would appear to be an exploration of the differences which can be found at the level of the state. There are serious difficulties with such an approach, however, the main danger being that the outcome is likely to lead to the discovery of 'peculiarities' or of 'idiosyncrasies' only, not of 'explanations'. Citizens' behaviour within each state is the result of long historical processes which were instrumental in the combined emergence of a large variety of factors: these typically cannot be disentangled easily; at least the precise impact of each of them seems almost impossible to measure. Yet this does not constitute a sufficient justification for avoiding examining the differences in attitudes to basic societal values which are found at state level. It was repeatedly noted that variations in these attitudes were large and that this was so with respect to the majority of the questions which were asked of respondents of the survey; these large variations from state to state are indeed at the root of the substantial spread and of the substantial overlap which was found to exist in previous chapters among the responses given in the various states when answers to the questions on basic societal values are analysed at the regional or sub-regional levels. These variations cannot simply be ignored: they have to be examined in some detail. This is the object of the present chapter.

To undertake the analysis, the chapter needs first to return to the two levels – regional and sub-regional – of the 'classical' 'explanations' given of the origins of basic societal values, as one needs to reflect on the reasons why 'explanations' at one or the other of these two levels are likely to be insufficient to account for the reality of basic societal value patterns. The chapter then has to examine the extent to which there is a sharp difference between the attitudes to basic societal values at the level of each country and the 'average' attitudes to basic societal values at the regional and sub-regional levels which were analysed in earlier chapters. The second section of this chapter therefore looks at the size of the variations from country to country and assesses whether this size is greater than the variations which are found, on average, between regions or between sub-regions.

Yet, while a detailed assessment of attitudes to basic societal values at the level of individual states quickly shows that there are substantial variations from state to state, this is not sufficient to provide a picture of these variations. Common characteristics also have to be discovered among these variations so that these can be classified and at least in part interpreted: otherwise all one would do is merely to list country idiosyncrasies. What one is looking for are therefore some types or patterns which will help to categorise and compare the attitudes of citizens at state level and to do so without having to move again to the level of regions or sub-regions: the third section of this chapter constitutes an attempt to undertake this task.

I

Why neither inter-regional nor intra-regional differences suffice to account for patterns of citizens' societal values

It has been widely regarded as almost axiomatic that value standpoints should be markedly different between East and West and also within each of these two regions. The literature does not make it entirely clear who is expected to hold these standpoints; it seems assumed that such attitudes are adopted because they are, so to speak, 'in the air'.

Neither of these views appears confirmed by the detailed empirical analysis of the answers of respondents, as we saw. To be precise, neither of these views appears *fully* confirmed by the empirical analysis, although there may be a partial influence of these factors, given that there are some differences in citizens' attitudes to basic societal values between the two regions as well as within sub-groups of countries in each of the two regions. Reflection is therefore needed as to what the reasons might be for the 'reality' being different from expectations. Reflection is also needed about the implications of that state of affairs, both for the way in which these 'classical' explanations should be treated and for the way in which any other explanations might be introduced.

The grounds which are regarded as accounting for the view that value standpoints are likely to differ between areas are basically of three kinds. The first ground is 'physiological', so to speak: it is based on the idea that the climate affects attitudes because people tend to react differently and (at least eventually) hold different views when it is hot or when it is cold, when it is typically sunny or when it rains frequently. The second ground can be described as broadly 'cultural': it is based on the idea that attitudes with respect to basic societal values differ because the views which prevail in different areas are not the same. The third ground is socio-economic and is part of modernisation theory: it views differences in the basic societal attitudes of those who live in the two areas as a consequence of the fact that 'development' did not take place at the same rate in these areas.

The grounds for variations between the two regions

Let us first review these grounds in the context of differences which are expected to be found between Western Europeans and East and Southeast Asians. The climatic ground cannot be expected to play a substantial part at this level, given that the climate varies markedly within each area, for instance between the North and the South of the regions. The 'cultural' grounds argument may play a major part, on the other hand: attitudes with respect to basic societal values are held to be different in the two regions because, for centuries, West and East have had little communication with each other and a whole set of views had been put forward separately in each area. The socio-economic ground also plays a large part as the two regions are regarded as not having developed at the same rate and in particular over the same length of time.

The 'cultural' or ideological basis of societal value distinctions between East and West

The notion that value distinctions exist between East and Southeast Asia and Western Europe for 'cultural' reasons is probably the ground which is most commonly put forward, at any rate in the society at large. As was indicated in previous chapters, it is based on a combination of historical and geographical arguments. The historical arguments have to do with the way in which philosophical and perhaps more specifically religious ideas are regarded as having spread in each area; the geographical arguments have to do with the view that the large distance between the two areas combines with the contiguity of the societies in each of the two regions to turn each area into what might be described as a 'value fortress'.

Neither set of arguments fits easily with the reality of historical or geographical developments. To be valid, the historical arguments postulate continuity and indeed uniform development in the cultural characteristics of each area. This is not what has happened in fact: the history of the West and that of the East both show many cultural twists and turns as well as many periods of cultural ambiguity. Neither the view that the West is individualistic nor the view that the East holds communitarian attitudes, for instance, has emerged in a straightforward manner in the course of the history of each region.

The geographical arguments are also difficult to sustain: the borders of each of the two areas are not defined precisely in fact and are not even definable precisely in theory. Where Western Europe ends has always been mysterious; where East and Southeast Asia ends seems to be somewhat easier to determine, given the enormous size of China, but the grounds on the basis of which Central Asia should not be included in the area are not altogether obvious. In reality both the historical and the geographical arguments on which the idea of the 'cultural' unity of each region is based are due to rather arbitrary abstractions which amount to putting forward those 'cultural' elements which happen to coincide with the point of view which is being presented and in discarding those elements which do not.

The socio-economic basis for value separateness between East and West

Prima facie, the socio-economic case for the value separateness of the two regions seems easier to sustain, as it is ostensibly based on empirical observations about the standard of living and welfare developments in the two regions. Thus, as a group, the countries of East and Southeast Asia can be regarded as being less 'developed' from a socio-economic point of view – or at least to have been less developed until recently – than the countries of Western Europe as a group. The historical basis for the case seems to be more 'testable' than the historical case which is made in the context of the 'cultural' argument: the socio-economic argument is indeed valid if it can be shown that the socio-economic development of the two regions has been different over time. The argument based on geography is also somewhat stronger in the case of the socio-economic development of the regions than in the context of the 'cultural' argument: one can in a sense 'carve up' an area of greater development and decide that it constitutes Western Europe!

From historical and geographical characteristics to value standpoints of citizens

The most serious problem with both arguments is a different one, however. These arguments are valid only if it can also be demonstrated that the citizens of the countries concerned hold the values standpoints which they hold *because* either a given state of 'cultural' development or a given state of socio-economic development has taken place. Yet, all that the 'cultural' argument may (or may not) show is that certain ideas 'have floated' in a given area, possibly for a long period of time and possibly in the whole of the area: it does not show that the citizens who live in the area also hold these ideas. The point seems even more obvious in the case of the socio-economic argument: unless the assumption is made that the basic societal values held by citizens are due to the socio-economic structure, there is no reason to connect the holding of these values to the state of socio-economic development.

Admittedly, it is probably believed that these arguments are plausible and even that they are based, to an extent at least, on evidence. It seems plausible to believe that those who live in a given area are influenced by the ideas which prevail in that area: opinion leaders affect the opinion of those who are led. It seems perhaps even more plausible to believe that attitudes of citizens are somewhat different in 'developed' and 'developing' areas: the ideas which Inglehart put forward and which were referred to in Chapter 1 to provide evidence of the 'materialism' of the poorer societies and of the 'post-materialism' of the richer ones (Inglehart, 1977, 1997).

Yet it is not because it is plausible that the views of the opinion leaders are shared by the led that these views *are* widely shared by the led and even more are shared always and uniformly. Nor is it because it appears to be the case that, to an extent, there are variations in values between richer and poorer countries that one can generalise and claim that the basic societal values of citizens will be the values which are 'in the air' or will be the values which are regarded as fitting best given states of socio-economic development.

Cultural and socio-economic arguments in connection with intra-regional differences

Thus neither the 'cultural' nor the socio-economic argument are strong enough to provide a firm basis for the view that different values will prevail in East and West, although this conclusion was able to remain untested so long as it was not possible to obtain empirical evidence about the values which do indeed prevail in East and West. The same difficulties arise if, instead of opposing East to West, one opposes groups of countries within East and Southeast Asia or within Western Europe. The 'climatic' argument does enter into the picture here, given that one of the main ways in which each of the two regions has been typically divided has been between North and South. Yet the climatic argument would become valid only if one were able to prove that the impact of the climate on individuals is so strong and so uniform that their attitudes are profoundly shaped as a result. The least that can be said is that the point is highly contentious.

At the regional level the cultural argument cannot easily be sustained either: if it does not obtain at the level of Western Europe as a whole, it is not clear why it would obtain at the level of sub-groups of nations within Western Europe, for instance between North and South. If it is true that there is neither a historical nor a geographical basis for the development of sets of Western European values, the same is equally true for the development of Northern or Southern values within Western Europe. The same conclusions can be drawn in relation to East and Southeast Asia: there is no satisfactory theoretical basis on which to claim that citizens of East Asia, for instance, will tend to hold values which differ from the values held by citizens in Southeast Asia.

Indeed, arguments based on cultural differences are likely to lead to an infinite regress. For instance, if religion is felt to be the main reason why there are cultural variations from one part of a region to another, that effect might not really take place at the level of a large sub-group within a region, but rather at a much lower geographical level, perhaps even at the level of villages. Indeed, even if the same religion covers a large area, that religion may not be perceived, understood or practised in one part of the area in the same way as it is in other parts. The history of religions and in particular of their interpretation by persons who are widely held to have the right or who have simply arrogated to themselves the right to undertake such interpretations shows that it is dangerous to claim uniform interpretations and, by way of consequence, uniform values without precise evidence that this is indeed the case.

Similar problems arise with the socio-economic argument – and with modernisation theory in general. To claim that a sub-group within a region is more developed than another sub-group is almost certainly always an oversimplification: some areas within the 'more developed' sub-group are most likely to be less developed than others. Italy is a particularly striking example given the sharp division between the highly developed North and the markedly less developed South; but similar conclusions need to be drawn about socio-economic variations in other countries.

Moreover, the general difficulty of linking particular cultural or socio-economic developments to the values held by citizens applies to the same extent and for the same reasons to sub-sets of regions as it does to a whole region. That some ideas are 'in the air' in a particular part of a region does not mean that those who live in that part will hold the values corresponding to these ideas; that a part of a region should enjoy a certain level of socio-economic development does not mean that those who live in that part will hold the values which are felt to 'coincide' with that particular level of socio-economic development. The flaws which characterise these arguments when made at regional level also characterise these arguments when made at the level of parts of regions.

A strong case for partial interpretations

Yet, the fact that both the case for value distinctions based on differences among regions and the case for value distinctions based on differences among sub-groups within regions suffer from the same kind of defects does not mean that either interpretation is wholly unsatisfactory and must be wholly discarded. In the course of the previous chapters, some variations in the basic societal values of respondents were found to occur at regional level: one may not claim that this is due to the cultural or socio-economic differences which may exist between these regions, but one has to note that there are regional variations. Some variations in the basic societal values of respondents were also found to occur at the level of sub-groups within each region: one may not claim that this is due to the cultural or socio-economic differences which may exist at the level of these sub-groups, but one has to note that these sub-regional variations occur. This suggests, not that both interpretations should be discarded, but, on the contrary, that both interpretations may well be valid simultaneously, albeit only partially.

Both interpretations should also be adopted equally, as they should be regarded as both being part of the 'explanation' of the overall phenomenon. These interpretations should not be regarded as hierarchically dependent on each other, as if the 'regional' interpretation provided a 'fundamental' view of the 'culture' of the area while the sub-groups would provide merely a sub-set (a 'sub-cultural refinement') of that 'fundamental' culture. As they are to be regarded as explaining the phenomenon merely partially, these two explanatory approaches are naturally not mutually exclusive: they provide elements of explanation of a highly complex phenomenon.

The question under investigation is the nature of the origin of the values held by individuals in two regions. Because we do not have evidence at the level of whole populations before the middle and in many cases the later part of the twentieth century, we cannot be expected to be able to determine with any degree of assurance what the development of these values has been in the past: we can only surmise what it might have been. When one has to surmise, the danger of oversimplification is always present. One must therefore compensate for such a danger in two ways, first by taking as many elements as possible into account and second by concentrating attempts at interpretation at the point in time where satisfactory evidence can be collected, that is to say, in this case, about the present and the very recent past.

In the context of basic societal values held by citizens, the evidence provided by the examination of current situations strongly suggests that these values do not necessarily originate from types of influence operating at a single level, but that they are the product of types of influence operating simultaneously at different levels. Some elements of that influence originate at the level of the region and some originate at the level of sub-groups within the region, but this is also likely to be at different levels within the region and not merely at a single one. It is not very useful to attempt to draw a list of what these different sub-regional levels might be: indeed, there will be significant differences from area to area. It suffices to note that the influence takes place at several and probably many levels. Thus the examination of the origin of attitudes with respect to basic societal values among the population is likely to be a continuing and indeed open-ended endeavour. The present study can be regarded only as part of such an endeavour: some elements likely to exercise influence are stressed; others may not be.

II

Large single country disagreements and relatively small regional or sub-regional disagreements among respondents about basic societal values

The scope of variations (the extent of spread) with respect to basic societal values from country to country and between regions and sub-regions

In the course of the previous chapters, we found substantial variations in the basic societal values of respondents between the two regions, among the subdivisions of these regions and from country to country. The variations are naturally different from question to question: they lead to the determination of the extent of *spread* across the countries of the study or across any sub-set of these countries. We noticed already that these variations – which spread – were much larger in many cases, in fact in most cases, between the countries than between the regions or sub-regions: thus the regional or sub-regional average markedly reduces and therefore partly conceals the size of the spread which exists at the country level. This is naturally to be expected with averages, but the extent to which this reduction occurs among the eighteen countries of the study is so substantial that it contributes to the general conclusion that basic societal values are perhaps less regional or even 'sub-regional' than national. Before examining the characteristics of this dispersion at the regional and sub-regional levels, it is therefore worth considering its amplitude at the country level (Table 6.1).

The extent of spread at the level of individual countries

Table 6.1 makes it possible to determine the extent to which the spread at the country level varies with respect to the attitudes of respondents to the basic societal values. It ranges from a minimum of 26 points in relation to the views about freedom of expression (Q.208b) to a maximum of 134 points in relation to the views about whether 'individuals should strive for their own good or for the good of the society' (Q.412g). As a matter of fact, one can subdivide the questions into three groups from the point of view of the spread of the attitudes to basic societal values. The dispersion is low (26 to 42 points) in three cases, those which relate to views about the freedom of expression, as we just noted, and to views about two socio-economic questions (but the spread is somewhat larger in these cases), that

Table 6.1 Range of dispersion between regions, sub-regions and countries (percentages)

Questions	Between regions	Between sub-regions		Between countries		
		East and Southeast Asia	Western Europe	East and Southeast Asia	Western Europe	Both
Human rights						
208b	13	2	1	17	15	26
208c	41	1	6	84	43	95
Average	27	2	4	51	29	61
Communitarian						
306e	50	18	15	79	57	103
306d	49	10	25	112	53	116
412d	9	37	19	63	58	68
412e	6	1	6	77	31	77
412c	37	4	10	106	51	117
412g	8	12	0	111	127	134
412f	37	16	51	57	37	70
Average	28	14	18	86	59	98
Socio-economic						
306a	0	3	7	40	21	42
306b	5	4	10	14	38	38
306g	31	10	25	64	54	91
412b	2	6	3	27	64	64
Average	10	6	11	36	44	59

Notes
208b Right to express one's opinion
208c Right to organise public protest meetings
306d Do what government wants
306e Government usually knows best
412c Women's primary role in the home
412d Important to achieve consensus
412e Give extra influence to older people
412f Public interest before family
412g Individuals should strive for their own good more than society
306a Competition good
306b Responsibility of government to provide jobs or social welfare
306g Society better if businesses free to make profits
412b Good environment more important than economic growth

which concerns competition (Q.306a) and that which concerns the responsibility of the government to provide jobs or social welfare (Q.306b). It is intermediate (64 to 77 points) with respect to four questions, one socio-economic (a good environment rather than economic growth (Q.412b)) and three communitarian (the influence to be given to old people, the role of consensus and whether the public interest should come before the family (Q.412e, d and f)). It is large or very large (91 to 134 points) with respect to the last six questions, the human rights question on the right to organise protest meetings (Q.208c), the socio-economic question dealing with the right to allow businesses to be free to make profits (Q.306g) and four communitarian questions, those dealing with attitudes towards the government (Q.306d and e) and those dealing with the role of women (Q.412c) and with the right of individuals to 'strive for their own good rather than for that of society' (Q.412g). Only with respect to the first group of three questions is there a broad consensus among the countries: this consensus covers near 'unanimity' with respect to one of these (the freedom of expression) and very strong positive support everywhere with respect to two socio-economic questions, on competition and on the responsibility of the government to provide jobs or social welfare – a matter which might have expected to lead to greater differences of opinion given that it is markedly controversial.

Comparing the extent of spread at the country-by-country level and at the regional and sub-regional levels

Meanwhile, at the regional or sub-regional levels, as Table 6.1 also shows, the spread is markedly more limited. At the regional level it ranges from being zero on the question relating to competition (Q.306a) to being 49 or 50 points on the two questions dealing with the attitudes citizens should have *vis-à-vis* the government (Q.306d and e). In six cases out of thirteen the spread is 9 points or less, in one case it is 13 points, in one case it is 31 points, and in the last five cases it is between 37 and 50 points. Not only is there a marked reduction in the amount of spread but also the number of cases in which the spread is low or very low increases from three to five.

As a matter of fact, there is only one exception to the general rule according to which spread is not only larger but also much larger at the country level than at the regional or sub-regional level: this is constituted by the 'human rights' question relating to the right to express an opinion (Q.208b). In this case the average difference between the two regions is 13 points only (East and Southeast Asian countries scoring −78 per cent and Western European countries −91 per cent): but, as we noted in several instances, the spread among all the countries is also low, at 26 points overall, being 17 points among the East and Southeast Asian countries (from −69 to −86 per cent) and 15 points among the Western European countries (from −80 to −95 per cent). As a matter of fact, while there is a rather smooth increase from −86 to −69 per cent among East and Southeast Asian countries, eight of the nine Western European countries score between −95 and −89 per cent, the lower minimum of −80 per cent being due to one country only, Spain.

In contrast to the responses to the human rights question related to the right to express an opinion, the spread on a country-by-country basis is much larger than at the regional or sub-regional levels in relation to the other twelve of the questions on basic societal values analysed here. This is even the case with respect to the two questions (on competition and on the responsibility of the government for jobs (Q.306a and b)) where the country-by-country spread was, as we noted, rather small: while the spread at the country-by-country level is 42 and 38 points on these questions, the inter-regional average spread is, respectively, nil and 5 points.

The contrast between the spread at the country-by-country level and at the regional and sub-regional levels is also typically large with respect to the other questions. For instance, in the case of the human rights question relating to the right of citizens to 'hold public meetings to protest against the government' (Q.208c), the country-by-country spread (95 points) is appreciably larger in East and Southeast Asia (84 points), though not in Western Europe (43 points), than the average difference between the two regions (41 points), Western European countries scoring on average −72 per cent while East and Southeast Asian countries score on average −31 per cent. This average summarises a 43 point spread among the Western European countries (from −47 to −90 points), but a much larger 84 point spread among East and Southeast Asian countries (from +6 per cent in Singapore and −2 per cent in Taiwan – a characteristic of that country which relates to those which were noted in Chapters 3 and 5 – to −78 per cent in Korea). As a matter of fact, the real spread may even be larger, since the question was not asked in China and some doubt therefore remains as to whether the citizens of that country might not feel, even more than the Taiwanese, that there should not be a right to 'hold public meetings to protest against the government'.

Among the communitarian questions, a large gap also exists between relatively small differences in the averages at regional and sub-regional levels and the variations from one country to the other in each region. This is, most interestingly, particularly so in the case of the two questions dealing with what 'should' be citizens' attitudes towards the government, despite the fact that, on these two questions, a substantial average difference occurs overall and in both regions, as we saw in Chapter 3. With respect to these two questions the difference between the average replies of respondents at the level of the regions is, respectively, 49 and 50 points. Respondents from East and Southeast Asia were found to be, on average, appreciably more likely than respondents from Western Europe to state that 'we should always do what the government wants' and that 'the government usually knows best' (Q.306d and e). Yet on these two questions, the country-by-country replies are markedly more spread out in East and Southeast Asia, though not in Western Europe, than they are at the average regional level: the country-by-country spread is, respectively, 112 and 53 points and 79 and 57 points.

This finding is important as it has some bearing on the interpretation to be given to 'Asian' or, for that matter, 'Western (European)' values. The two questions which have just been discussed, as well as the human rights question dealing with the right to organise protest meetings, have been shown in Chapter 3 to be those most likely to provide an empirical basis for the existence of a distinction between 'Asian' and 'Western (European)' values. This was because regional differences in the answers to these three questions had been found large enough to justify the conclusion that there were, if not two wholly contrasting cultures in the two regions, at least substantial variations in the reactions of citizens belonging to each of these two cultures: East and Southeast Asians could be regarded as being some-what, though admittedly only somewhat, more communitarian than Western Europeans. Yet, even this relatively modest conclusion may need to be revised in the light of variations from country to country, especially in East and Southeast Asia, since these variations indicate that there is no firmly entrenched view among the countries of the region (and indeed not among Western European countries either). It would seem therefore unjustified to place too much emphasis on the *average gap* between regions as country-by-country variations are markedly larger.

It was noted in Chapter 3 that the two questions concerned with attitudes to the government and the human rights question dealing with the right to protest were those which provided at least some evidence for the view that East and Southeast Asians and Western Europeans might have different value patterns. The answers to the other questions seemed to show, on the contrary, that differences at the level of average regional differences were rather small. As Table 6.1 shows, average regional differences with respect to the other five communitarian value questions (Q.412c, d, e, f and g) are indeed appreciably smaller (37 points in two cases, under 10 points in the other three). Yet with respect to all these questions, country-by-country answers are markedly spread out, this time in both regions and not just in East and Southeast Asia, although it is typically substantially larger in the latter region than in Western Europe, indeed over 20 points more overall (86 points against 59). With respect to these questions, the spread ranges from 31 to 127 points in Western Europe and from 37 to 112 points in East and Southeast Asia and except in one Western European case it is larger among Western European and among East and Southeast Asian countries than is the difference between the two regional averages. The country-by-country gap is also wider than the average difference between regions in the case of the attitudes to the four socio-economic questions analysed here.

Admittedly, the size of the spread among East and Southeast Asian countries is often rendered more pronounced by the behaviour of Japanese respondents, as these differ – a point already noted in Chapter 5 – in many instances in their views from the respondents of other East and Southeast Asian countries. This is not so, admittedly, with respect to the two human rights questions and it is so with respect to only one of the four socio-economic questions, that which relates to the value of competition, for which Japanese respondents are markedly less sanguine than other East and Southeast Asian respondents (Q.306a). The behaviour of Japanese respondents is idiosyncratic in the context of four of the seven communitarian questions, as we saw in Chapter 5: the only instances in that battery of questions in which this is not so are two questions, that which relates to the role of women and that which relates to the choice to be made between one's 'own good' and the 'good of society' (Q.412c and g). As a matter of fact, the position of Japanese respondents can be so different from that of other respondents of the region that it extends by 30 points on two questions (Q.412e and f) and by nearly 20 points in two others the spread which is found to exist among the other countries of the region.

Yet, although the attitudes of Japanese respondents differ to a substantial extent from those of other East and Southeast Asian countries and thus contribute to increase the country-by-country spread in the region, that country-by-country spread is none the less large in that region even if Japan is excluded, as it is in Western Europe on a country-by-country basis. Indeed, the spread of country answers would even be larger if the data had not been recoded in order to place those who agree with the statement presented to them in a single category instead of the two which separate those who 'agree strongly' from those who merely 'agree', those who disagree being also placed in a single category instead of two. There are substantially greater variations in the spread of the replies if both types of agreement and both types of disagreement are taken into account. The recoding was undertaken, as was noted in Chapter 2, in part to simplify analyses and to facilitate comparisons, but also because the distinction between 'agreeing strongly' and 'agreeing' (and between 'disagreeing strongly' and 'disagreeing') may not have an identical meaning across all the countries and among all the respondents, while the meaning given to 'agreement' and that to 'disagreement' are likely to be identical across the whole survey.

What has just been said about the contrast between regional averages and country-by-country variations can be extended to the sub-regional patterns of respondents' attitudes. These show how spread out with respect to most questions individual country attitudes are. The huge spread of answers to the question asking whether 'the public interest should always come before family obligations' (Q.412f) in both Western Europe and East and Southeast Asia is only the most extreme example of a phenomenon which occurs widely. While averages may show relatively little difference between the two regions and between those sub-groups within these regions which appeared in need of examination, variations from country to country within each region and within each sub-region can be very large.

The need to analyse attitudes of respondents to basic societal values on a country basis

If variations from country to country are large, but if one wishes to analyse regional or sub-regional patterns only, these variations do not need to be specifically examined. Indeed, the contrast between country variations and variations at a 'higher' level can be regarded as part of the evidence suggesting that there is no cultural gap between regions or between sub-regions: that point was made in the previous chapters. A spread of individual country results greater than the difference between regional or sub-regional averages means that there is little concentration of attitudes of the respondents at the regional or sub-regional levels. Such variations from country to country cannot simply be discarded as 'noise', so to speak, that is to say as if the global variations at the regional or the sub-regional level (the average variations at these levels among the individual countries, in effect) were the only ones giving a true picture of the reality.

There is no reason to discard distributions of answers at national level any more than to discard those obtained by averaging the national answers either on a regional or on a sub-regional basis. As a matter of fact, average regional or sub-regional distributions might perhaps more justifiably be discarded than national distributions, since they are in a sense more of a construct than are national results. Furthermore, it is not as if the national distributions were all widely spread out or at least spread out to the same extent across the range. As we saw, on the issue whether 'everyone should have the right to express an opinion...' (Q.208b), respondents of all the countries appear to be in close agreement, while on other issues, answers vary markedly from one country to another. If respondents from all the countries can be in near-agreement in some cases, differ somewhat in some others and differ markedly in yet others, the first task is surely to see whether some underlying patterns can be identified characterising the countries which are analysed here. It may not be possible in the process to provide explanations for the existence of these patterns, but some indications may be suggested of the reasons why respondents from the various countries react differently from each other irrespective of the regional or sub-regional groupings to which their countries belong.

III

Attitudinal variations at the country level

The attitudes of respondents to basic societal values must therefore be explored at country level after having been examined at regional and sub-regional levels. One might wish to undertake this exploration by using the questions themselves as the discriminating mechanisms and combine the results in the hope that patterns characteristic of each country will emerge. Yet, to be comprehensive, such an exploration would be laborious: it would entail examining 233 cases (thirteen questions for which replies come from eighteen countries, except for one question in China). When this is done, one would need to put the pieces together, so to speak, and find a way of reducing the information to a manageable level: this entails finding a means of grouping the cases without using regional or sub-regional variations as the instruments.

There are in reality two possible strategies. One consists in examining the extent to which, in each country, the replies to the questions are associated by means of factor analyses involving either all thirteen questions or merely the communitarian and human rights questions, if the socio-economic questions are regarded as belonging to a different 'realm'. One would then examine whether some patterns emerge and, if this is the case, group the countries on the basis of these patterns. Such an approach can help to show how related are the answers to the value questions at the country level, but it does not provide a measure or even a general sense of the spread of the answers in each case. Yet we do know that the spread at the level of individual country results is large: the spread must therefore be part of the overall assessment and it must be measured with respect to each question. Given that it is also valuable to discover how similar or different are the number and composition of the factors at play with respect to the eighteen countries, it seems necessary to use successively both approaches. In the first instance one should use the results of the factor analyses to determine the number and character of the dimensions according to which the various questions are spread among the countries of the study: a picture is provided in this way of the extent to which the various countries differ in terms of the way in which respondents associate the questions which were put to them. In a second stage, one can then use also the results of factor analyses to assess the spread with respect to each question by ranking country replies, not according to each question, but more parsimoniously according to those groups of questions which the factor analyses will have shown to be associated. These two approaches will be followed successively in this section.

The dimensions among which the answers to the questions fall in the various countries

To discover the number and character of the dimensions within which the questions on basic societal values fall in the countries of the study, factor analyses of all the questions were performed for each country. It would be surprising if the number and even more the composition of the factors should be the same for all eighteen countries: as a matter of fact, variations in number and composition will provide a rather more concrete picture of the way in which respondents perceive the nature of basic societal values. Three characteristics of these dimensions will help to provide that picture. First, the number of dimensions into which the thirteen basic societal values fall, a number which can be expected to vary from country to country, will show how closely connected or how disjointed these questions are in the minds of the respondents of particular countries. Second, by examining whether the answers to some questions tend to be located in the same dimension, in several, perhaps in many countries, one can discover how far the patterns which are observed in these countries are similar while those which emerge in other countries have different features. Third, one can then see whether the similarities within these patterns are sufficiently marked to justify the conclusion that genuine 'types' exist or whether there is a different pattern for almost every country of the study.

As we saw in Chapter 3, the answers to the thirteen questions fall within four dimensions when all the countries are analysed together as well as when they are examined at the level of each of the two regions, with the two human rights questions fully belonging to the same dimension, both in both regions and in each of the two regions (Q.208b and c), while the answers to the four socio-economic questions fall within one dimension only at the level of all the countries taken together and among East and Southeast Asian countries; among the Western European countries, on the other hand, these answers fall within two dimensions (Q.306a, b and g and Q.412b).

At the level of each country, however, the number of dimensions varies appreciably. When the thirteen questions are taken together, the number of dimensions into which the answers fall ranges from three to six. The extremes are constituted, on the one hand, by the Philippines and China – but, in the case of China, the analysis covers twelve questions only, since one of the human rights questions could not be asked – where answers fall within three dimensions, and, on the other, by France and Germany, where they fall into six. In between, there are five dimensions in nine countries and four dimensions in the remaining five. There is a marked regional contrast in this respect, the number of dimensions being appreciably smaller in the East and Southeast Asian countries. The thirteen questions fall into five dimensions in only three of the Asian countries (Singapore, Malaysia and Indonesia), while Spain is the only Western European country in which the thirteen questions give rise to four dimensions only.

There are also variations if the distribution of the answers to the four socio-economic questions and the distribution of the answers to the seven communitarian questions are examined separately. The answers to the four socio-economic questions fall within one dimension in three countries (all East and Southeast Asian), within two dimensions in fourteen countries and within three dimensions in Britain. The answers to the seven communitarian questions fall within two dimensions in ten countries and within three dimensions in eight countries, that distribution being also highly skewed on a regional basis: seven of the ten countries in which the communitarian questions fall into two dimensions are from East and Southeast Asia, while six of the eight countries in which the communitarian questions fall into three dimensions are from Western Europe. The three Western European countries in the 'minority' are Ireland, Italy and Spain; the two East and Southeast Asian countries in the 'minority' are Taiwan and Indonesia. If human rights and communitarian questions are then examined together, the answers to the nine questions fall within three dimensions in ten countries (seven of which are East and Southeast Asian) and within four dimensions in eight countries (six of which are Western European).

It is rather puzzling that the number of dimensions into which the answers to the questions fall should be larger in Western Europe than in

East and Southeast Asia. As a matter of fact, if there was to be a difference, the contrary might have been regarded as more 'normal': it might perhaps have seemed more difficult for respondents from East and Southeast Asian countries to come to terms with the location of either of the human rights questions, for instance, especially if one takes into account the point made at the end of Chapter 5 about the possible influence of the authoritarian character of the country on the attitudes of respondents in the polities concerned.

The nature of the division as well as the composition of the 'minority' in each case is puzzling as well. Thus, if answers given in most East and Southeast Asian countries tend to be spread over three dimensions only, it is not clear why Taiwan should be one of the two countries of the region in the 'four-dimension' 'minority'. In parallel, it is not clear either why Spain, and, if human rights and communitarian questions only are taken into account, Ireland and Italy, should be the three Western European countries in which the answers to the basic societal questions are spread over a smaller number of dimensions than in the other countries of the region. The socio-political characteristics of the three countries are not ostensibly simpler, to say the least, than those of the other countries of the region to which they belong.

There also appears to be a difference between the four socio-economic questions and the others. This is not only, or perhaps even so much, because the number of dimensions increases when all thirteen questions are analysed jointly. There is some increase, admittedly, of one dimension in nine countries (divided into four East and Southeast Asian and five Western European) and of two dimensions in six countries, two East and Southeast Asian (Singapore and Malaysia) and four Western European (Ireland, Italy, France and Germany), while there is no increase at all in three countries, all East and Southeast Asian, China, the Philippines and Thailand: this is particularly remarkable in the first two of these three countries, since the total number of dimensions within which the answers to the thirteen questions fall in these two countries is only three. On the other hand, it is somewhat puzzling that the number of dimensions should increase by two in six countries, with the result that, in France and Germany, the thirteen answers fall into six dimensions!

The dimensions of socio-economic questions

Meanwhile, the location of the four socio-economic questions within the overall dimensional space varies markedly. Thus, at the level of all eighteen countries taken together, the question relating to the choice between growth and the environment (Q.412b) belongs to a different dimension from the other three economic questions, but this is not so when the four socio-economic questions are examined on their own. Thus, too, the two questions relating to competition (Q.306a) and to the responsibility of the government for employment (Q.306b) are partly associated with the question concerned with the right of businesses to make as much profit as they wish (Q.306g) in East and Southeast Asia but not in Western Europe or overall. There is more: four different patterns are found at the level of individual countries. The question relating to the choice between growth and the environment (Q.412b) forms almost a dimension on its own in two East and Southeast Asian cases (Japan and Thailand). It is associated with the question relating to the responsibility of the state for jobs (Q.306b) in four Western European countries (France, Germany, Sweden and Italy) as well as overall for Western Europe. It is associated with the right of businesses to make as much profit as they wish (Q.306g) in seven countries (four Western European and three East and Southeast Asian) but, in Indonesia, the question related to the responsibility of the state for jobs stands in one dimension of its own, while the other three socio-economic questions are linked in the other dimension. Finally, in the British case, the support for competition (Q.306a) is associated with the support for the view that the state has a responsibility for jobs, while the responses to the other two questions constitute separate dimensions. These different patterns result in the socio-economic questions complicating the overall dimensional analysis and rendering the interpretation of the attitudes of respondents to these questions rather difficult.

Human rights and communitarian questions

There is greater consistency in the location of the nine questions relating to human rights and to communitarian value standpoints. These questions give rise to three dimensions at least and, in several cases, even to four, but country variations are smaller than with respect to the socio-economic questions. The main patterns are for the two human rights questions to be associated with each other and to form one dimension, although there are some exceptions; by and large, too, the answers to the communitarian questions fall into two or three dimensions. This leads in many cases to at least two questions being frequently associated with each other across the countries of the study and thus forming 'pairs'. Three characteristics of these pairs help to determine their robustness, the number of cases in which they occur, the number of cases in which they occupy on their own the whole or nearly the whole of one dimension and the number of cases in which they are associated with only one other attitudinal answer (Table 6.2).

The two human rights questions

Two pairs occur more frequently than the others: this is not altogether surprising given what has been pointed out in this and in previous chapters about the role of these questions in building the structure of the attitudes to basic societal values in the countries of this study. One of these two pairs is composed of the answers to the two human rights questions (Q.208b and c). The matter can only be observed for seventeen countries, since the question

Table 6.2 Cases of links between variables (number of countries)

	Links Occur	Do not occur	Entirely in one dimension		Alone or nearly alone	With one other variable	With more than more
			Yes	No			
East and Southeast Asia							
208b + c (out of 8 countries only)	5	3	3	2	4	1	0
306d + e	9	0	4	5	0	1	8
412d + e	6	3	2	4	0	0	6
Western Europe							
208b + c	9	0	5	4	6	2	1
306d + e	9	0	5	4	4	2	3
412d + e	7	2	3	4	1	0	6
Both regions							
208b + c (out of 17 countries only)	14	3	8	6	10	3	1
306d + e	18	0	9	9	4	3	11
412d + e	13	5	5	8	1	0	12

Notes
208b Right to express one's opinion
208c Right to organise public protest meetings
306d Do what government wants
306e Government usually knows best
412c Women's primary role in the home
412d Important to achieve consensus
412e Give extra influence to older people
412f Public interest before family
412g Individuals should strive for their own good more than society

relating to the right to organise protest meetings was not asked in China, but in sixteen of these, the answers to the two questions are associated in the same dimension; the seventeenth country is Taiwan. The fact that the answers to the two questions were not associated in that country partly accounts for there being four dimensions in Taiwan rather than three, though why the two questions are dissociated in that country is not immediately clear, although a suggestion as to what the reason might be was made earlier.[1]

There is thus a link between the answers to the two human rights questions in sixteen countries. That association takes place entirely in one dimension in nine countries and almost entirely in that one dimension in another two, while it is part of two dimensions in the other five[2]: this includes one case in which the incidence of one of the questions in the dimension is small. The distribution of the countries is skewed, in the same way as is skewed the distribution between 'three-' and 'four-dimension' countries. Six of the nine countries where the two questions are exclusively in one dimension and the two questions where they are nearly in one dimension only are Western European, the 'exception' being Ireland; only in three of the East and Southeast Asian countries, Japan, Korea and the Philippines, do the answers to the two questions fully belong to the same dimension. In Malaysia, Indonesia and Thailand, the two questions belong in part to one dimension and in part to others, while, in Singapore, although both questions are associated with each other in one of the dimensions, the association of one of these questions is not strong.

A substantial difference between East and Southeast Asian responses and Western European responses also emerges when examining whether the answers to the two human rights questions form a dimension on their own, nearly on their own or fully in combination with other questions. In four countries, all Western European, France, Sweden, Italy and Portugal, the two questions effectively constitute one dimension. In six other countries, three East and Southeast Asian, Japan, Korea and the Philippines, and three Western European, Britain, Germany and Greece, the answers to the two human rights questions are only associated in a minimal fashion with answers to some other questions. In Thailand, the association with other questions is a little stronger; in Ireland, Malaysia, Indonesia and even more Singapore, the association with other questions is substantial and/or one of both of the answers to the two 'human rights' questions are in part divided into two dimensions. The association between the two questions is thus substantial overall; but this association is particularly marked among Western European countries.

The two questions dealing with attitudes to the government

Among the seven communitarian questions, two are closely associated with each other and even seem to play a central part. Perhaps not surprisingly, these are the questions which concern the way in which respondents feel that citizens should relate to the government (Q.306d and e). That pair is even more closely linked than the human rights 'pair' in that the answers to these two questions form practically the core of one of the dimensions in both the 'three-dimension' and the 'four-dimension' countries. First, they belong entirely or almost entirely to the same dimension in twelve of the eighteen countries. Five of these are East and Southeast Asian and seven Western European: the distribution is thus once again skewed to an extent in favour of Western Europe, but not to the same extent as the equivalent distribution with respect to the two human rights questions. Second, in the other six countries, four East and Southeast Asian (Taiwan, Singapore, Thailand and Indonesia) and two Western European (Ireland and Spain), the answers to the two questions are also associated, though not as uniquely as in the case of the first group of countries; but there is no case in which there is no association at all between the two answers. Third, admittedly, there is no case in which the answers to these two sets of questions form a dimension on their own *alone*: however, in seven cases, one East and Southeast Asian (the Philippines) and six Western European (Britain, Ireland, France, Spain, Portugal and Greece), the two questions are associated with only very partial elements of the responses to other questions. The distribution is thus, here again, skewed appreciably in favour of the Western European countries. Finally, in eight cases, five from East and Southeast Asia and three from Western Europe, the answers to the two 'role of government' questions are associated only in a limited manner in the same dimension with the answers to other questions, while in the last three countries, all from East and Southeast Asia (Japan, Singapore and Thailand), the answers to these two questions are associated to a substantial extent in the same dimension with the answers to a number of other questions.

The association between the role to be played by consensus and the influence to be given to old people

A further set of two answers is also linked to an extent in the responses given at the level of individual countries. This pair is composed of the answers given to the questions asking what importance should be given to consensus in society and whether older people should exercise more influence (Q.412d and e). The answers to these two questions are associated to an extent in fourteen countries: in ten of them the association is very strong, while it is more limited in four; in four countries (three from East and Southeast Asia – China, Taiwan and Thailand – and in Portugal), the answers to the two questions do not belong to the same dimension at all. The marked link between the question asking about the role of consensus and the question asking about 'the influence which old people should hold' suggests that, in the minds of many respondents at least, these two characteristics correspond to a similar 'approach' to decision-making in society. In this case, the attitudes of respondents in Western European and East and Southeast Asian countries do not appear to differ: the link between the two questions is found in most countries in the two regions and the 'exceptions' to the link are also found in both regions.

The association of the answers to these two questions in the same dimension rarely means, however, that these two questions form the core of a dimension. This occurs only in Western European countries, principally in Germany and Sweden, as well as, but in association with one other question, in Britain, Ireland and France. Elsewhere, in particular in Italy but also in four East and Southeast Asian countries, Japan, Korea, Singapore and the Philippines, views about consensus and about old people are also associated in the same dimension with views about a substantial number of other basic societal values. Once more, respondents from East and South

East Asia are found to answer in a less 'streamlined' or 'structured' manner than respondents from Western Europe in the sense that their answers can be described as 'consistent' in terms of their 'dimensional location'.

The more limited – or even absence of – dimensional consistency with respect to the other three basic societal value questions

The way the other three questions combine with each other or with the questions which have been already examined is less definite. On the one hand, there is a substantial degree of association in the same dimension between the question dealing with the role of women and the question concerned with 'striving for one's own good' (Q.412c and g). Only in six countries (four of which are Western European) is there no association at all between responses to these two questions: the other twelve countries are evenly divided. In six of these (four of which are also Western European) the answers to these two questions are exclusively located or are located almost entirely in one dimension; in the other six (five of which are from East and Southeast Asia) the answers are located partly in one dimension but also partly in another. There are no cases in which these two questions form a dimension of their own, though this is close to being the case in Britain, France, Germany and Sweden. On the other hand, in China, the answers to the question whether the 'women's role is in the home' are associated negatively but exclusively with those to the question about the freedom to express opinions, which is the one human rights question being asked in that country (Q.208b). This is also the one case in which the question relating to the role of women is associated with another question only except for the question as to whether one should be 'striving for one's own good' (Q.412g).

The answers to the question relating to the choice to be made between the 'public interest' and 'family obligations' (Q.412f) are the ones which are least associated with the responses to any other question, although, as we saw in Chapter 2, at the regional level, that question is part of the same dimension as the question on consensus and the one relating to the influence which older people should have (Q.412d and e). These answers are also located exclusively or almost entirely in one dimension in two countries only, Britain and Spain. Somewhat surprisingly, the answers to that question are associated with the responses to the two human rights questions in Ireland. This suggests that, of all the questions, this is perhaps the one which is most 'country-idiosyncratic'. The interpretation of the role of the family may well vary appreciably, as we had occasion to note in Chapter 4, when it was found that the countries of the North of Western Europe differed from those of the South, but that, in both sub-regions, the answers of respondents were spread out widely across the range and that French respondents differed markedly from those of other countries.

Thus, if there is a 'structure' of the answers to that question and to an extent of the answers to the other two questions which have just been examined, it is not based on regional or sub-regional characteristics only, but it corresponds to attitudes which have developed in the context of the individual states.

In contrast with the four socio-economic questions, the questions concerned with human rights and the two communitarian questions concerned with 'the way citizens "should" react to the government' are those which lead most clearly to 'dimensional consistency' across and among the states which are the object of this study. Meanwhile, the two questions dealing with the role of consensus and with 'the influence which old people should hold in decision-making' also contribute, though to an extent only, to the building of a 'structured' set of dimensions. To a varying extent, admittedly, answers given by Western Europeans are less spread out across the dimensions than are the answers given by East and Southeast Asians. The analysis of the answers to human rights and communitarian questions on a country basis thus provides a basis for valuable distinctions to be made about the way the responses to these attitudinal questions are distributed.

Types of dimensional structure on a country basis

The association between replies to human rights and communitarian questions in individual dimensions can serve as a basis to determine whether the ways in which these questions are answered form recognisable types. As there is no consistency in the dimensional structure of answers to the socio-economic questions, however, it is not meaningful to take them into account to discover whether a number of types can be identified: it is better to concentrate on the communitarian and human rights questions only.

To determine what the pattern of the distribution of the answers to these questions may be, one can start from what might be regarded as the simplest arrangement, namely the one in which (1) the answers to both human rights questions (referred to in Chapter 2 as the *liberalism* questions) belong to and constitute alone one dimension (2) the answers to both questions relating to the attitudes to have *vis-à-vis* the government (referred to in Chapter 2 as the *government restraint* questions) belong to and constitute alone a second dimension and (3) the answers to the other five communitarian questions are jointly located in a third dimension. Where such a pattern prevails, the questions on human rights and on the attitudes to 'what the role of government should be' constitute the 'keys' to the structure of the system. These four questions have been regarded in this chapter and indeed earlier in this volume as different in character from the other five: it seems therefore logical that the simplest but also most 'streamlined' model should give a special place to these questions.

This pattern does indeed characterise four countries, Korea, the Philippines and, by and large, Italy and Spain, though some elements of the replies to other questions are associated with one of the two 'key' dimensions in these last two countries. In all four, it will be recalled, the nine communitarian and human rights questions give rise to three dimensions only. Interestingly, these four countries divide equally between East and Southeast Asia and Western Europe.

That simple pattern can be complicated somewhat in two ways without losing its general character altogether. It can first be rendered more complex by way of a division of the group of five questions which constitute the third dimension in the 'pure' type. This second type is found to apply to four countries, all of which are Western European. In Britain, France, Germany and Sweden, the last two dimensions are (fairly neatly) divided between, on the one hand, the answers to the question relating to the role of women (Q.412c) and to the question relating to whether individuals should 'strive for their own good or for that of society' (Q.412g) (described in Chapter 2 as the *social relations* questions) and, on the other, the three remaining questions (described in Chapter 2 as the *decision-making* questions).

A second variation from the 'pure' type characterises four countries, in two of which, Malaysia and Ireland, there are three dimensions only while, in the other two, Portugal and Greece, there are four dimensions. In these countries, the answers to the two 'key' questions can be said to be 'polluted' in that, in part, the answers to other questions also belong to one or both of these dimensions. Portugal and Greece are closest to the 'pure type' in that only one dimension, that in which the answers to the 'government restraint questions' are to be found, is 'polluted' in this way; in Malaysia and Ireland, on the other hand, both what is mainly the 'liberalism' dimension and what is mainly the 'government restraint' dimension are 'polluted'. Moreover, in the Irish case, the human rights question which relates to the right to organise protest meetings belongs in large part only to the 'government restraint' dimension. With this third type, one is therefore already at an appreciable distance from the original 'perfectly streamlined' structure.

Six countries remain, all of which are from East and Southeast Asia: in these the pattern of dimensions follows less closely or even not at all the characteristics of the 'pure' type. Japan is the country of the group in which that type is most nearly approximated, however, in that the answers to the 'liberalism' questions form the whole of one dimension, while the two 'government restraint' questions do not form a dimension on their own at all, but are associated with the answers to the questions relating to consensus, to the influence to be played by old people and to the choice to be made between the public interest and family (Q.412d, e and f). The answers to the questions relating to the role of women and to whether one should be 'striving for one's own good or for the good of society' (Q.412c and g) constitute the third dimension. Thus, the 'government restraint' questions do not appear to be regarded in Japan as 'key' questions needing to be separated from the others.

Yet the answers given by Japanese respondents bear some relationship with the 'pure' model as at least the 'liberalism' questions form a separate dimension. This is not the case in the last five countries. In two of them, Thailand and to an extent Singapore, the human rights questions belong to the same dimension, but the answers to these questions are also associated in part with the answers to other questions. Meanwhile, the answers to the questions relating to what 'the role of government should be' are divided between the last two dimensions which, moreover, include parts of all the other questions without much distinction being made between these questions. In Taiwan and Indonesia, the situation is the reverse, in that the 'government restraint' questions tend to form most of one dimension, but the answers to the human rights questions are divided between the other two dimensions together with the answers to all the other questions. Finally, in China, the answers to the human rights question which was asked in that country is associated (negatively) with the answers to the question related to the role of women, while the answers to the 'government restraint' questions are in a second dimension, but partially associated with answers to other questions, while the third dimension includes the rest of the answers (Table 6.3).

There are thus a number of ways, at the country level, in which the answers to the human rights and communitarian questions are linked to

Table 6.3 Four models of dimensions linking human rights and communitarian questions

---

1 *'Pure' model*
  Two key dimensions
    1 'Human rights'
    2 'Citizen and government'
  +1 for the rest
    3 All (or nearly all) other variables
  Countries S. Korea, Philippines, Italy, Spain

2 *Variation I*
  Two key dimensions
    1 'Human rights'
    2 'Citizen and government'
  +2 for the rest
    3 & 4 All (or nearly all) other variables
  Countries Britain, France, Germany, Sweden

3 *Variation II*
    1 'human rights' + others
    2 'citizen and government' + others
    3 or 3 and 4 the rest
  Countries Malaysia, Ireland, Portugal, Greece

4 *Variation III*
  'Human rights' divided, 'citizen and government' together
    Thailand, Singapore
  'Citizen and government' divided, 'human rights' together
    Indonesia, Taiwan
  China (one variable on 'human rights' only)
  Japan ('human rights' alone)

---

each other. In the majority of countries, however, most respondents appear to believe that the human rights questions form a 'pair' and the questions relating to the role to be ascribed to the government form another 'pair', although the arrangement is less tight in some of the countries where these pairs exist. The pattern is less uniform with respect to the other five communitarian questions; indeed, in a sizeable minority of countries, there is simply no consistency at all. A substantial difference can also be found between the two regions: for the respondents in the majority of the East and Southeast Asian countries, the part played by the two human rights questions and by the two questions relating to the role to be ascribed to the government is not apparently as central as it is for the respondents in the majority of Western European countries, perhaps because the Left–Right dimension plays less of a part in structuring political attitudes of citizens in East and Southeast Asia than it does in Western Europe. Moreover, there is no apparent consistency at all with respect to the answers to the four socio-economic questions and this lack of consistency affects Western European and East and Southeast Asian countries to the same extent.

A partial ranking of the country replies on the basis of the four dimensions of human rights and communitarian values

The 'types' which have just been identified relate to the way in which the replies to the nine human rights and communitarian questions are variously associated in a number of dimensions. They do not assess the extent to which, within the countries belonging to a given 'type', replies differ in terms of the strength of the support or opposition to a particular value. That is to say that they do not measure or even assess in any way the *spread* which might be there among the countries with respect to the answers given to particular questions. Yet, as was repeatedly noticed, that spread matters as it is large, in both regions, in connection with most questions. As a result, no fully realistic picture can be drawn of the way respondents from the various countries react to the questions which were posed to them merely by considering the number of dimensions of the answers to the human rights and communitarian questions in each country. In particular, it is not possible to assess realistically reactions to 'Asian values' across the eighteen countries as what is needed is a method which makes it possible to distinguish among the countries in terms of the strength of the association of the replies to particular questions. In order to move at least partially in that direction, an attempt has therefore to be made to obtain a measure of the spread of the answers given in the various countries, the key problem being that such a result must be obtained without needing to handle an unmanageably large mass of data which could not then easily be interpreted.

To avoid having to handle such an unmanageable mass of data, two difficulties have to be overcome. The first stems from the fact that even nine questions (assuming that one concentrates on human rights and communitarian questions) form too large a number to give the opportunity to 'have a feel' for the results simply by looking at them, for instance in a series of scattergrammes. Factor analyses provide at least a partial solution to this difficulty, as one can reduce the number of observations by looking at the combined answers falling into a single dimension. Moreover, it was found, at the level of the two regions, that no more than four dimensions covered the answers to these nine questions and it was also found in Chapter 2 that, whether when there are three dimensions only (in the case of East and Southeast Asia) or when there are four (as in the case of Western Europe), there is robustness in the dimensions, even if four, rather than three, have to be taken into account: these dimensions can thus be used to examine jointly the answers to the questions belonging to each of these dimensions, even though, at the level of each country, the distribution of the questions in the various dimensions may differ in part. This means looking jointly at the two human rights questions forming the 'liberalism' dimension (Q.208b and c), at the two questions concerned with the attitudes to hold *vis-à-vis* the government forming the 'government restraint' dimension (Q.306d and e), at the three questions concerned, respectively, with the role to be given to consensus (Q.412d), with the role to be given to older people (Q.412e) and with the relative importance of family and the public interest (Q.412f) which form the 'decision-making' dimension and at the two questions relating to the place of women in society (Q.412c) and to the choice to be made between striving for one's own good or that of society (Q.412g) which form the 'social relations' dimension.

The second difficulty to overcome concerns the ranking of the answers to the questions corresponding to the dimensions which have just been described. As ranking helps to assess spread, a formula, preferably a straightforward one, has to be adopted. The simplest method seems to be to relate to each other the answers to the questions belonging to the same dimension on the basis of percentages of agreement minus percentages of disagreement and to record the results in a two-dimensional space; in the case of the dimension of decision-making, there would have to be three such figures, since three questions are involved. To simplify, are recorded here only the position of the countries with respect to two of the three questions, the question on consensus and the question dealing with 'the influence which old people should hold'. This means that there are four figures overall.

On the basis of this formula, Figure 6.1 provides a picture of the relationship between rankings on 'liberalism' (Q.208b and c). Figure 6.2 provides a picture of the relationship between the rankings on attitudes on 'government restraint' (Q.306d and e). Figure 6.3 provides a picture of the relationship between rankings on the attitudes to consensus and rankings on the attitudes which one should have with respect to the role of old people in 'decision-making' (Q.412d and e). Figure 6.4 provides a picture of the relationship between rankings on attitudes concerning the role of women and attitudes relating to the preference to be given to 'striving for one's own good or being primarily concerned with the society' (the 'social

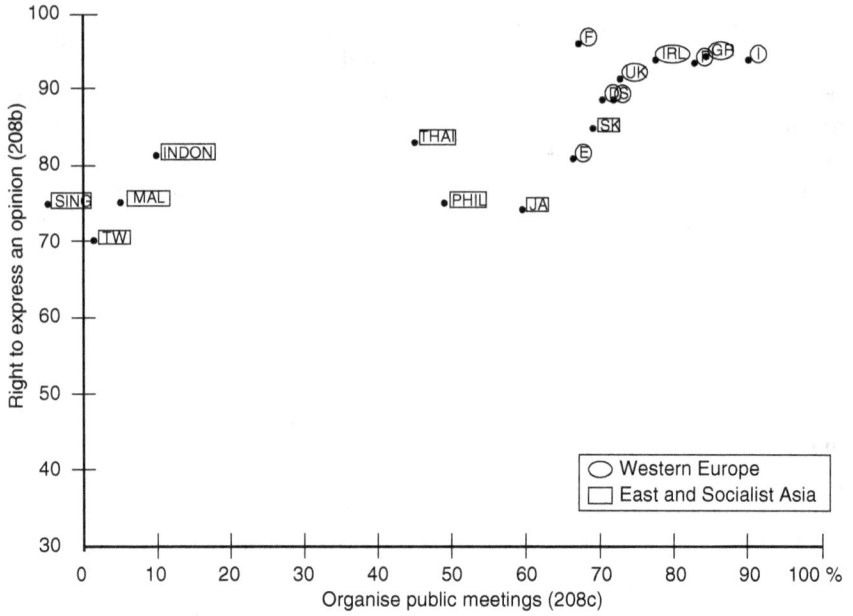

Figure 6.1 The relationship between responses on the two *liberalism* questions.

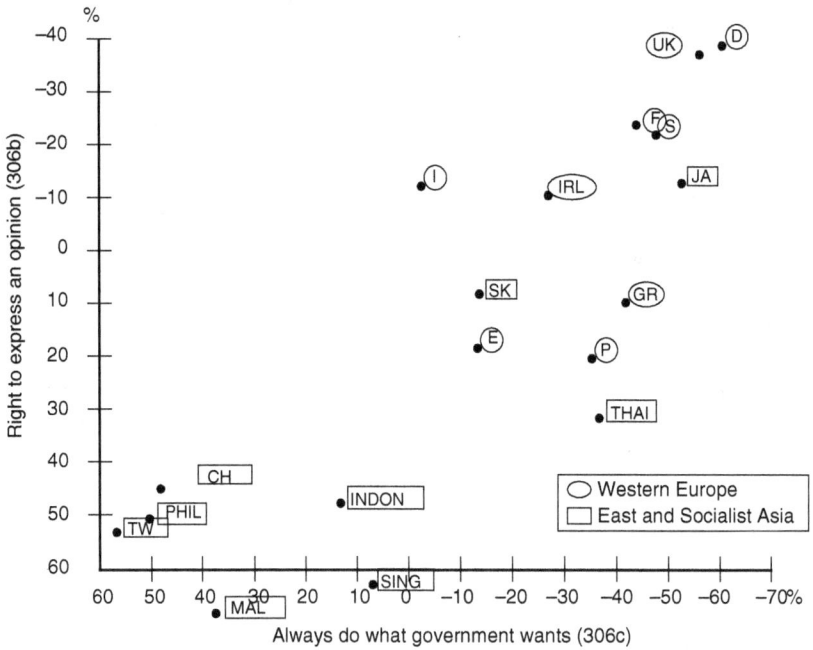

Figure 6.2 The relationship between responses on the two *government restraint* questions.

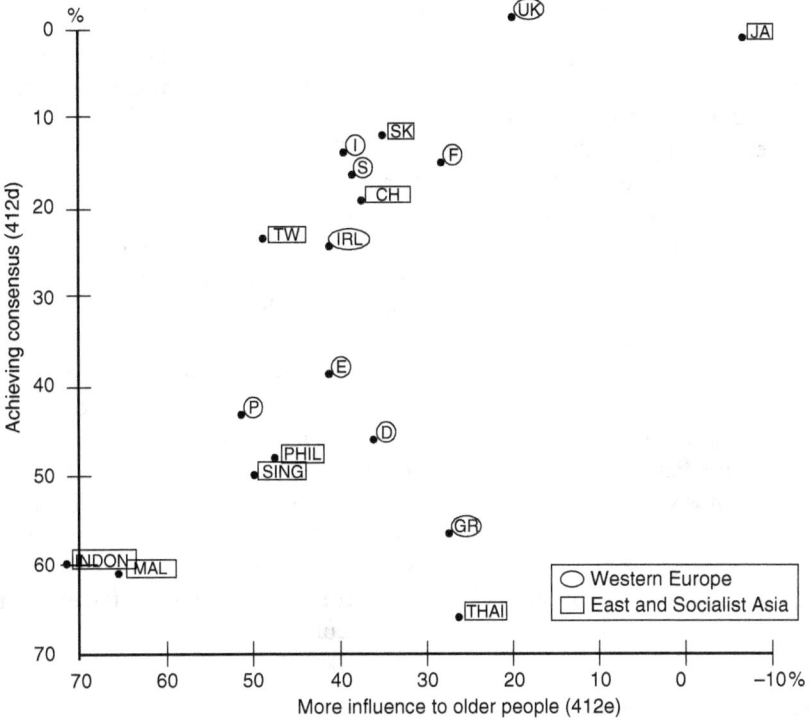

Figure 6.3 The relationship between responses on the two *decision-making* questions (consensus and influence which old people should have).

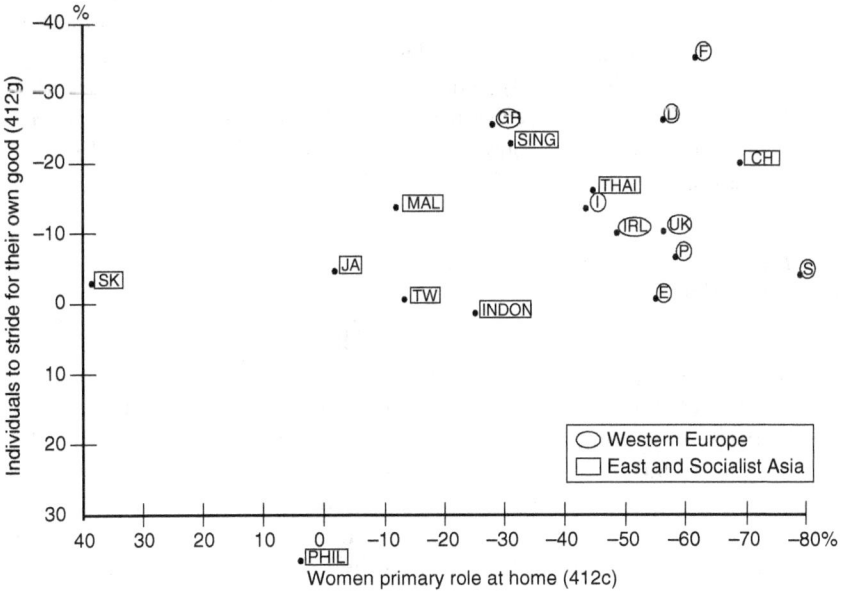

Figure 6.4 The relationship between responses on the two *social relations* questions.

relations' dimension (Q.412c and g)). In all four cases, there is a relationship between the two variables, as was to be expected given that these variables give rise to a common dimension.

These four figures show, at the level of individual countries, both the extent to which there is a similar tendency or not and the extent to which there is a limited inter-regional relationship. As was to be expected from what was found in Chapter 3, Figures 6.1 and 6.2 show that the inter-regional difference is strong, while it is weaker in the other figures, for example in Figure 6.3. Moreover, given that the relationship between the variable concerned with the choice 'between striving for one's own good and that of society' (Q.412g) and the other variable of the social relations factor, on the other, is negative, the direction of the regression line moves down from left to right in Figure 6.4 instead of up as it does in Figures 6.1, 6.2 and 6.3.

The four figures make it also possible to discover three key aspects of the relationships which give an image of the dispersion among the variables. These are (1) the extent to which the distribution is linear or not, (2) the nature of the groupings of the countries in the space, especially whether there is separation or concentration in the distribution of the countries and (3) the extent to which the same countries are found in particular positions in the space.

Is the dispersion linear?

A linear dispersion indicates that a monotonic relationship exists among the variables which belong to the factor under consideration. This is to an extent the case with respect to the 'liberalism' dimension (Figure 6.1); this is even more the case with respect to the 'government restraint' dimension (Figure 6.2); this is also the case, but less so, with respect to the 'social relations' dimension (Figure 6.4). The dispersion is not linear, on the other hand, with respect to the 'decision-making' dimension, at least in the context of the two variables (consensus and possible influence of old people) which are recorded in Figure 6.3.[3]

Are the countries associated to each other closely or separately?

There is no case in which the countries are all closely grouped to each other, the nearest example being that of the 'social relations' dimension which links attitudes concerning the role of women to attitudes relating to the choice between striving for one's own good and that of the society (Q.412c and g) (Figure 6.6): yet, even in this case, distances between the countries' position are relatively large. There is a partial linkage, however, with respect to the two human rights questions, as can be seen in Figure 6.1, and to a more limited extent with respect to the two questions on the attitude to have *vis-à-vis* the government, as can be seen in Figure 6.2, as some of the countries are close to each other and form a compact group, that group being rather distant from the other countries. This is less the case in the other two dimensions, as can be seen in Figures 6.3 and 6.4.

Which countries belong to the various 'sub-groups'?

Let us examine how the 'sub-groups' of countries are composed in each of the figures. In Figure 6.1, which provides a representation of the distribution of countries with respect to the 'liberalism' dimension, the countries are fairly neatly divided into three groups. At one end and well separated from the other countries, are four East and Southeast Asian countries (Singapore, Malaysia, Indonesia and Taiwan) (the attitudes of Chinese respondents are not recorded since the question on protest meetings could not be asked): these four countries are those in which the respondents take the least liberal line, especially with respect to the matter of allowing protest meetings. At the other end are also four countries, all Western European (Ireland, Italy, Portugal and Greece) in which respondents take the most liberal position, especially also on the question of allowing protest meetings. In between, but closer to the second than to the first group, is a mix of four East and Southeast Asian countries (Korea, Thailand, the Philippines and Japan) and of five Western European countries (Britain, Germany, Sweden, Spain and France). There are thus East and Southeast Asian countries at one end and Western European countries at the other: this indicates that 'Asian values' are supported by a majority of respondents in some countries of East and Southeast Asia, while 'Western values' are supported by a majority of respondents in some countries of Western Europe, but the fact that there are also many countries between these two groups also shows that, in many countries, the majority of respondents do not share either of the extreme standpoints.

The distribution of countries in Figure 6.2, which is concerned with 'government restraint' (Q.306d and e), has, not surprisingly, a somewhat analogous shape, at least in that at one end six East and Southeast Asian countries (the same four plus the Philippines and China) do not wish to restrain government markedly and in that there is a separation between these and the other countries. However, at the other end, the four Western European countries which most favour restraint on government, Britain, Germany, France and Sweden, are not very distant to some others, in particular Japan and Ireland. There is thus some similarity in the shape; there is also some similarity in the countries concerned at the Asian end, but not at the Western European end. What can therefore only be said is that four East and Southeast Asian countries are rather lukewarm on both liberalism and government restraint. On the other hand, there are East and Southeast Asian countries in the middle – Korea and Thailand, while Japan is close to the 'government restraint' pole; moreover, although none of the Western European countries is either very illiberal or substantially against government restraint, the positions which they occupy on the two dimensions differ substantially.

Figure 6.4 bears some relationship with the previous two cases in terms of the shape of the distribution, but the distribution of the countries in the space is very different. The extreme 'women in the home position', combined with a pro-self interest position, is held, at some considerable distance from each other, however, by Korea and the Philippines. As was noted earlier, there is no real separation among the other countries, but a group of four East and Southeast Asian countries (Japan, Malaysia, Taiwan and Indonesia) shares a middle-of-the road position on both variables, while the bulk of the countries are in a fairly large circle and include all the Western European and three East and Southeast Asian countries (Singapore, Thailand and China), the Philippines being markedly distant from all the other countries. Thus Malaysia, Taiwan and Indonesia are this time associated with Japan, while Korea is extreme, as least in terms of 'traditional' attitudes towards women. On the other hand, respondents from Singapore and even more from China are close to respondents from Western Europe in not agreeing with the view that the place of women is in the home. While a group of four East and Southeast Asian countries is fairly close together, it is not composed of the same countries as the compact group of countries from that region found in Figure 6.1.

The difference is also marked, perhaps even more marked, between the reactions to the 'decision-making' variables and the reactions to the variables which compose the three dimensions which have just been examined. In Figure 6.3, East and Southeast Asian countries are spread out, with Indonesia and Malaysia alone at the bottom left, while two groups of countries of that region are closely associated to two groups of Western European countries.

Overall, East and Southeast Asian countries are to be found at one end of the spectrum and Western European countries at the other: this suggests that there is indeed a contrast between the 'pro-Asian values' East with the 'anti-Asian values' West (Table 6.4). Yet only Indonesia and Malaysia are fully 'consistent' in this respect, as can be seen from the number of times

Table 6.4 Number of times a country is at the Asian and European ends of country groupings

| Number of times a country is at the | |
East and Southeast Asian 'end'	Western European 'end'
Indonesia 4	Britain 2
Malaysia 4	Sweden 2
Singapore 3	Japan 2
Taiwan 3	Germany 2
Philippines 2	France 2
Korea 1	Ireland 1
Japan 1	Italy 1
China 1	Portugal 1
	Greece 1
	China 1

in which the countries of the study are at one or the other of the two extreme positions in Figures 6.1 to 6.2.

(The only countries which do not appear in this list are Thailand and Spain, whose respondents hold a more 'middle' position on all questions.)

The difference between the two sides comes essentially from the score obtained by Indonesia and Malaysia, both of which are always part of the group which is at the 'Asian values' end, followed by Singapore and Taiwan, which are at that end in three cases out of four. There is greater 'turnover' at the Western values end, since no country finds itself more than twice in that position. The overall picture indicates that some of the East and Southeast Asian countries have a 'peculiar' relationship with respect to 'Asian values', as some Western European countries have with Western values. Since there are these peculiarities, belonging to a region cannot be the sole explanatory factor: the state would also appear to play a significant part.

No simple overall formula links countries to region: country patterns are thus in many respects 'idiosyncratic'. First, configurations vary from being linear to being rather widely dispersed in the space and from being fairly regularly spaced out to being separated by substantial gaps. The simplest and most easily recognisable of these structures is that which relates to the two dimensions of 'liberalism' and of 'government restraint' (Figures 6.1 and 6.2). In these two cases, the shape of the distribution is broadly linear *and* there is a gap between two groups of countries. The first group includes a number, four in the first case, six in the second, of East and Southeast Asian countries; the rest of the countries are in the second group. With respect to these two dimensions, as we know, the association between regional distribution and 'pro-Asian values' positions is the most clear-cut.

On the other hand, that association becomes much thinner in connection with the other two dimensions: the pattern of the distribution of countries is then not linear and countries are spread out more widely across the two-dimensional space. There is then also less of a gap between the groups or, if there is a gap, countries are dotted about over a large part of the whole space. There is still a tendency for a number of East and Southeast Asian countries to constitute a bloc or 'cluster' at one end, but that bloc is then an 'island' separated from several other 'islands' which include either Western European countries or countries of both regions. There is thus more of a mix, although the mix is generally limited to a minority of the East and Southeast Asian groups. It is therefore in part because the distance between that rather compact 'cluster' of East and Southeast Asian countries and the rest of the countries is smaller that, ultimately, the difference between the two regions is not very large.

Overall, the nature of the distribution of the East and Southeast Asian countries in the space is different from that of the Western European countries. In East and Southeast Asia, there is a 'cluster' of a number of countries (usually about four), located at one end of the space and separated from the rest of the countries of either region, with the other countries of the region being sometimes at considerable distance from that 'cluster', but the country composition of the cluster at one end of the space varies appreciably among the four dimensions. It can include nearly all the countries of the region, including in one case Japan, with two exception only, those of Thailand, which never occupies a polar position, and of Korea, whose respondents are particularly 'traditional' with respect to the role of women (Figure 6.4). Only two countries are always part of the cluster, however, Malaysia and Indonesia, a somewhat surprising 'pair': these are the two countries whose respondents support most consistently a 'pro-Asian values' position, though with the proviso that the respondents of both these countries also take a most 'anti-Asian values' position with respect to the choice between striving for one's own good rather and that of the society (Q.412g).[4]

The way Western European countries are distributed in the space is different. There is no cluster, but a rather amorphous and 'nebulous' set, a set which is amorphous and nebulous because countries are not located in any systematic manner with respect to each other and are also in general rather distant from each other. There is only one exception, that of the 'decision-making' dimension, in which seven of the nine countries belong to one of two groups, each of these including or being close to East and Southeast Asian countries: this distribution is due in large part, but not exclusively, to sharply distinct attitudes among respondents of Western European countries with respect to the consensus question. With respect to the other three dimensions, Western European countries are appreciably less likely to include a set of countries which react in the same fashion with respect even to two dimensions, let alone with respect to more than two. Thus the Western European countries are often distant from each other and at least some of the East and Southeast countries tend to become mixed with the somewhat 'nebulous' set which the Western European countries constitute: more than in the case of East and Southeast Asia, this distribution poses therefore the question of the extent to which specific characteristics of individual countries play a part in accounting for the way in which respondents react to 'Asian values'.

* * * * *

The examination of the answers to the basic societal values questions at the level of individual countries shows that there are substantial variations at that level over and above any variations which have been found to occur at the level of regions and of subdivisions of regions. There are regional differences since the extent to which there is pattern consistency depends in part on the region to which a country belongs, as is particularly the case in connection with the human rights questions and the questions concerned with 'government restraint': but this is true only in part. Indeed, even on these issues, the regional impact never leads to a straightforward division pitting the countries of one region against the countries of the other. There are at least 'minority' countries in the two regions and these behave in the same way as the 'majority' of the other region.

The fact that important differences emerge at the level of individual countries indicates that, as was already pointed out in the introductory chapter, nation-states have at least a significant effect on the attitudes of citizens. That this should be the case may not be surprising, but exactly how and why this effect occurs is less obvious. Even if it seems unlikely that an answer to that question can be given in this volume and while another volume looks more closely at the relationship between *The State and the Citizen*, it is surely important to examine already, in the concluding chapter, some of the reasons which may play a part in this respect and, more generally, to assess what the significance of 'Asian values' may be in a context in which reactions to these values appear to vary sharply according to particular issues.

7   Conclusion

The inquiry which has been conducted here has identified problems about political culture, which are specific to the two regions examined in this study as well as problems which relate to the general characteristics of political culture. The specific problems have been mentioned throughout this volume: the starting points of the analysis were the strongly worded statements made by some Asian politicians as well as by scholars and other commentators from both Asia and the West. It had been said that basic societal values were profoundly different in the two regions and, according to some, that they were different because they were superior. We need to return to the findings which have emerged from the survey of the citizens of the eighteen countries analysed here to bring together some of the key points which have emerged. We need also, however, to broaden the context of the discussion and consider what the study of the attitudes of these citizens from the two regions suggests about the notion of 'Asian values' as it is usually referred to. This concluding chapter looks successively at these two aspects.

I

What can and cannot be justifiably stated about similarities and differences in the political culture of the two regions

The analysis of the eighteen country data leaves a number of questions only partly answered and rather difficult to interpret; it does answer some questions, however. The questions which are answered can at least help to settle some of the controversies which had arisen as a result of what were purely speculative remarks, since no empirical base had previously been at the disposal of scholars. Before examining what has not been settled, which will naturally lead to the consideration of the general questions which this study poses, we need to summarise what appears to be settled. These points relate to what are probably the two key aspects of the problem, namely the substance of the findings and the levels – regional, sub-regional or state – at which similarities and differences can be found to emerge.

The substance of the differences: a division of opinion, but not a contrast

The study was based on thirteen questions, seven communitarian, two human rights and four socio-economic. These divided into four factors which were labelled in Chapter 2, namely attitudes to the 'political system', to the 'decision-making', to 'individualism' and to 'socio-economic governance'. As the analysis progressed, however, it emerged that the four socio-economic questions did not constitute a homogeneous dimension, at any rate when they were examined jointly with the other questions, despite the fact that, on their own, at any rate overall and in the nine East and Southeast Asian countries, they did. On the other hand, factor analyses limited to the nine communitarian and human rights questions identified dimensions which were more 'resistant'. Three factors were discovered when all eighteen countries were examined jointly; these same three factors, each of which covering the same questions, were identified when the nine East and Southeast Asian countries were examined separately: there were four factors when the Western European countries were examined separately, but the only difference was that in East and Southeast Asia, five communitarian questions belonged to the same factor, while in Western Europe they were split into two factors. On this basis, the nine communitarian and human rights questions could be said to be divided into a '*liberalism*' factor, a '*government restraint*' factor, a '*decision-making*' factor and a '*social relations*' factor.

The key question was whether the results of the survey of the eighteen countries did or did not suggest that there was a major division of opinion between respondents of the two regions with respect to these nine questions, indeed as well as with respect to the four socio-economic questions. The simplest answer is that there is some division of opinion, but whether that division of opinion is a major one is at least arguable.

What is straightforward is the following. On one of the human rights questions (that which deals with the freedom of expression (Q.208b)) and on two socio-economic questions, those which deal with competition and with the responsibility of the government to provide jobs (Q.306a and b), there are very large overall majorities in both regions. On two other questions, a relatively small overall majority of the respondents (between 58 and 53 per cent) agree in both regions with the proposition put to them, namely that older people should have more influence (Q.412e) and that a good environment is better than economic growth (Q.412b). There is no overall majority in either region (while a large group of respondents 'neither agree nor disagree' or do not know) about whether one should strive for one's own good or for that of the society (Q.412g). Finally, on the question concerned with consensus (Q.412d), there is the smallest possible overall majority in favour of the proposition among East and Southeast Asian respondents (51 per cent) and no overall majority in the other region: however, as

45 per cent of the Western Europeans take the same view, it is difficult not to treat that case as one of equality among the two regions. Thus, in seven out of thirteen questions, three socio-economic (out of four), one human rights (out of two) and three communitarian (out of seven), there is, in reality, no difference between the attitudes of respondents in the two regions (Table 7.1).

The other side of the picture is therefore constituted by six questions: but these cases are not entirely straightforward, in large part because of the substantial proportion of respondents who do not take a definite position. In no case is an absolute majority of respondents in one region pitted against, so to speak, those in the other region. The six questions fall into three categories: (1) in four cases, there is an absolute majority for the proposition in one region, but no absolute majority against it: only a minority of respondents takes the opposite view; (2) in one case, there is an absolute majority on both sides in favour of the proposition (as it is presented, that is to say in this case against the 'pro-Asian values' position),

Table 7.1 Distribution of 'pro-' and 'anti-Asian values' standpoints (percentages)

	East and Southeast Asia			Western Europe		
	'Pro' AV	'Against' AV	Neither or DK	'Pro' AV	'Against' AV	Neither or DK
208b	4	82	14	2	93	5
208c	21	52	27	7	79	24
306e	56	17	27	30	41	29
306d	42	31	27	16	54	30
412d	51	14	35	45	17	38
412e	58	16	26	53	17	30
412f	29	42	29	48	24	28
412c	30	46	24	16	69	15
412g	34	31	35	39	28	33
306a	85	4	11	85	4	11
306g	52	20	28	35	34	31
306b	86	2	12	84	5	11
412b	58	14	28	58	12	30

Notes
208b Right to express one's opinion
208c Right to organise public protest meetings
306e Government usually knows best
306d Do what government wants
412d Important to achieve consensus
412e Give extra influence to older people
412f Public interest before family
412c Women's primary role in the home
412g Individuals should strive for their own good more than society
306a Competition good
306g Society better if businesses free to make profits
306b Responsibility of government to provide jobs or social welfare
412b Good environment more important than economic growth

but that absolute majority is much smaller in one region than in the other; (3) finally, in one case, there is no absolute majority for either proposition in either region, but the difference between the size of these 'minorities' is very large.

The first situation is that of the two 'government restraint' questions (Q.306d and e): a majority of the Western Europeans is against the view that one should do what the government wants, but only a minority of all the respondents from East and Southeast Asia feel the contrary. The situation is the reverse with respect to whether 'the government usually knows best'. That last situation also characterises the replies to the only socio-economic question which has not been mentioned so far, namely the question concerned with whether businesses should be free to make as much profit as they wish (Q.306g). Finally, a very large majority of the Western European respondents (69 per cent) oppose the view that 'the place of women is at home', while only 46 per cent of the East and Southeast Asian respondents share this attitude (Q.412c).

The second category is composed of the human rights question concerned with the right to organise protest meetings (Q.208c): there are absolute majorities in both regions in favour of the proposition, but in Western Europe it is overwhelming (79 per cent) while in East and Southeast Asia it is very small (52 per cent): the gap of 27 per cent is about the same as the gap between the respondents of the two regions with respect to the four questions which have just been examined.

The third situation is constituted by the question relating to the choice between the family and public interest (Q.412f). There is no absolute majority either for or against the proposition, but the predominant viewpoint is different in the two regions: 48 per cent of the Western Europeans feel that the family should come first, while 42 per cent of the East and Southeast Asians feel that the public interest should come first.

There are thus almost as many questions in which there is a difference between the two regions as there is where the reaction is the same: this suggests a division of opinion on regional lines. However, that division of opinion is in no case 'overwhelming': it ranges between 17 and 27 per cent. This clearly does not justify the conclusion that there is something approaching consensus, but this clearly does not justify either that there is a truly sharp contrast. Admittedly, the questions on which there is such a division of opinion are the majority of the communitarian questions (four out of seven) and it includes one of the two human rights questions, while there is much less division of opinion on socio-economic issues. Moreover, it might be claimed that these questions are particularly important in the context of the relationship between individuals and the state. Yet it is also the case that on one of the communitarian questions, that which is concerned with the choice between the family and the public interest, it is in East and Southeast Asia that the answers are most 'modern' and, therefore, that the position of the respondents of that region cannot be considered as providing support for Asian values. In the end, it is because of views about the right to organise protest meetings, about 'government restraint' and about the place of women in society, as well as about the freedom to be allowed to business firms, that the case for an attitudinal difference between respondents of East and Southeast Asia and those of Western Europe can be made – and yet, in all these cases, the gap between the respondents of the two regions is unquestionably not overwhelming. On the two 'government restraint' questions, for instance, while there is an absolute majority (and a fairly small one at 54 and 56 per cent) in one region, the respondents of the other region are relatively evenly divided – 42 to 31 per cent in one case, 30 to 41 per cent in the other; meanwhile, between 27 and 30 per cent 'neither agree nor disagree' or do not know. The large group of what must be regarded as 'abstainers' – between a quarter and a third of the respondents on ten questions in East and Southeast Asia and on nine questions, identical except for one, in Western Europe – makes it difficult to conclude that the two regions are truly opposed to each other in terms of their political culture.

Is the division of opinion exclusively or even primarily due to inter-regional differences? Do 'sub-regions' play a part?

The problem is further complicated by the fact that it is not at all obvious that the division of opinion which exists at the regional level can be directly attributed to regional factors alone. Country results are not clustered around the regional average in the overwhelming majority of cases: indeed they are only clustered around the average on the questions in which there is an overwhelming majority in both regions in favour of the same proposition. What one finds on the contrary is a substantial dispersion and that dispersion leads very often to a noticeable overlap of country results of the two regions. It is therefore only natural that one should wish to examine whether other 'causes' might not account for the divisions of opinion among the two regions, hence the search for the possible effect of 'intra-regional' distinctions and of distinctions at the level of each country.

The view that there were profound divisions in climate, history, customs and habits, socio-economic development, especially between North and South, in both regions, constituted a *prima facie* case for looking at intra-regional distinctions, especially in Western Europe, but in East and Southeast Asia as well. These divisions may well have been expected to lead to a contrast between the societies of the two sub-regions.

Yet, when the attitudes of respondents to the communitarian, human rights and socio-economic questions are examined in detail, little does emerge which supports the view that differences in attitudes to basic societal values could be linked to respondents belonging to one rather than another of the sub-regions. As Chapters 4 and 5 showed, there is no clear evidence on the basis of which to claim that the political culture differed between North and South in Western Europe or between the 'Chinese' and the 'Malay' group of countries in East and Southeast Asia: a substantial spread remained within each 'sub-region' and there was often overlap between the countries of the two 'sub-regions'.

In Western Europe, despite the 'classical' suggestion that Southern Europe could be culturally different from Northern Europe because of the existence of a link between religion and socio-economic development, one could not trace any consequences of that link at the level of the basic societal values of respondents. This could of course be because the decline of religiosity almost everywhere and the spread of socio-economic development across large parts of Southern Europe at least did result in greater homogeneity of the whole of the Western European region by the end of the twentieth century than had been the case 100 or even 50 years previously: but, at any rate by the beginning of twenty-first century, the claim that Southern Europe was (or was still) culturally different from Northern Europe could not be substantiated.

Moreover, a further difficulty stems from the fact that the geographical boundaries of the 'sub-regions' are somewhat arbitrary. This is so in Western Europe, where there might be reasons to locate, not just France, but Italy or Ireland in one or the other of the two sub-regions, on grounds of historical development, religion or socio-economic development. This is even more so in East and Southeast Asia where the boundary between 'sub-regions' is rendered almost impossible to draw because of the great mass of China, on the one hand, and of the extent to which there is a Chinese 'diaspora' across Southeast Asia, on the other. The 'Malay sub-region' thus becomes somewhat 'porous', so to speak, and its contours are therefore more arbitrary than the Southern 'sub-region' is in Western Europe. It makes no sense, on ethnic and on socio-economic grounds to consider Singapore as part of the 'Malay sub-region'; even locating Malaysia fully in that sub-region is somewhat hazardous. As a result, one is constrained to consider the countries on a case-by-case basis: but, if this is to be the approach, it seems better to move directly to an examination of differences on a country basis.

Moreover, the examination of patterns in the sub-regions already provided evidence suggesting that the attitudes of respondents in at least some countries were difficult to interpret except on the basis of specific single country interpretations. This was found to be so in particular with respect to France and Japan. We found in Chapter 4 that it was difficult, if not downright impossible, to classify the attitudes of French respondents with respect to a number of questions without assuming that these were country-idiosyncratic. Indeed, Italy was found to be idiosyncratic as well in relation to some of the answers.

In Chapters 5 and 6, Japanese responses proved to be so different from those of the other East and Southeast Asian countries, in particular in terms of their dispersion from the average of the region, that it seemed valuable to test whether the dispersion of the answers from the countries of the region remained sizeable even when Japan was excluded: this was indeed found to be the case, but the Japanese responses did make a substantial difference and this therefore did indicate that these responses were, in part at least, country-idiosyncratic. The pattern of attitudes of Taiwanese respondents was also found to be, in several respects, difficult to interpret. The need to examine country patterns does therefore stem, at least in part, from the fact that a number of examples showed that the attitudes of respondents could not be explained by reference to regional or sub-regional characteristics only.

Variations at the level of states and their impact on differences across the two regions

As we saw all along this volume, the greater part of the variations in the attitudes to basic societal values occurs at the level of the individual states: these variations account for the spread of countries across the space and for the substantial amount of overlap which was also found to exist among countries of the two regions. When faced with these findings, one is none the less tempted to draw away from any interpretation which would appear to give prominence to the view that the countries are the key protagonists, as such an interpretation seems almost inevitably to lead to a mere description of individual cases, and thus that descriptions replace attempts at providing explanatory models. That danger exists: yet variations from country to country are so large with respect to the findings with which this volume is concerned that it seems simply unrealistic to neglect the problem which the distribution of these findings poses.

Chapter 6 endeavoured to identify underlying structures at country level by analysing the patterns of distribution of the countries with respect to the four dimensions within which, in both East and Southeast Asia and Western Europe, the answers to the communitarian and human rights questions can be located. No simple overall framework was found to account for these patterns; some regularities did emerge, however, but the limits of these regularities also help to identify 'peculiar' characteristics of individual countries, both within each region and between the regions.

With respect to the large majority of questions – in effect with respect to all the communitarian questions and one of the human rights questions, the exception being the human rights question dealing with the freedom of expression (Q.208b) – answers from the countries of both regions are spread out: however, the way they are spread out differs in the two regions. By and large, in East and Southeast Asia, there are 'clusters' composed of four or even, in one case, six countries at one end of the range of the distribution of the eighteen countries; however, this also means that the countries of that region which do not belong to the cluster – at least three out of the nine – are spread out towards the middle or even at the other end of the range. It was also found that, except for Malaysia and Indonesia, the countries belonging to these 'clusters' varies from dimension to dimension.

There is no similar clustering among the Western European countries: these are typically widely spread out, though, again in general, not spread out to such an extent that they come close to be in that part of the space where East and Southeast Asian clusters are located. There is arguably only one case when Greece and one case when France are in that position.

As far as East and Southeast Asian countries are concerned, three conclusions can be drawn, all three of which raise the question of the part played by country characteristics. First, there are, so to speak, the cases of the two countries, Malaysia and Indonesia, whose respondents take more of a 'pro-Asian values' position than might have been expected, even if they also take an 'anti-Asian values' position with respect to the question concerned with the choice between public interest and family (Q.412f) and with respect to the question concerned with the choice between striving for one's own good and that of the society (Q.412g). The explanation may be due to a characteristic common to both countries: they are indeed the only ones among those studied here which are essentially Moslem countries. Yet their social structure and the history of their political system have been sufficiently different to cast some doubt as to whether their Moslem character constitutes the key to the similarity of the attitudes of their citizens with respect to basic societal values.

Second, since it is the case that the 'clusters' of East and Southeast Asian clusters are not composed of the same countries according to all four dimensions, majority support for 'Asian values' is partial, not consistent, except perhaps in the cases of Malaysia and Indonesia. The cluster of 'pro-Asian values' countries includes Singapore and Taiwan with respect to the *liberalism* dimension and China and the Philippines join the group in relation to the *government restraint* dimension. In the case of the *decision-making* dimension, Indonesia and Malaysia are joined by Singapore and the Philippines only, indeed at some distance, when the question on consensus is associated to the question on 'the influence which old people should have'. Finally, in the *social relations* dimension, Indonesia and Malaysia are joined by Japan and Taiwan. These variations in the composition of the clusters of countries which hold a more 'pro-Asian values' position cannot easily be explained, if at all, at the level of general trends. We did note earlier in this chapter as well as in previous chapters that the attitudes of Taiwanese respondents may have to do with worries about instability, especially in relation to the liberalism and the government restraint dimensions, these being in contrast with the behaviour of Taiwanese citizens with respect to their political system since the mid-1990s at least. More generally, the question of the 'partial' support for 'pro-Asian values' positions – a kind of 'a la carte' attitude on the part of the citizens of some of the countries – does raise general questions which need to be addressed and which shall be raised in the next section.

Third, there seems little doubt, however, that, alongside the notion that the support for 'pro-Asian values' position has to be regarded as 'partial' rather than comprehensive in many, if not in all countries, specific country characteristics are also at play. This is the case for almost every country. The case of Japan has already been mentioned at some length in earlier chapters. The same occurs in Taiwan, where respondents are less liberal in their attitudes than might have been expected from their behaviour; the situation is not very different in the Philippines, not just because the respondents of that country, while holding liberal attitudes, do not, any more than the Taiwanese, support the notion of government restraint; but they are also the ones who hold the most 'pro-individual' position of all the respondents of the survey, another aspect on which they are unquestionably 'idiosyncratic'. It was further pointed out earlier that Korean respondents held peculiarly 'traditional' views about the place of women in society.

While, indeed possibly as, it is difficult to find clusters which include exclusively Western European countries, except to an extent in the 'liberalism' dimension and, but even less, in the 'government restraint' dimension, the question of the location of these countries in the space raises questions about the idiosyncratic character of the attitudes of the respondents in almost all cases. The French support particularly the freedom of expression, but are more lukewarm about the freedom to hold protest meetings; they are among those respondents, together with the British, the Germans and the Swedens, who most wish to restrain governments: the combination of these three sets of attitudes is not immediately self-explanatory, while it is perhaps more understandable, given the centralisation characteristics of their country, that the French should also be the respondents who favour most the public interest and least the family. France is the country which is possibly the most 'idiosyncratic' from the point of view of the response of its citizens; but in all the other Western European countries analysed in this study, issues of this kind can be raised about each dimension. This is so, even if, on the whole, Western European countries are located typically at some distance of whatever cluster of the East and Southeast Asian countries happens to hold the most 'pro-Asian values' position in a given dimension.

II

'Asian values': from conceptualisation to empirical reality

What adopting a 'pro-Asian values' position could realistically mean

This study started on the basis of the implicit assumption that 'Asian values' constituted a syndrome of attitudes, a syndrome which had been elaborated by thinkers and by politicians and which was held to be adopted by citizens, if not in all Asian countries, at least in the countries on the East and

Southeast of the continent. The extent to which people held these values was not discussed by those who stated that they were the values of the area: this was not done either in terms of the proportion of people who were expected to hold these values, let alone of the strength with which these values were being held; nor was there any discussion as to whether the syndrome constituted by these values was truly comprehensive in that these values were all held simultaneously.

Yet all three points, the proportion of people holding the values, the strength of the belief in these values and whether there was a joint acceptance of all that these values covered, could be expected to be controversial as one begins to unfold – to 'deconstruct' – the problems posed by these values. To these questions another was to be added, namely whether these values were held by people other than Asian citizens and in particular by Westerners: since it was claimed that these values were 'Asian' and that they were emphatically regarded as not being 'Western', it was manifestly not just important but indeed logical to find out whether Westerners did hold values which were opposed to those held by Asians.

It was obvious that any attempt to examine whether citizens of East and Southeast Asia held what had been labelled 'Asian values' would immediately raise questions about the 'degree' to which this was the case, either in terms of proportions of people who held them or in terms of the forcefulness, so to speak, with which these values were held by those who held them, as well as about whether all these values were held together or about the extent to which viewpoints were different or similar among Westerners. As a result, by the very fact that an effort was made to test whether these values were being held, one was already limiting their scope. For merely to raise the questions which have just been raised means answering that it was simply impossible that all should hold equally forcefully everything that was described as 'Asian values'; it seemed indeed equally impossible that one should find no-one, in the West, who held such values. The empirical examination of the extent to which 'Asian values' positions were held in East and Southeast Asia were shared in the population necessarily meant, to a degree at least, relativising these values, a characteristic which does apply to the analysis of the spread of any sentiment within any population.

Given the fact that it would be simply absurd to expect everyone to hold all Asian values, in a forceful manner, in East and Southeast Asia, in contrast with the attitudes adopted in the West, the realistic questions had therefore to be posed differently. What was to be asked was whether the proportions of supporters of these values in East and Southeast Asia were sufficiently large, especially in comparison with the views on these matters among Westerners, and whether the extent to which the support given to all these values was sufficiently wide to allow for the conclusion that East and Southeast Asian citizens adopted these values while Westerners did not. The answers emerging from this study are that this is not the case: the proportions of supporters of these values in the East were not found to be very large; in the West they were not found to be insignificant; support was more likely to be partial than comprehensive.

These conclusions, which result from a detailed examination of a series of complex answers to a questionnaire lead directly to a number of questions about what can and what cannot be expected to be found when a series of abstract statements about social and political life are presented to a sample of citizens; these conclusions are indeed probably at the root of what are at best misunderstandings and at worst profound oppositions between 'normative theorists' and empiricists. It would clearly be better were it to be the case that the more realistic standpoint was accepted by all: this is unlikely to occur, however, despite the fact that human experience does show that the unanimity basis on which absolute statements are based never comes to be correct when these statements are put to the test. As a result, what has not been settled so far are the questions of *threshold* – and these may not be settled as long as the view is held that value standpoints can be held unanimously and equally strongly by a whole population. In the case of 'Asian values', but probably in the case of the distinction of any set of values, questions of threshold are the translation on the 'realistic' plane of the three points made earlier: this means that one must have an idea of the proportions of supportive respondents needed for values to be considered to be widely spread; one must also have an idea of the proportions of respondents from other cultures who feel differently about the values held by the citizens of the culture under examination; finally, one must have an idea of the proportions of the respondents of the culture under consideration who hold all these values jointly if the values are to form, so to speak, a coherent whole. Let us examine these three questions in turn.

The threshold of support required for values to be regarded as adopted by a population

It seems difficult to claim that a set of values is supported by a population unless an *absolute majority* of that population holds these values. This question was not examined, let alone resolved, in the discussions about 'Asian values': the content, not the extent of support was considered, as is in the logic of the approach of normative theorists. Yet the requirement of an absolute majority support must be regarded as a minimum.

In the East and Southeast Asian case, this minimum is far from having been reached, except with respect to the socio-economic questions. With respect to the nine communitarian and human rights questions which have been the object of this study, the proportion of supporters of the 'Asian values' position is 36 per cent, while the proportion of supporters of the four socio-economic questions is 70 per cent: it is particularly large, as we saw, on the question concerned with competition but on the question concerned with the need for the government to provide jobs for the citizens; it is also over 50 per cent in the other two socio-economic questions. One can therefore conclude that this set of four value standpoints are held by the population in East and Southeast Asia. On the other hand, the support for the 'Asian values' standpoint on human rights is not only particularly low at 13 per cent, but even on the seven communitarian questions, it is only 43 per cent. Thus, on these nine questions, the minimum threshold cannot be deemed to have been passed. It cannot therefore be stated that this set of nine value standpoints are held by the population in East and Southeast Asia.

A substantial part of the problem is due, as we had several occasions to point out, to the proportions of respondents who stated that they 'neither agreed nor disagreed' being substantial and being generally over a quarter. This means that, for supporters to constitute an absolute majority, there have to be at least two supporters for every opponent of the 'Asian values' standpoints. This is often not likely to be the case with respect to value standpoints in general; indeed it is probably less so than in the case of attitudes about sentiments about the policies of a government, for instance.

One might of course regard those who do not express an opinion as not counting, in the way abstention (normally) does not count, for instance, at an election. This does not seem to be correct in the context of the values of a community. Those who 'neither agree nor disagree' with the question posed cannot be considered as 'non-existent': they exist and, in the particular case of this study, they do not think that 'Asian values' are sufficiently prominent in their consciousness for them to be prepared to show support.

Overall, the requirement of an absolute majority threshold is in reality both relatively severe and relatively limited. It is relatively limited – and thereby realistic – in that a positive support is asked of only half the population, with the corollary that there might be a substantial minority opposed to these views. It is relatively severe, on the other hand, in that what is required is an overall majority of all the citizens, as should be the case when one refers to the values which members of a society are held to support. Yet, as a matter of fact, such a requirement may be insufficient – indeed too weak – in the case of a polarised country where the proportion of 'abstainers' is very low and the supporters are confronted to a large minority of opponents.

In principle, for the analysis to be complete, the question of the strength of the support must be examined alongside the question of the extent of that support. This was scarcely tested in the case of the values studied here, in large part because, as was noted in Chapter 3, the proportion of 'strong' supporters and of 'strong' opponents was in general small. Yet the matter may well be important, for instance, when a 'thermometer' is being used to determine the degree of support of citizens for a particular question. As was pointed out in Chapter 2, this was felt to be inappropriate in the case of this survey, as the 'culture' of respondents may be very different when it comes to determining whether a value is held 'very' strongly rather than just strongly: but the fact that the proportions of citizens who stated that they held a given value 'very strongly' were small does provide further evidence for the claim made earlier that 'Asian values' could not be said to be truly supported by the respondents of East and Southeast Asia as a whole.

The threshold of support required in two populations
for values to be regarded as adopted by one
population but not by the other

It is surely not sufficient to discover that a given population supports a set of values for one to be able to conclude that these values are characteristic of that population: there must also be evidence that that population is the only one which supports this set of values. In the case of the study undertaken here, such a requirement means that one must find out whether Westerners do not support 'Asian values' positions; indeed, to be precise, one must find out whether the level of support for 'Asian values' positions among Westerners (specifically here Western Europeans) is significantly smaller than it is among East and Southeast Asians, given that, realistically, it would be absurd to imagine that no Western European at all would hold such positions. The question which arises is therefore what the size of the gap should be between East and Southeast Asian and Western European positions on 'pro-Asian values' positions. Where an absolute majority of citizens in one population supports a given set of values, it seems reasonable to suggest that not more than a quarter of the other population should hold the same values: in the case which is examined here, where the support for 'Asian values' is low among East and Southeast Asians, the support for 'Asian values' positions among Western Europeans should be appreciably lower. It seems reasonable to suggest that it should not be more than half the support for Asian values positions among East and Southeast Asians.

As a matter of fact, this requirement is far from being met, except with respect to the two human rights questions when these are taken jointly: in this case only 5 per cent of the Western Europeans take a 'pro-Asian values' position, while 13 per cent of the East and Southeast Asians do so. On the other hand, when all nine communitarian and human rights questions are examined jointly, the proportion of Western Europeans who hold a 'pro-Asian values' position is 28 per cent, while, as we saw, it is 36 per cent among East and Southeast Asians and, among the seven communitarian questions alone, the 'pro-Asian values' position is 35 per cent among Western Europeans and 43 per cent among East and Southeast Asians. Those who support these values among Western Europeans are thus not a negligible group at all: we had indeed noticed in Chapter 3 that this was the case even on the two 'government restraint' questions, where the gap is only 'just' sufficient, as 48 per cent of the East and Southeast Asians support the 'pro-Asian values' position against 23 per cent of the Western Europeans (as a matter of fact, the support for the opposite of 'Asian values' is only 47 per cent among Western Europeans). Moreover, there is almost no gap at all with respect to the four socio-economic questions: while these are supported by 70 per cent of the East and Southeast Asians, they are supported by 66 per cent of the Western Europeans, almost all that difference being due to the fact that Western Europeans are markedly more lukewarm about the idea of letting businesses make all the profits they wish (Q.306b). Thus, Western Europeans agree almost entirely with East and Southeast Asians about socio-economic standpoints and the gap between the respondents from the two regions is too small on communitarian values to be able to conclude that there is a profound difference, overall, between these two regions on these values.

The question of partial support for Asian values

It was pointed out that East and Southeast Asians appear to adopt an 'a la carte' notion of Asian values since the countries which form clusters in that region differ from one dimension to another. Indeed, the fact that the answers to the nine human rights and communitarian questions give rise to at least three dimensions does suggest that respondents are unlikely, on the whole, to take a comprehensive view of the concept. Yet this state of affairs is in manifest contradiction with the view expressed by those who expounded the concept of Asian values and according to whom that concept is a syndrome of views which relate to the role of the individual in family and state. There is no suggestion that some relationships should be regarded as more important than others or that some could be dropped.

Admittedly, it could be felt that, in practice, at any rate for the leaders who stressed the importance of these matters, what did count most were attitudes to the government and, as a matter of fact, to those human rights which are regarded by Westerners as essential. Such a cynical interpretation of the scope of 'Asian values' may well be realistic in terms of what the leaders who support Asian values have tended to feel: it is plausible that the other elements, relating to the family, the role of older people, the position of women, might interest these leaders less or less directly. Yet such a view cannot easily be openly sustained, since it reduces the concept of 'Asian values' to being merely a defence of political authoritarianism: for, if the dimensions which we referred to as 'liberalism' and 'government restraint' are what Asian values are to be restricted to, the case for a philosophical justification of these values becomes weak in the extreme, indeed borders on the non-existent.

As a matter of fact, as we have seen, East and Southeast Asian countries would not pass the threshold which has been discussed earlier, not just on the two human rights questions, on which East and Southeast Asian countries score 13 per cent, as we noted, but on all four questions related to 'liberalism' and 'government restraint', where the score for the countries of the region is 30 per cent. As a matter of fact, the proportion of respondents who take a 'pro-Asian values' position on consensus and on the influence to be given to old people is higher than on each one of the liberalism and government restraint questions.

This does not mean that there is anything 'wrong' in respondents holding attitudes which are only 'partially' in tune with the broader concept of 'Asian values' as it was analysed in Chapter 2. What it means is that the notion of a 'syndrome' of Asian values is markedly less widespread than the proponents of the overall concept suggested; this indicates that, at a minimum, what the concept might cover has to be somewhat rethought and the relative impor-tance of its components has to be assessed. Such rethinking must none the less not result in giving so much importance to 'anti-liberal' and 'anti-government restraint' positions compared to the other standpoints that, in effect, the notion becomes tantamount to what was just pointed out to be a serious potential danger, namely that it is essentially a defence of authoritarianism.

The concept of Asian values does therefore encounter what is perhaps its greatest difficulty at that point. If it is to be regarded as 'respectable' as a model, that concept has to cover matters going well beyond the question of the (rather obedient) relationship between the citizen and the state. The concept has indeed to be broader for both internal and external use: the fact that there is an 'a la carte' element suggests that there are countries – Japan, Korea and Thailand, to be sure, as well as to an extent the Philippines – which are simply outside the scope of these values unless these constitute an overall presentation of the relationship between individual and society. Thus the problem which the supporters of the notion of 'Asian values' have to overcome is not only that the proportion of citizens who support these values, both in general and in detail, is rather small, but that the overall economy of the concept is at best rather shaky.

Is East and Southeast Asia united in terms of its political culture?

The question of the partial support given to 'Asian values' leads directly to the further question of the existence of East and Southeast Asia as a socio-political cultural unit. The contrast between Western Europe and East and Southeast Asia was noted earlier: although the answers of Western European respondents are markedly spread out and give rise to what was described earlier as an amorphous and nebulous configuration, there is among them paradoxically more cultural unity as a result. Variations have to do with the 'idiosyncratic' character of each country's respondents with respect to each question, except in the case of freedom of speech, where there is, indeed, unity. There is clearly a need to explore the reactions of Western Europeans to basic societal values in greater depth and beyond what the data provided by a survey such as the one which was undertaken here: but such an exploration has to be at the level of each country, while the notion that all Western European countries have a common socio-political culture, admittedly somewhat loosely defined, does have some reality.

The situation is different in East and Southeast Asia. The existence of clusters of countries already suggests that, with respect to each dimension, certain attitudinal characteristics lead to distinctions among which countries belong to a group and which do not. In particular, the fact that Indonesia and Malaysia share apparently special but also relatively common 'pro-Asian values' positions with respect to all four dimensions means that these two countries are in some sense different from the rest of the region in terms of the attitudes of their respondents: there are no similar 'pairs' in Western Europe. At the other end of the scale, it is generally believed that Japanese respondents are likely to react differently to basic societal values from respondents from other East and Southeast Asian countries for a variety of rather obvious reasons. As a matter of fact, while this is broadly true, this is not only or perhaps even so much because Japanese respondents do not hold 'pro-Asian values' positions: it is in many ways because Japanese respondents hold rather idiosyncratic positions and, in particular, often prefer not to adopt a position. Moreover, not only the respondents from Japan, but those from Korea and, in most cases those from Thailand, as well as even to an extent those from the Philippines hold views which are distinct from those of the countries of the region which belong to a cluster and, among these, those of Malaysia and Indonesia in particular. The region is thus profoundly split in terms of its reactions to basic societal values: the split may not be on geographical lines, as we noticed in Chapter 5; but that split does exist. It is therefore a manifest exaggeration to see the region as a socio-political cultural unit. Perhaps 'Asian values' are not prevalent because that concept is based even more on a myth than the concept of Western values.

* * * * *

The countries of the 'Pacific rim' have succeeded, in a little more than a generation, to develop economically so strongly that they are truly unrecognisable. This has been said to have been due, according to many, to a 'spirit' uniquely shared by these countries. As a matter of fact, the extent to which economic development has taken place in the area has varied markedly: the image of the flying geese is appreciably more realistic than would be the image of a movement having taken place in parallel everywhere from the same starting point and at the same speed. It might therefore be hypothesised that, by osmosis or sheer imitation, the success of Japan and of the other early 'flying geese', usually referred to as the 'dragons', might have also led to the gradual spread of certain standpoints and indeed values across the regions.

Whether such a spread of values did occur – or indeed is occurring – cannot be tested with the instruments which we have at our disposal, since we do not know what were the values prevailing in the countries of the area in the earlier period: we can only register what can be detected now. What can be detected now is that there are manifest differences in the socio-political culture of the countries of East and Southeast Asia. Yet it is not immediately clear either that the lines along which these differences occur correspond to the lines of the successive waves of 'flying geese', except that in two countries which are among the last of the 'flying geese', Malaysia and Indonesia, respondents take many socio-political cultural positions which are rather similar.

The aim of this work was not originally only nor indeed even primarily to examine how far the political values of East and Southeast Asians were similar to each other: it was to see to what extent the values of these citizens were similar to or different from those of Western Europeans. The answer is unquestionably more mixed than is usually believed: it is more mixed than is usually believed because, almost certainly, differences in socio-political values across the world are less sharp than most of us, on the basis of engrained dichotomous intellectual habits, are prepared to expect. Among the lessons which a study such as this does provide is that 'profound' differences in the socio-political culture of the 'common man and woman' are typically not as profound as one readily assesses them to be. Distinctions are more about nuances than about contrasts. One must therefore be prepared to recognise that it is over these nuances that the variations in the socio-political culture of citizens need to be examined.

Appendix I
Characteristics of the Asia–Europe Survey

The Asia–Europe Survey (ASES) is an eighteen country cross-national survey conducted in summer 2000 for the democracy project funded by the Japanese Ministry of Education and Science (#11102001, with principal investigator, Takashi Inoguchi, for the period between 1999 April and March 2002). Its aim is to examine, through randomly sampled national surveys of countries of Asia and Europe, how democracy (or quasi-democracy) functions in response to various domestic and international stimuli, especially focusing on the rise of civil society and the deepening of globalisation. The sample size is about 800 in each country, the sampling method is national random sampling and face-to-face interviewing was conducted except for Japan. The country surveys were coordinated by the Nippon Research Center, Tokyo, and conducted by Gallup International coalitions. (See details in Appendix I.)

The eighteen countries surveyed are: Japan, South Korea, China, Taiwan, Singapore, Malaysia, Indonesia, Thailand and the Philippines from East and Southeast Asia, and the United Kingdom, Ireland, France, Germany, Sweden, Italy, Spain, Portugal and Greece from Western Europe. (See their profiles in Appendix II.) The questionnaire was designed in English language first. It went through two devices to improve its quality, (1) back translation and (2) focus group experiments. Back translation was indispensable as the Asia–Europe Survey used many languages sometimes even for just one country. Focus group experiments were no less indispensable. Budget limitation allowed us to do it only in Ireland and in Japan prior to the finalisation of the questionnaire in English language. To give a dramatic example, the local language questionnaires used in China, Taiwan and Singapore included those in Chinese but the three Chinese language questionnaires in these three countries are noticeably different from one another for various reasons. The cross-national surveys like this demand overall unobtrusiveness and cultural sensitivity as reflected in linguistiscally properly composed questions and properly contextualised questions.

The questionnaire consists broadly of five areas, (1) identity (2) trust (3) satisfaction (4) beliefs and actions and (5) socio-economic attributes. By identity is meant what is primarily important in relating oneself to a larger social entity. By trust is meant what is reliable in terms of affection, utility and system. By satisfaction is meant the overall gratification in life in terms of various values such as affection, health, wealth, power, knowledge and respect. Across the five areas, the two major thrusts of the Asia–Europe Survey, that is, the rise of civil society and the deepening of globalisation, are reflected in the questionnaire.

The Asia–Europe Survey is one of the largest cross-national surveys done since the classical Almond–Verba civic culture survey done *c.*1960. Needless to note, the Euro-barometer survey has been on the scene since the 1970s. But it is conducted by the transnational administrative-political institution. The World Values Survey has been continuously conducted since more than two decades periodically with the current wave being conducted in more than seventy countries. The World Values Survey is primarily academic. More regionally confined cross-national surveys are not in shortage now. The Latino-barometer the Afro-barometer, the New Democracy barometer and the East Asia barometer are such examples. Those surveys run by the Center for the Study of Developing Societies, New Delhi, is another example. The AsiaBarometer survey covering the entire sub-regions of Asia, East, Southeast, South and Central Asia, has been on the scene since 2003.

The beauty of the Asia–Europe Survey is the fact that it surveys two of the most dynamic regions of the world embedded with very different cultural contexts and historical countours. It allows us to contrast the two regions as well as to compare among the eighteen countries and among different subgroups in terms of respondents's attributes and responses. It allows us to bring in new regions to the survey rich regions of the world, that is, North America and Western Europe. The region of Asia is arguably the least surveyed area in the world in that it has been heavy in one country focused surveys and that regional surveys have not been regularly conducted until the AsiaBarometer survey and the East Asia barometer arrived at the scene in the 2000s.

A few examples of questions included in the Asia–Europe Survey are given below:

1   Many people think of themselves as being part of a particular nationality, for example, as French or American or Japanese or whatever. Do you think of yourself as (JAPANESE) or as belonging to another nationality, or do you think of yourself in this way? (Circle one answer)

   (i)   I think of myself as (JAPANESE)
   (ii) I think of myself as another nationality
   (iii) No, I do not think of myself in this way.

2   Now, could you tell me how much confidence you have in each of the following? There may be one or two items on the list that you haven't thought much about. If so, just tell me and we'll go to the next item. (Circle one answer for each statement)

(i) the (NATIONAL PARLIAMENT – INSERT ACCORDING TO COUNTRY)
(ii) the political parties
(iii) the (JAPANESE) government
(iv) the law and the courts
(v) the main political leaders in (JAPAN)
(vi) the police
(vii) the civil service
(viii) the military
(ix) (JAPANESE) big business
(x) the mass media.

3 All things considered, how satisfied are you with your life as a whole these days? (Circle on answer)
   Very satisfied, satisfied, neither satisfied nor dissatisfied, dissatisfied, very dissatisfied

4 For each of the following, could you please tell me whether or not it applies to you. (Circle one answer for each statement)

(i) I have a family member or relatives living in other countries (Applies or Does not apply)
(ii) I travelled at least once in the past three years, for business or holiday purposes (Applies or Does not apply)
(iii) I use the Internet at home or school/work (Applies or Does not apply)
(iv) I have friends from other countries (Applies or Does not apply)
(v) I often watch foreign entertainment programs on TV (Apply or Does not apply)
(vi) I often watch foreign news programs on TV (Apply or Does not apply)
(vii) I use email to communicate with people in other countries (Apply or Does not apply)
(viii) My job involves contacts with organisations or people in other countries (Apply or Does not apply)
(ix) I receive an international satellite or cable TV service (Apply or Does not apply).

Sources

Asia–Europe Survey Web Page (www.asiaeuropesurvey.org). Please contact Prof. Takashi Inoguchi (tinoguc@tamacc.chuo-u.ac.jp) for any inquiry.

Takashi Inoguchi (2004) *Kokumin Ishiki to Globalism* (Globalism and Awareness of the Citizens), Tokyo: NTT Publishing.

Takashi Inoguchi and Jean Blondel (2002) 'Political cultures do matter: citizens and politics in Western Europe and East and Southeast Asia', *Japanese Journal of Political Science*, 3: 2(November), 151–71.

Appendix II
Profiles of the eighteen countries of the Asia–Europe Survey

Selected indicators	Japan	Singapore	Korea, Rep	Malaysia	Thailand	Philippines	China	Vietnam	Indonesia
HDI rank	11	25	28	61	73	84	85	108	110
Human development index (HDI) value 2003	0.943	0.907	0.901	0.796	0.778	0.758	0.755	0.704	0.697
Freedom House Index (1 = democratic/7 = non)	1.5	4.5	1.5	4.0	2.5	2.5	6.5	6.5	3.5
GDP per capita (ppp US$) 2003	27,967	24,481	17,971	9,512	7,595	4,321	5,003	2,490	3,361
GDP growth (annual %)	2.66	2.46	3.10	5.31	6.87	4.70	9.30	7.24	4.88
Life expectancy at birth (years) 2003	82.0	78.7	77.0	73.2	70.0	70.4	71.6	70.5	66.8
Adult literacy rate (% ages 15 and above) 2003	N/A	92.5	97.9	88.7	92.6	92.6	90.9	90.3	87.9
Combined gross enrolment ratio for primary, secondary and tertiary	84	87	93	71	73	82	69	64	66
Total population (millions) 2003	127.7	4.2	47.5	24.4	63.1	80.2	1,300.0	82.0	217.4
Physicians (per 100,000 people) 1990–2004	201	140	181	70	30	116	164	53	16
Infant mortality rate (per 1,000 live births) 2003	3	3	5	7	23	27	30	19	31

Under-five mortality rate (per 1,000 people) 2003	4	3	5	7	26	36	37	23	41
Cellular subscribers (per 1,000 people) 2003	679	852	701	442	394	270	215	34	87
GDP per capita annual growth rate (%) 1990–2003	1.0	3.5	4.6	3.4	2.8	1.2	8.5	5.9	2.0
Employment by economic industry activity (%)									
Agriculture									
Women 1995–2002	5	(.)	12	14	48	25	N/A	N/A	43
Men 1995–2002	5	(.)	9	21	50	45	N/A	N/A	43
Industry									
Women 1995–2002	21	18	19	29	17	12	N/A	N/A	16
Men 1995–2002	37	31	34	34	20	18	N/A	N/A	19
Services									
Women 1995–2002	73	81	70	57	35	63	N/A	N/A	41
Men 1995–2002	57	69	57	45	30	37	N/A	N/A	38
Urban population (% of total) 2003	65.5	100.0	80.3	63.8	32.0	61.0	38.6	25.8	45.5
Electricity consumption per capita (Kilowatt-hours) 2002	8,612	7,961	7,058	3,234	1,860	610	1,484	392	463

(Appendix II continued)

Appendix II (Continued)

Selected indicators	Sweden	Ireland	United Kingdom	France	Italy	Germany	Spain	Greece	Portugal
HDI rank	6	8	15	16	18	20	21	24	27
Human development index (HDI) value 2003	0.949	0.946	0.939	0.938	0.934	0.930	0.928	0.912	0.904
Freedom House Index (1 = democratic/7 = non)	1.0	1.0	1.0	1.0	1.0	1.0	1.0	1.5	1.0
GDP per capita (ppp US$) 2003	26,750	37,738	27,147	27,677	27,119	27,756	22,391	19,954	18,126
GDP growth (annual %)	1.58	3.70	2.22	0.47	0.26	– 0.10	2.43	4.28	– 1.20
Life expectancy at birth (years) 2003	80.2	77.7	78.4	79.5	80.1	78.7	79.5	78.3	77.2
Adult literacy rate (% ages 15 and above) 2003	N/A	N/A	N/A	N/A	98.5	N/A	N/A	91.0	92.5
Combined gross enrolment ratio for primary, secondary and tertiary	114	93	123	92	87	89	94	92	94
Total population (millions) 2003	9.0	4.0	59.3	60.0	58.0	82.6	42.1	11.1	10.4
Physicians (per 100,000 people) 1990–2004	305	237	166	329	606	362	320	440	140
Infant mortality rate (per 1,000 live births) 2003	3	6	5	4	4	4	4	4	4
Under-five mortality rate (per 1,000 people) 2003	3	6	6	5	4	5	4	5	5

Cellular subscribers (per 1,000 people) 2003	980	880	912	696	1018	785	916	902	898
GDP per capita annual growth rate (%) 1990–2003	2.0	6.7	2.5	1.6	1.5	1.3	2.4	2.1	2.1
Employment by economic industry activity (%)									
Agriculture									
Women 1995–2002	1	2	1	1	5	2	5	18	14
Men 1995–2002	3	11	2	2	6	3	8	15	12
Industry									
Women 1995–2002	11	14	11	13	20	18	15	12	23
Men 1995–2002	36	39	36	34	39	44	42	30	44
Services									
Women 1995–2002	88	83	88	86	75	80	81	70	63
Men 1995–2002	61	50	62	64	55	52	51	56	44
Urban population (% of total) 2003	83.4	59.9	89.1	76.3	67.4	88.1	76.5	60.9	54.6
Electricity consumption per capita (Kilowatt-hours) 2002	16,996	6,560	6,614	8,123	5,840	6,989	6,154	5,247	4,647

Source: World Bank, *World Development Indicators*, http://publications.Worldbank.org/WDI/ United Nations, *Human Development Report*, 2005 HDI rank (from 1 to 173)/HDI value Freedom House, *Freedom in the World* 2005, A12/

Appendix III
Recodes undertaken for Chapter 3

Educ 4 categ: Recode of Q.510

    1–2 = 1
    3   = 2
    4   = 3
    5–7 = 4

Age collapsed: Recode of Q.507

    1–3   = 1
    4–6   = 2
    7–9   = 3
    10–13 = 4

Livstandards new: Recode of Q.516

    1–2 = 1
    3   = 2
    4–5 = 3

Occcupation: The recode was complex, given the fact that occupations did not have the same significance in every country. The overall recoding led to the creation of four variables, two large, non-manual (40 per cent) and manual (23.4 per cent), two much smaller, farmers (2.7 per cent) and 'other' (1.2 per cent). There was also a marked percentage of missing answers (32.7 per cent).

Public v. private: Recode of Q.513

    1–3 = 1
    4–5 = 2
    6   = 3

Relpractice: Recode of Q.504

    1–2 = 1
    3–4 = 2
    5–6 = 3
    7   = 4

The Gender (Q.506) and Foreign Minister (Q.103) questions did not have to be recoded.

Sources

Asia–Europe Survey Web Page (www.asiaeuropesurvey.org). Please contact Prof. Takashi Inoguchi (tinoguc@tamacc.chuo-u.ac.jp) for any inquiry.

Takashi Inoguchi (2004) 'Kokumin Ishiki to Globalism' *Globalism and Awareness of the Citizens*, Tokyo: NTT Publishing.

Takashi Inoguchi and Jean Blondel (2002) 'Political cultures do matter: citizens and politics in Western Europe and East and Southeast Asia', *Japanese Journal of Political Science*, 3: 2(November), 151–71.

Notes

1 Introduction

1 The question has naturally been the object of highly controversial debates for generations, but it has come to be 'rejuvenated', so to speak, in the 1990s, as a result of a number of works, and in particular those of Huntington, about what 'civilisations' are and how distant they are from each other. See in particular Huntington (1996).
2 Inglehart's analysis in his 1997 volume does purport to be worldwide: some of the problems of that analysis are examined later in this chapter. This is irrespective of the fact that the study relates to forty countries only, in the context of the 'World value survey', and that it is based on a sample of countries which is far from representing accurately the various continents.
3 Inglehart's studies are primarily based on the use of batteries of attitudes to specific issues. This author's well-known 'postmaterialist' 'syndrome' has been constructed on the basis of reactions to twelve specific issues, indeed referred to by the author as 'items' (1977, 40–53). They consist of wanting more say on jobs, wanting a less impersonal society, stating that ideas count, supporting more say in government, favouring freedom of speech, and wanting more beautiful cities (these being the 'post-materialist' attitudes), while feeling that rising prices should be fought, wanting strong defence forces, favouring economic growth, favouring a stable economy, wanting a fight against crime and maintaining order form the set of 'materialist' attitudes.
4 See Chapter 2 and the bibliography at the end of this volume for a presentation of some of the literature on the characteristics of the 'Asian values' notion.
5 The literature on managerial culture is vast. Being undertaken by social psychologists, that literature is normally emphasising values in the firm and around rather than socio-political values in general, Hofstede's pioneering work being in part an exception. An idea of the vast literature on the subject is given in the bibliography following the paper by Brodbeck *et al.* at pages 27–9. For a general presentation of the development of analyses of this kind, see Smith *et al.* (1996).

2 The nature and content of the notion of 'Asian values'

1 See Chan (1997).
2 See Chapter 4 for a development of this theme.
3 See Chapter 5 for a development of this theme. The impact of these 'idiosyncratic' attitudes of Japanese respondents will be examined further in Chapter 5 of this volume and in chapter 5 of the volume on *The State and Citizens in Western Europe and East and Southeast Asia*.

4 See for instance Chatterjee (1993), 236.
5 It is important to notice that both one of the decision-making variables and one of the social relations variables are *negatively* associated with the other or others in the corresponding dimension: this means that, while there is association and a dimension, those who take a 'pro-Asian values' and those who take an 'anti-Asian values' position in the case of the other variables take a converse position in the case of these variables. In concrete terms, this means that, for instance, those who hold the view that consensus should prevail (a 'pro-Asian values' position) also tend to hold the view that the public interest should be preferred to the family (an 'anti-Asian values' position). Similarly, those who hold the view that 'a women's place is in the home' (a 'pro-Asian values' position) also tend not to hold the view that one should strive for one's self but for the society (an 'anti-Asian values' position). The fact that these associations should be the ones which characterise the decision-making and the social relations variables has obviously an important bearing on the extent to which respondents from the two regions hold or do not hold 'pro-Asian values' positions.
6 A problem remains, however. Answers relating to the human rights questions are negatively loaded when they form part of the same factor as the government restraint questions: this is to be expected, since respondents then support an 'Asian values' position, both on human rights (by being negative on the two questions once recoded) and on government restraint (by being positive on the two questions). There is a difficulty, however, with respect to the two communitarian questions concerned with the choice between the public interest and family obligations (Q.412f) and with the choice between striving for one's own good and that of society (Q.412g). That difficulty stems from the fact that to take a negative standpoint on these questions, once recoded, means adopting what can be regarded as an 'anti-Asian values', not a 'pro-Asian values' position. Someone who favours, for instance, giving more power to old people (a 'pro-Asian values' position) also favours the public interest rather than family obligations: but this is not the 'pro-Asian values' position, any more than striving for one's own good is the 'pro-Asian values' position. What the case is, apparently, that respondents combine 'pro-Asian values' positions on the other communitarian questions and perhaps on some aspects of human rights with more individualistic and less marked 'pro-family' attitudes than the 'Asian values' position would have suggested. The point is mentioned here without being discussed as this section is merely concerned with the presentation of the factor analyses: the examination of the consequences of this point is left to the detailed analysis which is undertaken in the following chapters.

3 How opposed are 'basic societal values' in the two regions

1 The impact of these 'idiosyncratic' attitudes of Japanese respondents will be examined further in Chapter 5.
2 It may well be that the reactions of Taiwanese citizens have to do with the fact that party competition brought with it a feeling of that the result was a degree of instability in political life of which these citizens were not accustomed and with which they felt uneasy.

4 A common political culture in Western Europe?

1 Simon de Montfort and his crusade against the 'Albigeois' in the early thirteenth century provide a clear example of colonisation of parts of what became since Southern France by the French Kings.

2 In his Preface to the 1976 edition of Weber's work on *The Protestant Ethic and the Spirit of Capitalism*, Giddens notes that 'To be at all satisfactory, it [Weber's thesis] would involve considering the status of the companion studies of the "world religions".... No author has yet attempted such a task, and perhaps it would need someone with a scholarly range approaching that of Weber himself to undertake it with any hope of success' (1976, 12).

3 Weber takes great pains to show that predestination, more than any other doctrine, was able to produce a spirit of enterprise. The feeling that success in life was a proof that one was one of the elect was critical. 'That worldly activity should be considered capable of this achievement, that it could, so to speak, be considered the most suitable means of counteracting feelings of religious anxiety, finds its explanation in the fundamental peculiarities of religious feeling in the Reformed Church' (1976, 112).

5 A common political culture in East and Southeast Asia?

1 The attitudes of Taiwanese respondents are markedly different, on many questions and in particular in relation to the government, from those of Japanese and South Korean respondents. It was pointed out in Chapter 3 that this may have to do with the fact that the change in the character of the political system may have created a degree of instability which has worried some citizens: yet it remains remarkable that Taiwanese respondents should be, overall, less support-ive of liberal-democratic standpoints than respondents of the other countries, including Indonesia, which became fully liberal-democratic between the 1980s and the end of the twentieth century.

2 The question is discussed in the volume on *The State and Citizens in Western Europe and East and Southeast Asia*.

6 Political culture at the level of individual states

1 See Chapters 3 and 5 for an account of the attitudes of Taiwanese respondents with respect to human rights and the 'role of the government' questions.

2 In a number of countries, the human rights or the 'role of government' questions form one factor on their own; in other cases, these factors also include either one further question or more than one.

3 Relationships are somewhat more complex if one attempts to examine the spread with respect to the other two questions which are part of the 'decision-making' factor, but the overall conclusion remains, namely that the relationship between the answers to these questions is not linear.

4 They also occupy an anti-'Asian values' position with respect to the choice between the public interest and the family (Q.412f).

Bibliography

G.D. Almond and S. Verba (1963) *The Civic Culture*, Princeton, NJ: Princeton University Press.

G.D. Almond and S. Verba, eds (1990) *The Civic Culture Revisited*, Boston, MA: Little, Brown.

B.R.O.G. Anderson (1991) *Imagined Communities: Reflections on the Origin and Spread of Nationalism*, New York, NY: Verso.

L. Barzini (1984) *The Italians*, Harmondsworth, Middlesex: Penguin books.

D.A. Bell and Joanne R. Bauer, eds (1999) *The East Asian Challenge for Human Rights*, Cambridge, New York: Cambridge University Press.

R. Benedict (1946) *The Chrysanthemum and the Sword; Patterns of Japanese Culture*, Boston, MA: Houghton Mifflin Company.

J. Blondel, R. Sinnott and P. Svensson (1998) *People and Parliament in the European Union*, Oxford: Oxford University Press.

F.C. Brodbeck, Michael Frese, Staffan Akerblom, Giuseppe Audia, Gyula Bakacsi, Helena Bendova, Domenico Bodega, Muzaffer Bodur, Simon Booth, Klas Brenk, Phillippe Castel, Deanne Den Hartog, Gemma Donnelly-Cox, Mikhail V. Gratchev, Ingalill Holmberg, Slawomir Jarmuz, Jorge Correia Jesuino, Revaz Jorbenadse, Hayat E. Kabasakal, Mary Keating, George Kipiani, Edvard Konrad, Paul Koopman, Alexandre Kruc, Christopher Leeds, Martin Lindell, Jerzey Maczynski, Gillian S. Martin, Jeremiah O'Connell, Athan Papalexandris, Nancy Paplexandris, Jose M. Prieto, Boris Rakitski, Gerhard Reber, Argio Sabadin, Jette Schramm-Nielsen, Majken Schultz, Camilla Sigfrids, Erna Szabo, Hank Thierry, Marie Vondry-sova, Jurgen Weibler, Celeste Wilderom, Stanislaw Witkowski, and Rolf Wunderer (2000) 'Cultural variation of leadership prototypes across 22 European countries', *Journal of Occupational and Organisational Psychology*, 73, 1–29.

R. Buswell, ed. (2004) *Encyclopedia of Buddhism*, 2 vols, New York: Macmillan Reference USA.

J. Chan (1994) 'The Asian challenge to universal human rights: a philosophical appraisal', in James T. H. Tang, ed., *Human Rights and International Relations in the Asia-Pacific Region*, New York: St. Martin's Press.

J. Chan (1997) 'An alternative view', *Journal of Democracy*, 8(2), 35–48.

P. Chatterjee (1993) *The Nation and Its Fragments*, Princeton, NJ: Princeton University Press.

W.T. De Bary (1998) *Asian Values and Human Rights*, Cambridge, MA: Harvard University Press.

D. Easton (1965) *A Systems Analysis of Political Life*, New York, NY: Wiley.

R.A. Fox (1997) 'Confucian and communitarian responses to liberal democracy', *The Review of Politics*, 59(3), 561–92.

F. Fukuyama (1995a) 'Confucianism and democracy', *Journal of Democracy*, 6(2), 20–34.

F. Fukuyama (1995b) *Trust*, London: Hamish Hamilton.

L. Harrison and S.P. Huntington, eds (2000) *Culture Matters*, New York: Basic Books.

G. Hofstede (1980) *Culture's Consequences*, London and Los Angeles, CA: Sage.

G. Hofstede (1997) *Cultures and Organisations*, New York: McGraw Hill.

S.P. Huntington (1991) 'Democracy's third wave', *Journal of Democracy*, 2(1), 12–34.

S.P. Huntington (1996) *The Clash of Civilisations and the Remaking of World Order*, New York: Simon and Schuster.

R. Inglehart (1977) *The Silent Revolution: Changing Values and Political Styles*, Princeton, NJ: Princeton University Press.

R. Inglehart (1990) *Culture Shift in Industrial Society*, Princeton, NJ: Princeton University Press.

R. Inglehart (1997) *Modernisation and Postmodernisation*, Princeton, NJ: Princeton University Press.

R. Inglehart and W.E. Baker (2000) 'Modernisation, cultural change, and the persistence of traditional values', *American Sociological Review*, 65, 19–51.

B. Kausikan (1997) 'Governance that works', *Journal of Democracy*, 8(2), 24–33.

D. Kelley and A. Reid, eds (1998) *Asian Freedoms*, Cambridge: Cambridge University Press.

H.D. Klingemann and D. Fuchs, eds (1995) *Citizens and the State*, Oxford: Oxford University Press.

T. Koh (1993) 'The 10 values that undergrid East Asian strength and success', *International Herald Tribune*, 11–12 December.

J.E. Lane and S. Ersson (2002) *Culture and Politics*, Aldershot, Hants: Ashgate.

Lee Kuan Yew (2000) *From Third World to First: The Singapore Story 1965–2000*, New York: Harper Collins.

S.M. Lipset (1960, new edn 1983) *Political Man*, London: Heinemann.

Mab Huang (2000) 'Debating Asian values: saying too little or saying too much', *PROSEA Research Paper*, # 31, pp. 1–20.

K. Mahbubani (2002) *Can Asians Think? Understanding the Divide Between East and West*, South Rouyalton, VT: Steerforth press.

A. Milner (2000a) 'What happened to Asian values', in G. Segal and D. Goodman, eds, *Toward Recovery in Pacific Asia*, London: Routledge, pp. 56–68.

A. Milner (2000b) 'ASEAN + 3, "Asia" consciousness and Asian values', *PROSEA Research Paper*, #39, October, 15.

A. Milner and M. Quilty, eds (1997) *Asia in Australia: Comparing Cultures*, Melbourne: Oxford University Press.

C.S. Montesquieu (1748) *The Spirit of Laws*, 2 vols (1878 edn), London: Bell & Sons.

M. Ng (1997) 'Why Asia needs democracy', *Journal of Democracy*, 8(2), 10–23.

R. Nozick (1977) *Anarchy, State and Utopia*, Cambridge, MA: Perseus Books.

J.S. Nye, Jr, P.D. Zelikow and D.C. King, eds (1997) *Why People Do Not Trust Government*, Cambridge, MA: Harvard University Press.

S. Parman (1998) *Europe in the Anthropological Imagination*, Upper Saddle River, NJ: Prentice-Hall.

W.L. Parrish and C. Chi-hsiang Chang (1996) 'Political values in Taiwan: Sources of change and constancy', in Hung-mao Tien, ed., *Taiwan's Electoral Politics and Democratic Transition*, London: Sharpe, pp. 27–41.

S.L. Popkin (1979) *The Rational Peasant: The Political Economy of Rural Society in Vietnam*, Berkeley, CA: University of California Press.

R.D. Putnam (1993) *Making democracy Work*, Princeton, NJ: Princeton University Press.

L.W. Pye (1985) *Asian Power and Politics*, Cambridge, MA: Harvard University Press.

B.M. Richardson (1974) *The Political Culture of Japan*, Berkeley, CA: University of California Press.

S. Ronen and A.I. Kraut (1977) 'Similarities among countries based on employee work values and attitudes', *Columbia Journal of World Business*, 89–96.

J.C. Scott (1976) *The Moral Economy of the Peasant: Rebellion and Subsistence in Southeast Asia*, New Haven, CT: Yale University Press.

D.A. Segal (1991) 'The European', *Anthropology Today*, 7(5), 7–9.

A. Sen (1999) 'Democracy has a universal value', *Journal of Democracy*, 10(3), 3–13.

P.B. Smith, S. Dugan and F. Trompenaars (1996) 'National culture and the values of organisational employees', *Journal of Cross-Cultural Psychology*, 27(2), 231–64.

R.H. Solomon (1971) *Mao's Revolution and the Chinese Political Culture*, Berkeley, CA: University of California Press.

G. de Stael (1810) *De l'Allemagne*, 3 vols, 1813 edn, London: John Murray.

F. Toennis (1885, London edn 1955) *Community and Association*, London: Routledge and Kegan Paul.

T. Vanhanen (1997) *Prospects of Democracy*, London: Routledge.

T. Vanhanen (2003) *Democratisation*, London: Routledge.

M. Weber (1951) *The Religion of China*, New York: Free Press.

M. Weber (1976 edn, but first published in English in 1930) *The Protestant Ethic and the Spirit of Capitalism*, London: Allen and Unwin.

M. White (1987) *The Japanese Educational Challenge: A Commitment to Children*, New York: Free Press.

K.A. Wittfogel (1980) *Oriental Despotism*, New Haven, CT: Yale University Press.

R.E. Woliver and R.B. Cattell (1981) 'Reoccurring national patterns from 30 years of multivariate cross-cultural studies', *International Journal of Psychology*, 16, 171–98.

Yi-Huah Jiang (2000) 'Asian values and communitarian democracy', *PROSEA Research Paper*, #32, pp. 1–16.

Index

Note: Page numbers in italics indicate figures and tables.

absolute monarchies 67
administrative centralisation 76
Afro-barometer 166
Almond, G. 1, 15; and Verba, S., civic
    culture survey 166
America/n: culture 71; freedom, style
    of 92
Amnesty International 92
Anderson, B. 92
anti-'Asian values' position 44,
    175 nn.5, 6, 176 n.4; in West 144
ASEAN 94
Asia/Asian 91; crime-rate figures 92;
    and European countries, type of
    relationship between background
    variables and societal values *61*;
    and European respondents,
    cross-tabulation *60*; exceptionalism
    23; financial crisis in late 1990s 22,
    23; societies, nature and role of
    human rights in 29
AsiaBarometer survey 166
Asia–Europe Survey (ASES) 165;
    characteristics of 165–7; profiles of
    eighteen countries of 168–71;
    questionnaire 165
Asian Challenge to Universal Human
    Rights, A Philosophical Appraisal 30
Asian Power and Politics 91
Asian values xv, 6, 30, 63, 161; based
    on communitarianism 77;
    characteristics 28; citizens, in East
    and Southeast Asia 21; from
    conceptualisation to empirical reality
    156–63; constituting syndrome of
    attitudes 32–4, 156; debate on 21;
    described in the literature 26–7;

in East and Southeast Asia 8;
    historical origins of debate on 21–3;
    on human rights and on government
    restraint 175 n.6; movement 20;
    nature and content of notion of 20;
    need to understand 22;
    notion of 39; operationalising 31;
    as opposed to 'Western values' 79;
    paradoxical aspect of emphasis
    on 23; partial support for 161–2;
    positions, support for and
    opposition to 46, 175 n.6;
    questionnaire 31–9; socio-economic
    standpoints of 30; tradition of
    'communitarian' spirit 92
attitudes: to basic societal values 16,
    112; of citizens to democracy and
    society in both East and Southeast
    Asia and the West xv, xvi; of citizens
    vis-à-vis government 58; to 'good
    society' 16; to government, question
    dealing with 49, 132–3; of
    respondents to basic societal values
    on a country basis, need to analyse
    125; variations to basic societal
    values at country level 126–7
Austria 12
authoritarian/ism 109; character of
    country, influence of 129;
    regimes 110

Baker, W.E. 5
barbarians 66
Barzini, L. 70, 71
basic societal attitudes 86–8; of
    Western Europeans and of East and
    Southeast Asians, comparing 65

basic societal values questions 56;
attitudes of respondents to 100–1;
of citizens in East and Southeast Asia
and in Western Europe 62; differences
in attitudes to 152; dimensional
consistency 134; of European citizens
65; inter-regional differences 41, 42;
large single country disagreements
and relatively small regional or
sub-regional disagreements 120–6;
at level of individual countries 146;
overall reactions to 42; overlap in
responses of interviewees 54–6;
pattern, demographic characteristics
and knowledge of politics 59–60;
spread at country-by-country level and
at regional and sub-regional levels,
comparing 122; spread at level of
individual countries 120–2; in the
two regions, recodes undertaken
for 60, 172–3
Bauer, J.R. 89
Belgium 13, 15, 74, 76; Catholicism
and Protestantism in 73
Bell, D.A. 89
Benedict, R. 92; study on minds
of Japanese during Second World
War 92
Blondel, J. xvi, 15, 173
Borneo 107
Britain/British 12, 64, 80, 83, 85, 95,
133; consensus and influence which
old people should hold 133;
liberalism 143; 'public interest' and
'family obligations', choice between
134; restraining government 156;
striving for one's own good 134; on
women, role of 134
Brodbeck, F.C. 10, 174 n.5
Buddhism 96, 97, 104; spread of 97;
traditions 94
Burma 9; under British rule 96
Buswell, R. 97

Calvinism 72; doctrine 73
Cambodia 92
Canada 12
capitalism 74
capital punishment 92
Catholicism/Catholic 74; Church 67;
Europe 72; Italy 73;
Low Countries 73
Catholic–Protestant divide in Europe
80, 85–6; North–South division 73

Cattell, R.B. 10
Center for the Study of Developing
Societies, New Delhi 166
Chan, J. 22, 25, 28, 29, 30, 174 n.1
Chang, C. Chi-Hsiang 62
Charles the Great 66
Chatterjee, P. 175 n.4
China/Chinese 5, 9, 32, 94, 95, 97, 98,
104, 105, 109, 111, 128, 131;
businessmen 93; communities in
Malaysia and Singapore 97;
consensus, role of 133;
'diaspora' across Southeast Asia
153; economic growth, rapid 22;
human rights 29; influence which
old people should hold 133;
liberalism government restraint
dimension 155; record in field
of human rights 25; striving
for one's own good 134;
Western influence in 96;
women in the home 144;
women, role of 134
Christians 97
citizen/s: analysis of political culture
of 15–18; attitudes towards
government 123; behaviour within
each state 113; in East and
Southeast Asia holding 'Asian
values' 157; historical and
geographical characteristics to
value standpoints of 116; political
culture(s) in Western Europe, 'shape'
of 77–80; societal values
inter-regional or intra-regional
differences, patterns of 114; and
society, relationship 30;
socio-political culture(s) in East and
Southeast Asia, 'shape' of 100–11;
of the two regions, pattern of
values characterising 40;
of Western Europe, basic societal
values 39
The Civic Culture 1, 13, 15;
intellectual contribution of 2
The Civic Culture Revisited 1
civilisations: assumptions about 19;
clash of xv; Eastern and Western,
Western idea of differences in 23,
49; Huntington on 174 n.1
climate 68–70, 78; role of 75;
significant effect on Western European
culture 69; in socio-political culture in
East and Southeast Asia 94

'collective' or 'communitarian' view of society 7
colonialism/colonial 74; inferiority 75; legacy 68; nationalism 70–2; rule 96; or semi-colonial past 78
colonisation 99; large impact of 95
communism: fall of 4; impact of 9
communitarian and human rights questions 90, 127, 149, 160; dimensions linking questions, four models of *137*; East and Southeast Asia and Western Europe 136; four dimensions, partial ranking of country replies 138–42; three dimensions only 136
communitarianism 28, 31, 78, 79, 93; character of society 26; heritage, determining content of 28–9; matters 56; syndrome 32; values 49, 50, 60, 82, 103
communitarian questions 30, 37, 38, 48, 58, 123, 124, 159; Asians on 57; 'classical' questions 47; 'pro-Asian values' position among Western Europeans and East and Southeast Asians 82, 103, 160; respondents 42
competition question 36, 43, 46, 130, 158; Japanese on 103, 124; maximum overlap in East Southeast Asia 55, 124, 158; Taiwanese on 110
Confucianism 20, 22, 26, 27; and 'communitarianism' as bases of Asian values 26–7; as origin of 'Asian values' syndrome 96
consensus 141; and influence to be given to old people 133–4
Constantinople, fall of 66
convergence 4–6, 8, 10; aspects of economic development 7; of citizens' values across world 1, 6, 7; over time 3
countries: association to each other 142–3; belonging to various 'sub-groups' 143–6; first-level linkages between 56, 57; 'forced' character of groupings 12
Cuban War 96
culture/cultural: differences among geographically contiguous countries 13; distinctiveness, gradation in extent 56–9; patterns, distinct 51–2; and socio-economic

arguments for intra-regional differences 117–18
cultural-cum-legal-cum-institutional factors 91
Culture's Consequences 10, 16, 17

debate: on Asian values as part of general debate on cultural specificity of values 23–6; on common East and Southeast Asian culture 91
decision-making 38; factor 149, 176 n.3; process of 31; questions, relationship between responses *141*
democracy/democratic 94; participation 2; stability 2; in the Western sense 2
Democracy as a universal value 24
Democracy, Governance and Economic Performance xv
'democratisation, 'waves' of 4
Denmark 12, 64
dimensions/dimensional: of answers to questions in various countries 127–9; of human rights and communitarian values, partial ranking of country replies on basis of 138–42; linking human rights and communitarian questions, four models of *137*; structure on country basis, types of 135–8
dragons 163

East and Southeast Asia/Asians 5; citizens on 'basic societal values' 18; common socio-political culture 63, 89, 91–3, 102–3; communitarian and human rights questions 158; countries, conclusions 155; countries in Inglehart's study 11; countries subgroup 143; economic and social change 6; family and public interest, choice 151; government restraint questions 151; human rights questions 138, 151; North–South division 99; political culture of citizens in countries of 1; position on 'pro-Asian values' positions 160; problems 4; responses extent of difference from Western European responses 56; role to be ascribed to government 138;

East and Southeast Asia/Asians
(*Continued*)
  socio-economic questions 135, 158;
  as socio-political cultural unit 162;
  on socio-political culture 40;
  sub-regional cultural areas in 90;
  support for 'Asian values' standpoint
  on human rights 159; two clearly
  defined cultural groups 103–8;
  and Western Europe, difference
  between 16
East Asia barometer 166
Eastern and Western civilisations,
  chasm between 23
Eastern European countries 5
Eastern intellectuals 23
Easton, D. 15
East Timor 92
East–West divide 88, 111
economic and social development 113
economic questions 57
Edict of Nantes 73
England 66, 73, 74
Eurobarometer: series 65; survey 166
European/s: in China 23; citizens 65;
  colonisation in the Third World 70;
  elites, Europeanness of 9, 65, 72,
  76, 91; feeling, emergence of 67;
  political culture 72
European Community, integration of
  national markets in 77
'Europeanisation' process in the
  European Union 76
European Union 15, 24, 71;
  development of 76

family: Britain, 'public interest' and
  'family obligations', choice between
  134; French respondents, 'public
  interest' and 'family obligations'
  choice 134, 156; Ireland, 'public
  interest' and 'family obligations',
  choice 134; position of individual in
  31; and public interest, choice 151;
  Spain, 'public interest' and 'family
  obligations', choice 134; Western
  Europe, family and public interest,
  choice 151
Far East 23
financial crisis in Asia 22, 23
Finland 11, 12
flying geese 93, 98, 99, 163; model
  109; successive waves of 164
Formosa *see* Taiwan

Fox, R.A. 27
fragmentation: of culture 68; of
  political units in Europe's centre 66;
  of Western European political
  culture 65
France/French 12, 66, 67, 71, 74, 80,
  84, 86, 95, 128, 133, 155, 156;
  Calvinist Protestants 73; Catholicism
  86; consensus and influence which
  old people should hold 133; culture
  67; human rights questions 132;
  kings 67; liberalism 143; literature
  67; Louis XIV 73; Protestantism 73;
  respondents, different from other
  Western European countries 153;
  respondents, 'public interest' and
  'family obligations' choice 134, 156;
  responsibility of state for jobs 130;
  Revolution 68; striving for one's
  own good 134; support for freedom
  of expression 156; women,
  role of 134
freedom of expression 48, 50, 149; of
  opinion *53, 55, 57, 59, 81, 106,
  121, 122, 126, 131, 134, 150*
'free thinking', centres of 67
*From Third World to First, The
  Singapore Story 1965–2000* 92
Fukuyama, F. 27

Gallup International 165
geographical conditions 99, 113
geographical contiguity: boundaries of
  'sub-regions' 153; of groups 12;
  of political culture 11–13;
  search for 3
Germany/German 12, 66, 69, 70, 74,
  76, 80, 83, 84, 85, 128; Catholicism
  and Protestantism 73; government
  restraint 156; influence which old
  people should hold 133; liberalism
  143; Lutheran 73; as major industrial
  power 72; responsibility of state for
  jobs 130; striving for one's own good
  134; women, role of 134
Giddens, A. 176 n.2
globalisation 1; debate on 24
global variation at regional or
  sub-regional level 126
Goodman, D. 28, 89
'good society', views about 15–18
government: need to provide jobs for
  citizens 158; role of 135, 138,
  176 n.2; *see also* state

government restraint questions 38, 136, 143–6, 149, 161; 'pro-Asian values' position, percentage support of East and Southeast Asians and Western Europeans 160; relationship between responses *140*

Greece 66, 70, 76, 80, 83, 84, 133, 136, 155; liberalism 143

Hegel 91

Henri IV 73

Hofstede, G. 10, 11, 16, 77, 89, 93, 174 n.5; analysis 11; data 17; presentation 12; *see also Culture's Consequences*

Hong Kong 24

Huang, M. 28, 29, 30

human rights 29–31, 60, 77, 79, 90, 135; and Asian values 25, 29; issues 47; values 49

human rights questions 37, 48, 57, 122, 123, 130, 138; communitarian and socio-economic questions by country, spread of answers *50*; communitarian and socio-economic questions, divided between East and Southeast Asia, spread of answers *106*; and communitarian questions 38, 39, 130–2, 135; difference between East and Southeast Asian responses and Western European responses 132; East and Southeast Asian countries 161; or 'role of government' questions 176 n.2; Western Europeans 160

Huntington, S. 27, 174 n.1

India 13, 23, 96

individualism 7, 17, 79; societal values of Westerners 27

individual states, political culture at level of 113

Indochina, under French rule 96

Indonesia 9, 95, 96, 98, 105, 107, 164; Asian values 145; businessmen, systematic analysis of modes of behaviour of 93; *decision-making* dimension 155; human rights questions 132; liberalism 143; 'pro-Asian values' position 146, 155, 163; responsibility of state for jobs 130; *social relations*

dimension 155; women in home position 144

industrialisation 78; and socio-economic development 97–8; spread of 75

industrial revolution and its effect on North–South divide 74–5

Inglehart, R. 5, 6, 10, 12, 93, 117, 174 nn.2, 3; 1977 study based on Western European countries 5, 11

Inoguchi, T. xvi, 165, 167, 173

inter-regional differences: in division of opinion 152–4; extent of 46; in 'uncommitted answers' 44–7

intra-regional differences 51; overlap 55; spread 53

Ireland 80, 83, 85, 86, 133, 136; Catholicism and Protestantism 73; consensus and influence which old people should hold 133; human rights questions 132; liberalism 143; 'public interest' and 'family obligations', choice 134

Ireland, Republic of 80

island countries 99; two types of 95

Italy/Italian 12, 66, 70, 76, 80, 83, 84, 85, 135, 153; division into two political cultures 71–2; effects of industrialisation 74; human rights questions 132; influence which old people should hold 133; liberalism 143; respondents 88; responsibility of state for jobs 130

Japan/Japanese 5, 23, 25, 89, 93, 95, 97, 98, 104, 105, 109, 136, 146, 156; Asian values, concept of 162; basic societal values 163; capital 9; consensus influence which old people should hold 133; as economic leader 9; human rights questions 132; 'idiosyncratic' attitudes of respondents 124, 175 n.1; liberalism 136, 143; Ministry of Education and Science xv, 165; model of industrial management 7; occupation of both Taiwan and Korea 96; respondents 108, 125; responses, different from other East and Southeast Asian countries 153; *social relations* dimension 155; Western influence in 96; women in the home position 144

Jiang, Yi-Huah 27, 28, 29, 31

Kabashima, Ikuo xvi
Kausikan, B. 24, 25, 89
Kelly, D. 89, 91
Koh, T. 89
Kojima, K. xvi
Korea *see* South Korea
Kraut, A.I. 10, 11
Kwon, H. 89

Latin American countries 5, 12, 14, 17
Latino-barometer 166
Lee Kuan Yew 22, 28, 58, 92, 93, 96
liberal democracy: or authoritarian character of the polity 112; and authoritarian rule, distinction 111; countries, attitudes of respondents 109; spread in region 98–9
liberalism 37, 38, 94, 135, 136, 143–6, 149, 161; questions, relationship between responses *140*
liberal modernity 27
libertarianism 93
Lipset, S.M. 4
literature: 'Asian values' in 26–7; on difference between East and Southeast Asia and Western Europe 16, 18, 114; on managerial culture 174 n.5; on Western Europe 78
local language questionnaires 165
Locke 70

Mahathir Mohammad 28, 29, 58, 96
Mahbubani, K. 22, 89
Malaya under British rule 96
Malaysia 13, 22, 28, 95, 98, 104, 107, 109, 136, 164; Asian values 145; Chinese and Malay cultural background, distinction 111; Chinese sub-region 104, 105; *decision-making* dimension 155; human rights in 25, 29; human rights questions 132; liberalism 143; Malay population, ethnically 97; Malay sub-region 104, 105, 153; 'pro-Asian values' position 146, 155, 163; *social relations* dimension 155; women in home position 144
management: literature on managerial culture 174 n.5; studies 11; 'supra-national' managerial cultures 12;
Marsh, I. xv, xvi
Marx, K. 91
masculinity 17

materialism 12; of poorer societies 117
Mexico 2
Michigan election studies 31
Middle Ages 67
Milner, A. 22, 23, 28, 93
Mitteleuropa 71, 72
modernisation 4–6
modernisation theory 2, 4; problems 118
modernity 1
Montaigne 91
Montesquieu, C.S. 69, 70
Montfort, S.de 175 n.1
Moslem countries 155
Muslims: dominance 94; in Malaysia and Indonesia 97

Napoleon 71
nationalism 68
national political cultures, shaping of 75–7
Netherlands 11, 12, 74, 95; Catholicism and Protestantism 73
New Democracy barometer 16
new nations 2
Ng, M. 24, 25
Nippon Research Centre xvi, 165
non-communitarianism 78
Northern and Southern Western Europe: division in 12, 76, 78, 80; political cultures of 9; spread of answers to human rights, communitarian, and socio-economic questions, divided *81–2*
Nozick, R. 93

old people, influence in decision making 133, 135, 139, *141*, 175 n.6
opinion, right to express *53, 55, 57, 59, 81, 106, 121*, 122, *126, 131*, 134, *150*
Oriental Despotism 91

'Pacific rim' countries 163
papacy 66
Parrish, W.L. 62
partial interpretations, case for 118–20
participation: explosion, two forms of 2; state 2
Philippines 9, 89, 93, 95, 96, 98, 105, 109, 128, 133, 135, 156; Asian values concept 162; Christians in 97; consensus and influence

which old people should hold 133; *decision-making* dimension 155; human rights questions 132; liberalism 143; *liberalism government restraint* dimension 155; women in the home position 144

political authoritarianism 161

political change 99

political culture: accounting for economic and social change 6–7; across regions, differences in 3; of citizens across political systems 3; of citizens and 'objective' social and economic change 8; of citizens, uniform within each region 8; as distinct from economic and social change 7–8; East and Southeast Asian citizens, empirical knowledge of 90; 'inductive' approach to 19; Northwestern Europe 71; of the two regions, similarities and differences 148; united, in East and Southeast Asia 162–3; Western European citizens, empirical knowledge of 90

political socialisation and administrative centralisation 75–7

Popkin, S. 92

Portugal 66, 71, 76, 80, 83, 96, 136; consensus and influence which old people should hold 133; effects of industrialisation 74; human rights questions 132; liberalism 143

post-materialism/post-materialist 12; of richer societies 117; syndrome 174 n.3

post-modernisation 4–6

post-modernity 1; values 11

power distance 17

predestination, doctrine of 72

preferences of respondents, overall distribution of 44–6, 47

prisoners 92

'pro-' and 'anti-Asian values' standpoints, distribution of *150*

'pro-' and 'anti-communitarian' positions 79

pro-Asian values 44, 156; East 144; position 24, 31–4, 79, 145, 175 n.5

Protestant–Catholic distinction 75

The Protestant Ethic and the Spirit of Capitalism 72, 176 n.2

Protestantism 24, 72, 73, 74; ethic of 72–4, 91

Putnam, R.D. 71; modes of behaviour of North and South 71

Pye, L.W. 7, 9, 91; on the many political cultures of Asia, East, Southeast and South 91

Quilty, M. 93

recodes undertaken for basic societal values in the two regions 172–3

regional political culture: controversy about the existence of 8–10; in East and Southeast Asia 20; or sub-regional 10–11; value distinctions based on differences 118

Reid, A. 89, 91

religion/religious 78; affiliation 99; and ethnic differences 96–7; practices 113

religiosity, decline of 153

Renaissance 73

respondents who do not express an opinion 33, 42–4, 46–7, 149, 152, 159; large proportion 47

responses of interviewees, wide spread in 52–4

Revocation of the Edict of Nantes 73

Richardson, B. 92

rights: of businesses to make profit 130; to express an opinion *53, 55, 57, 59, 81, 106, 121,* 122, *126, 131,* 134, *150*; to organise protest meetings 131; *see also* human rights

Roman empire 66

Rome and the papacy 73

Ronen, S. 10, 11

Scandinavian countries 17, 64; cultural area 11

Scotland 73

Scott, J. 92

Second World War 92, 98

Segal, G. 28, 67

semi-authoritarian countries, attitudes of the respondents 109

Sen, A. 24

Shintoism 97

Siam *see* Thailand

Singapore 23, 24, 28, 95, 96, 98, 104, 109, 123, 133, 145; consensus and influence which old people should hold 133; *decision-making* dimension 155; frequency of executions in 92; human rights 29;

Singapore (*Continued*)
  human rights questions 132, 137;
  leaders 22; liberalism 143;
  pro-Asian values 155; record in field
  of human rights 25; women in the
  home position 144
Sinnott, R. xvi
Smith, P.B. 10, 17, 175 n.5
socialisation 76
social psychologists 11
social relations 38; factor 149;
  questions 37; relationship between
  responses on the two questions *141*
society, position of individual in 31
socio-economic development, link
  between religion and 153
socio-economic questions 36, 38, 39,
  48, 77, 79, 90, 127, 129, 149;
  dimensions of 129–30; East and
  southeast Asians 161; human rights
  and communitarian questions,
  overall inter-regional differences
  47–51; Western Europeans 161
socio-economic values 31, 60; 'Asian
  values' on communitarian and
  human rights 30; distinctions
  between East and West, 'cultural' or
  ideological basis of 115–16
socio-political values of citizens 1–18
Solomon, R. 92
Southeast Asian patron–client
  systems 9
South Korea 105, 109; 5, 9, 25, 89,
  95, 97, 98, 104, 135; Asian values,
  concept of 162; consensus and
  influence which old people should
  hold 133; human rights questions
  132; liberalism 143; respondents
  176 n.1; women in home position
  144; women, role of 146, 156
Spain 66, 71, 76, 80, 83, 87, 122, 133,
  135; conquistadores 71; effects of
  industrialisation 74; liberalism 143;
  'public interest' and 'family
  obligations', choice 134
spirit of capitalism 91
The Spirit of Laws 70
Stael, Madame de 69
state: attitudes relating to support
  for 15; as basic unit of analysis in
  political culture studies 13–15; in
  education of children 14;
  strengthening of power of 66;
  'weight' of 14; West and in

East and Southeast Asia 14;
  see also government
*The State and Citizens in Western
  Europe and East and Southeast Asia*
  174 n.3, 176 n.2
The State and the Citizen 147
sub-cultures 9; below level of the
  state 13
sub-regional cultures 11; distinctions
  90; in East and Southeast Asia 101;
  groupings, validity in East and
  Southeast Asia and in Western
  Europe 94; political, limits of
  11–13; sub-groups within,
  value distinctions based on
  differences 118
sub-regions: in division of opinion
  152–4; variations within 113
Suharto, fall of 98, 109
superiority of 'Asian values' 22, 96
Sweden 80, 83, 84, 85; government
  restraint 156; human rights
  questions 132; influence which old
  people should hold 133; king 67;
  liberalism 143; responsibility of state
  for jobs 130; striving for one's own
  good 134
Switzerland 12, 13, 67

Taiwan/Taiwanese 25, 89, 95, 97, 98,
  104, 105, 109, 110, 123, 131, 145,
  156; attitude of respondents
  176 n.1; citizens, reactions of
  175 n.2; consensus and influence
  which old people should hold 133;
  difficulty in interpreting responses
  154; liberalism 143; *liberalism
  government restraint* dimension 155;
  respondents on human rights and
  'role of the government' questions
  176 n.1; *social relations* dimension
  155; Western colonisation in 96;
  women in home position 144
Thailand 9, 12, 95, 96, 98, 104, 109,
  133; Asian values, concept of 162;
  businessmen, systematic analysis of
  modes of behaviour of 93; consensus
  and influence which old people
  should hold 133; human rights
  questions 132, 137; liberalism 143;
  women in home position 144;
  women, role of 146
Third World 14, 71; effects of
  industrialisation 74

threshold of support required for values adopted by population 158–60
time as factor of 'development' 3
totalitarian participation 2
triumphalism 22

uncertainty avoidance 17
uniform regional cultures 12
United Provinces 67
United States 71; number of prisoners in 92
University College Dublin xvi
University of Sydney xv
University of Tokyo xvi
urban proletariat 74

value/s: 'Asian' or 'European' 42; in East and Southeast Asia, specificity of 21–3; fortress 115; held by individuals, origin of 119; patterns 52; reasons for standpoints differing between areas 115; systems 17; universalistic vision of 23; variation between the two regions 115; Western 20, 21, 22, 63
Vanhanen, T. 4
variations at level of states and their impact on differences across the two regions 154–6
Verba, S. 1, 15
Vietnam 9, *168*

Weber, M. 72, 91,176 nn.2, 3; analysis of 'Protestant ethic' 74
West, common political culture 9
Western Europe: basic societal values 162; 'basic societal values', variations from state to state 88; citizens, values 18; common socio-political culture 64–8, 80–3, 162; 'communitarianism' human

rights and socio-economic standpoints 88; cultural area 67; culture divided by climate 68; 'decision-making' dimension 146; and East and Southeast Asia, substance of difference 149–52; family and public interest, choice 151; government restraint questions 151; human rights questions 138, 151; 'liberalism' dimension 156; North–South division in patterns of political culture 83; political culture of citizens in countries of 1; on 'pro-Asian values' position 160; role of government 138; socio-economic questions 135; Southern 'sub-region' in 153; sub-groups 143; two fundamentally distinct political cultures 72
Westernisation 96
White, M. 89, 92
'white collar' middle class 74
Wittfogel, K.A. 91
Woliver, R.E. 10
women: Britain, on role of 134; in China, role of 134, 144; in France, role of 134; in Germany, role of 134; in Indonesia, in home position 144; in Japan, in the home position 144; in Korea, role of 144, 146, 156; in Malaysia, in home position 144; in Philippines, in home position 144; role of 125; in Singapore, in home position 144; in Taiwan, in home position 144; in Thailand, role of 144, 146; 'traditional' attitudes towards 144
work culture in Europe 10
World Values Survey 89, 166

Ying-shi Yu 29

For Product Safety Concerns and Information please contact our EU
representative GPSR@taylorandfrancis.com
Taylor & Francis Verlag GmbH, Kaufingerstraße 24, 80331 München, Germany